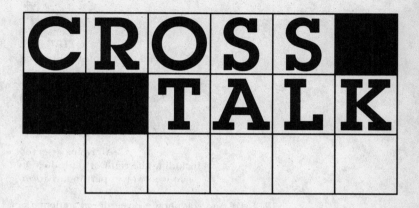

EUGENE T. MALESKA

A FIRESIDE BOOK
Published by Simon & Schuster
New York   London   Toronto   Sydney   Tokyo   Singapore

FIRESIDE
Simon & Schuster Building
Rockefeller Center
1230 Avenue of the Americas
New York, New York 10020

FIRESIDE and colophon are registered trademarks
of Simon & Schuster Inc.

Designed by IPA
Manufactured in the United States of America

10   9   8   7   6   5   4   3   2   1

Library of Congress Cataloging-in-Publication Data

Maleska, Eugene T.
Crosstalk : letters to America's foremost crossword puzzle authority /
Eugene T. Maleska.
p.   cm.
"A Fireside book."
Includes index.
1. Crossword puzzles.   2. Maleska, Eugene T.—Correspondence.
3. Crossword puzzle makers—United States.   I. New York Times.
II. Title.
GV1507.C7M344   1993
793.73—dc20
93-15814
CIP

ISBN: 0-671-70875-9

This book is dedicated with love to my wife Carol.

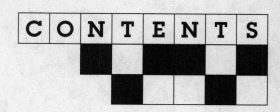

CONTENTS

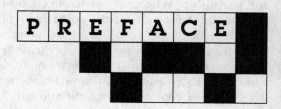

PREFACE

Crossword puzzles have been my passion for more than sixty years. I started solving them in high school and began constructing them in college. By now dozens of interviewers have reported the fact that my first attempt at the craft was a birthday present to a lovely coed who eventually became my first wife. Her first name, Jean, was 1 Across.

After graduation, I became a teacher of Latin and English. Simultaneously, I tried to make a little extra money by selling my wares to crossword puzzle magazines for $1.50 apiece. But my real goal was to crash the gates of the *New York Herald Tribune*. After forty rejections, I was finally admitted in 1940. Not only was I paid the handsome sum of $5 for a daily puzzle, but my name was printed above the clues. "O frabjous day! Callooh! Callay!" I had finally convinced the editor that my good puzzles were the original efforts of a neophyte who had practiced carefully for four years before diving into the pool.

A few years later another thrill was granted to me. The featured puzzle of the Sunday *Herald Tribune* was mine! Then in 1942 the *New York Times* began to publish crossword puzzles in the Sunday *Magazine*. I was among the first to knock on the door and was soon admitted by a gracious lady named Margaret Petherbridge Farrar.

Success in my hobby was matched by good fortune in the New York City school system. There, I rose in rapid steps from teacher to principal to community superintendent in the East Bronx. When I retired in 1971, a brand-new middle school was named for me—a unique event; never before had a living person been given such an honor.

Meanwhile, my relationship with Mrs. Farrar grew from one of respect of a disciple for a mentor to one of mutual admiration and friendship. Whenever she felt overworked, she hired me as a ghost editor for some of the pocketbook puzzles. As she grew older, she made me co-editor of the amazingly popular series called the *Simon & Schuster Crossword Puzzle Book*. When she died, I became the sole editor; shortly thereafter, I appointed John Samson as my co-editor. At this point, the series numbers more than 175 and continues to be the most successful sequence in the history of crossword puzzles.

Simon & Schuster also published seventeen volumes of my *Crossword Book of Quotations* and six volumes of cryptic puzzles, in which I tried to eliminate the Britishisms that had confused Americans who attempt those tricky creations.

Will Weng, who had succeeded Margaret Farrar as editor of the puzzles of the *Times,* chose me to take his place when he retired in 1977. I approached the new post with confidence because in all my years as editor of Simon & Schuster puzzle books, no letters of complaint about my work had ever been sent by solvers.

What a rude awakening! During my first few weeks as a *Times* editor, letters from angry fans demanded that Mr. Weng return. In discouragement I told him about the barrage of brickbats. But he quickly assuaged my hurt feelings and told me that he had been similarly assailed by solvers who missed Margaret Farrar. "*Times* fans are unusual," he said. "They like to write. But the complaints will die down once they get used to you."

His assessment and his prediction were both correct. The letters continued to pour in through the next decade even though the irate objections to my style of editing had decreased to a small trickle. And since I considered it to be a part of my job to answer all fan mail, I found myself devoting one eight-hour day each week to correspondence with all sorts of solvers.

One day it occurred to me that the fans fell into four categories: Sleepers, or Angels; Leapers; Squawkers; and Gotchas. I began to save the most interesting or unusual letters. That procedure, in turn, led to the decision to write this book, *Crosstalk*.

Crosstalk was a joy to write. I hope it will give equal pleasure to my readers.

I am grateful to all the fans who have shown such deep interest in the puzzles. Finally, I extend my sincere appreciation to Pamela Parsons for typing the manuscript for this book.

Pax, amor et felicitas,
E. T. M.

INQUIRING
MINDS

Ever since I became a crossword puzzles editor, I was made keenly aware that thousands of solvers have an insatiable appetite for correct information. And even when the answers to their questions are supplied, some of them still want to know why. This large group of fans has a wide range of interests starting with such aspects of language as etymology, orthography, diction, and vocabulary. Beyond those spheres, these fans probe into areas like history, geography, literature, mythology, the Bible, music, current events, flora, and fauna.

What I like most about these aficionados is that they are not eager to pounce upon me when I've made a mistake or when they merely think that they have spotted an error. Among them are my beloved Sleepers—people who cannot believe I could have made a mistake.

A prime example of a Sleeper sprang up when I erroneously placed the statue of Eros in Trafalgar Square. A nice woman from Wisconsin asked me: "When did they move the little fellow from Piccadilly Circus?"

Let's start with questions of a general nature.

Grading the Difficulty

Astute solvers of daily *Times* puzzles have made an interesting discovery. For example, here's a letter sent to me by J.R. in 1989.

> We here at the London Bureau of *World Monitor* have had an argument for sometime over your puzzles which appear in *The International Herald Tribune.*
> Can you write and tell me if the puzzles get progressively harder from Monday to Friday?
> I know you must be very busy, but a reply would be greatly, greatly appreciated. Thank you.

In my reply I noted that *The International Herald Tribune* apparently does not publish my Saturday puzzles. Otherwise, the people at the bureau would have been aware that those puzzles are sometimes even harder than the Sunday ones. In essence, I try to start with easy puzzles on Mondays and gradually increase the difficulty so that the Saturday crosswords are real toughies.

Why? In a way, the practice started with Margaret Farrar in the 1950s. When difficult 15-by-15 puzzles came across her desk, she published them on Saturdays because people had the whole weekend to solve them. Also, avid addicts would have access to reference books at their homes or in public libraries on Saturday mornings.

Will Weng continued the practice and usually tried to make the Monday puzzle as simple as possible so as not to make that "blue" day even more unpleasant.

When I took over, I merely refined the process. Tuesday's crossword would be easy, too, but a bit harder than Monday's. Conversely, the Friday puzzle would be almost as challenging as its successor. Finally, I attempted to publish medium-difficulty puzzles on Wednesday and Thursday.

The chief method for controlling the degree of difficulty resides in the choices of clues. Here are some examples:

Solution	Monday Clue	Saturday Clue
ROAM	Wander	Spatiate
TEASE .	Vex; badger	Chivy or chevy
REAR	Place for a caboose	Perform a pesade
URN	Vessel for flowers	Ossuarium
HAM	He overacts	Gammon

IMPOSSIBLE DREAM

R.A.C. of Macon, Georgia, recently inquired as follows:

> Do you know of any Cross Word Dictionary that lists mostly people, living and dead, real or fictional, etc.—authors, playwrights, painters, characters in plays, books, etc. I am 83 years old and cross words are about the only entertainment I am able to engage in.

Unfortunately, even the best encyclopedias and almanacs cannot meet Mr. C.'s request. My suggestion to crossword addicts is that they make greater use of their local public library. If they are not able to visit the building, they should ask questions on the phone. Most librarians are delighted when requests for help are made.

Another recommendation is to follow a procedure I have used for many years. Friends and relatives are urged not to buy me clothes or gadgets or other presents on my birthday or at Christmas. Instead, I let the word go forth in advance that I need certain reference books. Using this method, as well as funds of my own, I have acquired such valuable reference books as the following:

Columbia Encyclopedia
Cyclopedia of Names (three volumes)
Webster's Biographical Dictionary
Webster's New Geographical Dictionary
The Reader's Encyclopedia

Baseball Encyclopedia
The Dictionary of Greek and Roman Mythology
Encyclopedia of the Opera
The Concise Oxford Dictionary of Ballet
Sports Dictionary
Tune In Yesterday (re radio)
The Book of Who
Rock On
International Encyclopedia of Film
The Filmgoer's Companion
Roget's International Thesaurus
TV Movies and Video Guide
The Synonym Finder
Abbreviations Dictionary

Additionally, I have collected several atlases, books of quotations, pop music books, a thesaurus of slang, tomes on art and classical music, many dictionaries of various foreign languages, a few Bibles, current and past almanacs, books on flora and fauna, trivia volumes, a directory of television shows, and the complete works of Shakespeare.

Of course, the average solver does not need as many reference books as a crossword puzzle editor or constructor; nevertheless, every aficionado of the black-and-white squares should be encouraged to build a personal library.

Tangentially, let me make three points:

1. I admit I'm prejudiced against crossword dictionaries.
2. If solvers consult reference books to find answers to clues in puzzles, they are not cheating. After all, the constructors and editors resort to such books regularly.
3. I am not in favor of the 900-number idea for completing the solution to a puzzle. In cases where bets are made, it incites cheating.

Costly Club

Apropos of the foregoing, back in 1983 C.B. informed me that she belonged to a club which charged "a certain amount of money for each error and/or blank box."

The club had fined Mrs. B. for crossing *appenage* with *theme* when my printed answer contained *appanage* with *thema*.

Since some unabridged dictionaries accept *appenage* as a second spelling and allow *theme* as a "series of notes constituting the subject of a musical composition," my decision was in favor of the defendant.

If you have never come across *appanage,* one of its many definitions is "whatever belongs rightfully or appropriately to one's station in life." It can also mean "extra money; perquisite." Thus, a tip is a waiter's *appanage.*

Mnemonics

Mrs. F.G.C. of Wilmington, Delaware, is one of many solvers who were startled when I defined VIOLET as "part of Roy G. Biv." She wanted to know what was Mr. Biv's association with the flower.

Actually, the clue refers to an old memory aid I used when I was studying for a high school exam. The colors of the spectrum are:

*R*ed   *O*range   *Y*ellow   *G*reen   *B*lue   *I*ndigo   *V*iolet

Similarly, when ERIE was defined as "The fourth of HOMES," many fans who had never heard the mnemonic for the Great Lakes were confused.

Statue, Atlas?

The heading should really read "Where You, *Atlas?*" but the old joke was hard to resist. Anyway, Mrs. G.W.W. of East Lansing, Michigan, wrote:

> I've waited a week, but can't get over the feeling of uneasiness. Am I growing old?
> The May 12 puzzle had as 110 Down "Statue in Rockefeller Center" and the answer is ATLAS. Since my childhood, I've thought of the gold statue in the plaza as "Prometheus Unbound." Where is Atlas? Can somebody tell me?"

The statue of Atlas at Rockefeller Center is located outside 630 Fifth Avenue.

What the Dickens!

In 1985, R.J.S. of Rockville Centre, New York, wrote to me as follows:

> Although I am relatively new to crossword puzzles, I am an avid Dickens reader. I recently completed *Barnaby Rudge* and when I came upon 26 Down ("Dolly Varden, e.g.") on Sept. 14, I thought it would be a breeze.
>
> The answer TROUT was a stunner—too arcane for me. Does it relate to fishing? Please let me know the derivation of the answer.
>
> Thank you.

Personally, I shared Mr. S.'s wonderment. How had the gaily dressed coquette in Dickens's book become a fish? A trip to an unabridged dictionary enlightened me: The trout has an olivaceous hue, marked by round red or orange spots.

On my trip I also learned that the Dolly Varden was a nineteenth-century clothing style for women. Finally, it's a colorful crab!

Snared by a Drum

Another 1985 Sunday puzzle was entitled "Buffoon's Bestiary." The last part of each main entry was a member of the animal kingdom.

R.E.L. sent an inquiry all the way from Barcelona:

> . . . the definition "food fish that beats time" turned out to be TRAP DRUM. That one shook us, but good, especially because we hit on *bass drum* as the logical solution. What possible relationship does *trap* have with "food fish"?

To tell the truth, I can see why my overseas solver was confused. Most people have heard of the bass drum, but not the trap drum. What Señor L. failed to realize is that a drum is not just a percussion instrument. It's also a food fish.

MIDDLE-NAME MUDDLE

In a 1985 puzzle, the clue for SIMPSON was "Middle name accidentally given to President Grant." That statement caused many letters.

Grant was baptized Hiram Ulysses Grant, but he transposed the two names to create Ulysses Hiram Grant when he grew up. Subsequently, a congressman who recommended the young man for admission to West Point accidentally changed *Hiram* to *Simpson*. Grant accepted the U.S.G. monogram—maybe because it looked more patriotic then U.H.G. (which could be transposed UGH)!

On a few occasions, when *Hiram* appears in a puzzle that I am editing, I have rejected the following possible definitions:

A king of Tyre
Author Haydn
College in Ohio
Royal friend of Solomon
Mr. Walker of liqueur fame

Instead I have caused havoc among fans via a clue that reads "First name of our 18th president."

Who He?

Presidential monograms often appear in puzzles. The most popular ones are F.D.R., H.S T. (note: no period after the S), D.D.E., and J.F.K.

But some are unfamiliar. For instance, during President Ford's administration, OMAHA NEB was defined as "Birthplace of G.R.F." If R.M.N.'s successor had seen my "who he?" mail, he would have been embarrassed. But he's not the only one. During the early eighties, many fans asked me to identify R.W.R. and even today some don't recognize G.H.W.B. or W.J.C.

And then there's OPAL, which I once defined as "A stone for J.E.C." because it's the birthstone for October—the month in which President Carter was born. Three or four inquiries resulted.

In a punny puzzle by C.J. Angio, the word JAG appeared. It

was defined as "Pres. who seems to be on a spree." Today, a possible alternate is "Pres. who is catty." Poor Garfield!

Here's an inquiry from Mrs. K.S. of Chicago.

> I would like to know the name of Napoleon Bonaparte's horse. I tried everywhere to get this information—no luck. Could you help me?
> Thank you.

I have no idea why Mrs. S. was bothered by not knowing the name of Bonaparte's steed, but I was able to supply the information with the aid of *Roget's International Thesaurus*. Care to know? Napoleon's horse was named Marengo.

A Winner from Wynne

Here's a letter from J.L.K. of Buffalo, New York:

> I wonder if you have any idea when the first crossword puzzle originated and who was the originator? I would appreciate any information that you might have.

It was a pleasure to inform Mr. K. that crossword puzzles were invented in December 1913 by Arthur Wynne, an editor at *The New York World*.

Claire and Carol

In 1983 I received an interesting letter from Ms. Claire T.N. of Phoenix.

> I have been working your puzzles—at least attempting to— for many years. I have never doubted the definitions. Strange as many have been. I'm sure you have rooms full of dictionaries from all over the world and some very rare ones indeed.
> But having lived with my name for half a century plus, I'm sure somewhere along the way I would have become aware that the name Claire is also an oyster pond. Never have I heard the name described as one in all that long time.
> Could it be a proper name of a pond—like Walden or

Golden—somewhere along your eastern shore or in upstate New York known only to a few Easterners? Or is it truly a small "c" *claire?* If so, where did you find it?

In my reply, I referred Ms. N. to *Webster's Third.* In that tome the definition for *claire* is "a small enclosed pond for growing or observing the growth of oysters."

Carol, of course, is a song of joy—especially a Christmas air. But it is also a seat in a bay window, according to *The Random House Dictionary of the English Language, Second Edition* (hereafter referred to as *Random House, Second*). Incidentally, the seat is similar to a carrel, which is a cubicle for reading or studying in a library.

Who Is Silvia?

From Mercer Island, Washington, comes L.M.H.'s inquiry.

Re the crossword puzzle in the *Seattle Post-Intelligencer* for Jan. 28, 1987, the mother of Romulus and Remus comes out ILIA. Wm. Rose Benet's *Readers' Encyclopedia* says she was Rhea Silvia. How come?

To be brief, *Ilia* is an epithet for Rhea Silvia, just as *Parthenia* is another name for Athena.

Prolific but not Terrific

A.L. of Elizabeth, New Jersey, certainly had good reason to send an inquiry. Her letter reads:

In Thursday, October 30 *Times* puzzle, item 2 Down asks for a "composer of 43 operas." Luckily I had Friday's *Times* and looking for the solution found the composer to be PAER. I checked with my *Larousse Encyclopedia of Music,* but no such composer is listed. Being a music lover—and especially an opera buff—I find it hard to figure how I would have missed out on a composer who composed 43 operas. If you would give me the source of your information I would be most appreciative.

David Ewen's *Encyclopedia of the Opera* declares that Ferdinando Paer (1771–1839) "wrote forty-three operas, all of them now forgotten." Enough said!

Steal from Steele?

An English dramatist named George Lillo popped up in a 1986 puzzle. The clue was: "He wrote *The Christian Hero*." F.H. of the Bronx and S.G. of Fort Lauderdale were mystified because they knew that Richard Steele had produced a devotional manual having that name.

A quick trip to my reference books solved the problem to some extent. Steele's publication date was 1701. Lillo's play was staged in 1735. My guess is that the drama was based on the manual. If some erudite readers know better, please let them come forward.

She "Needed" That?

A crossword puzzle editor never knows what kind of question will be asked in the next batch of mail. For instance, here's part of a letter from E.M.C. of New York City.

> I need to know what name is given to two words of the same spelling that are pronounced totally differently—i.e., *minute* and *minute*.

I never found out why Ms. C. "needed" the information. Was it because she needed to win a bet or was she participating in a puzzle contest? Anyway, I revealed to her that the word she was desperately seeking is *homograph* (from the Greek—"written the same"). *Webster's Third* says it's "one of two or more words spelled alike but differing in derivation or meaning or pronunciation."

Loosely speaking, *homographs* and *homonyms* are the same. However, purists make a distinction. They hold that a *homonym* is a word that is the same as another in sound but different in meaning, origin, and usually spelling.

Super-purists also distinguish between a *homonym* ("same name") and a *homophone* ("same sound"). The latter extends to the sounds of letters as well as words. For example, the *c* in *century* and the *s* in *sun* are *homophonous*.

What's a #?

Nancy Joline, one of the world's best puzzle constructors, tells me that a Canadian acquaintance of hers calls a # an *octotharp*. That word is not in any American dictionary. Can any reader out there shed light on the subject?

Lucky R.S.N.!

In February 1985 a marvelous daily *Times* puzzle was submitted to me. The only problem was that one of the small entries was R.S.N. Those letters could possibly be an abbreviation for *reason,* but since I had recently defined WMT as "Auth. of *Vanity Fair,*" I decided to search for a writer's monogram. Lo and behold, in a volume of *Books in Print,* I found that Robert Stuart Nathan had written a novel called *Amusement Park.* Hurrah! R.S.N. deserved some publicity.

Here's the letter that Mr. Nathan wrote to me on the day the puzzle was published:

Dear Mr. Maleska:

This morning I was having a little difficulty with "having a handle," 13 Across, when I looked at 3 Down and discovered— shock, double-take, what?—that the answer was me, or my initials, rather.

I'm of course pleased to be oddly immortalized this way. But as a novelist of something less than great renown, I can't for the life of me figure out how it happened. I wonder if you might be able to take a moment and tell me how you happened to choose me for a clue.

Thank you very much.

The above incident reminds me that a contribution to the Sunday *Times* puzzle page contained the word HARA. Since I had used HARA-kiri so often, I probed my mind for another definition. It occurred to me that O'Hara is a common name. Then why not Hara? Voila! In *The New York Times Directory of the Theater,* I found an actress named Mary Hara. She had appeared in almost a dozen plays, including three Shakespearean tragedies. Okay. In she goes!

A few days after the puzzle was published, I received a long appreciative letter from M.H. She said that she is an avid solver and that she almost fainted when the answer for 5 Down turned out to be her surname.

Foreign Invaders

Some fans maintain that crossword puzzles should never contain foreign words. I disagree, but I urge constructors to limit the number of such entries and to restrict them to commonly known words.

At any rate, some fans are baffled when non-English clues and answers are used. For instance, L.G. wrote: "What the aitch is MESE? Also, what the aitch is *marzo* or *maggio*?"

MESE was the word to be filled in. It means "month" in Italian. The two clues can be translated into "March" and "May."

S.S. of New York City says she thinks in English, not in French. Hence, she thinks that we should indicate that words like *éclat* and *sans* and *nonpareil* are French. But, Mrs. S., please remember that we have incorporated those Gallic words into our language.

P.O., also from the Big Apple, wonders if the plural of *curriculum vitae* should be *curricula vitarum*. No, Mr. O., the lexicographers agree on *curricula vitae*.

Puzzled Future Puzzler

Thirteen-year-old S.P. of Hicksville, New York, recently sent this inquiry.

> Dear Mr. Eugene Maleska,
>
> I'm sorry to bother you, but I have a project for school and I'm told that you may well be the only person able to help me.
>
> I must construct a crossword puzzle and the answers, and to my dismay, I can't find any "how to" references.
>
> How is it done? How can I do it? What's the secret to the designs on both upper left and right and matching lower left and right?
>
> HELP!   PLEASE!
>
> What do you need from me to get this info from you? Any specific info will be helpful.

This was an easy one to answer. My young correspondent was told to go to a public library and borrow *A Pleasure in Words*. In that book of mine, Chapter 16 is "How to Construct Crossword Puzzles."

The same advice was given to G.H. of San Jose, California. His amusing letter reads as follows:

> Fear not! This is *not* a "Gotcha" letter.
> For some time, I have wanted to learn how to construct a crossword puzzle. (A while ago, I even made the silly mistake of starting to make a puzzle—by devising clues and answers *first,* then realized that I had no idea how to fit the answers into spaces. I felt somewhat like the backyard mechanic who tears apart an engine, without knowing how to put it back together.)
> Can you recommend any material on puzzle construction?

Can't Understand the Cant

The use of slang, colloquialisms, and idioms is a sure way to elicit interrogation. For example, in the lingo of the street *gawp* means "to stare slack-jawed." That definition comes from *Webster's New World Dictionary, Second College Edition,* which shall be referred to hereafter as *New World.*

G.K. of Willimantic, Connecticut, wondered if I would print a correction, and L.S.L. of West Orange, New Jersey, wrote:

> I think you are bending your literary (or crossword) license to an extreme by the solution of 38 Down "stare slack-jawed" as GAWP. My dictionary calls for *gawk.*

In another puzzle, BAT was clued as "Lost weekend." V.L. of Glendale, California, said that she and her friends wondered if they were looking at a misprint.

Here again, "slanguage" confused some people. A bat is a binge. "Lost weekend" referred to Charles Jackson's best-seller in which the protagonist went on a drunken spree.

A daily *Times* puzzle contained ACK EMMA, which was defined as "Before noon, in England." P.W. of New York City was among the many solvers who asked for an explanation.

The answer comes from *Webster's Third.* British signalmen use "ack" to mean *A* and "emma" to mean *M.* Thus "ack emma" is A.M.

The Flit that Fled

More than a half-century ago, an insecticide called Flit was very popular. The advertisement for the product usually depicted a frightened woman being bothered by an insect, such as a bee, while her husband looked on in surprise.

"Quick, Henry, the Flit!" the woman shouts.

In 1989, HENRY was an entry in a puzzle by one of my veteran constructors. She defined the word as "Flit-fetcher of yesteryear."

C.A.W. of Detroit was among the many younger solvers who asked: "What is a flit-fetcher and who is this Henry?"

April Fool!

Margaret Farrar, the first of the *Times* puzzles editors, usually published a tricky crossword on April 1. Her successor, Will Weng, continued the practice and so did I when I took his place in 1977.

Experienced *Times* solvers are ready for tomfoolery on the first day of what T.S. Eliot called "the cruellest month." But the problem is that the *Times* syndicates the puzzles to scores of other newspapers which must wait at least a few weeks before publishing the crosswords. Thus, an April 1 puzzle might crop up as late as May in another newspaper.

Among the many letters that pour in as a result of that situation is the following typical example, written by E.F.V. of Phoenix, Maryland.

> May I have a moment of your time to inquire into the definition of the following words—
>
> TNEMEGAGNE
> REVODNEB
> YGOLOHCYSP
>
> They really have me stumped. They are not in my dictionary—can't even give creditability to a "tongue in cheek" meaning. They appeared in the Baltimore morning *Sun,* Wednesday, May 13th—answers in Thursday, 14th.
>
> I hope you'll reply—word games are my hobby.

As some of you will see, the three words in question are spelled backward.

Letters Re Letters

Sometimes the use of letters rather than whole words can cause a modicum of confusion. For example, here's an inquiry from Mrs. K.M.B. of New York City:

> Would you be kind enough to explain the definition of "the whole bit" as ATOZ (9-14-89)? I have been unable to find the latter in dictionaries.
>   Thank you in advance for your trouble.

ATOZ, of course, is not a word. A TO Z is the answer.

The foregoing reminds me of the time ATOM was described as "First half of the alphabet." Read it as "A to M."

From time to time criticisms come in when constructors resort to entries using alphabetic sequences. Thus, RST is defined as "Q-U connection" or GHI is clued as "Trio after F."

People who object apparently have never attempted to create a publishable crossword puzzle. A measure of elasticity should be acceptable as long as it is fair to the solver. By the way, I like the above clue for GHI much more than "A butter made in India." That GHI is a variation of *ghee!*

Combining Forms

Every passing year brings at least a half-dozen letters inquiring about combining forms. For instance, in 1989 M.F. and H.R. of the University of Stony Brook, New York, wrote:

> We enjoy doing your crossword puzzles but have a question about a clue that appears frequently. We would appreciate an explanation and some examples of "comb. form."
> After asking several people, we are even more confused about its exact meaning than before. Please put our minds to rest.
> Thank you for your time and effort.

Yes, it is difficult to define a combining form. Most dictionaries give convoluted, abstruse explanations. Perhaps the best is *New*

World, Third. Let me quote: "a word form that occurs only in compounds and derivatives, and that can combine with other such forms or with affixes to form a word."

New World, Third gives *anthropo* ("man") and *centric* ("having a center") as an example of two combining forms uniting to create a single word: *anthropocentric.*

Many people, including some crossword editors and constructors, fail to distinguish a prefix from a combining form. That is like equating a pawn with a bishop or knight in chess. In other words, combining forms are bigger and stronger than mere prefixes.

Most combining forms come from Greek. Here are a few examples:

Phon, phono	Sound
Cac, caco	Bad
Hier, hiero	Sacred

A combining form sometimes becomes a word: *centric,* for instance. Sometimes it becomes the major part of a word, as in *anthropoid.* Prefixes and suffixes cannot make that boast.

Coming to Our Census

In 1987, P.H.C. inquired as follows:

> Needless to say, my husband and I enjoy your crossword puzzles. However, we are wondering just how many crossword puzzle fans there are in this country? Have you any statistics on this?

The last time puzzlers were polled was by the Gallup organization almost thirty years ago. At that time, the total number of solvers was approximately fifty million. Tackling crosswords is, by far, the most popular indoor leisure-time activity. Scrabble, bridge, poker, and mah-jongg must all take a back seat while the black-and-white squares game drives onward and upward. I believe that the number of solvers has possibly grown to sixty million. I receive letters from people from all over the United States and Canada.

Mr. Gallup, please take another poll.

No Need for Speed

A little hard data would also be welcome on another unresolved matter, raised in a recent letter from R.H.B. of Smithsburg, Maryland.

> A few months ago a contestant on the television show "Jeopardy!" said it took him 4 or 5 minutes to solve the *New York Times* crossword puzzle.
>
> I've found that on my best day I can't even write that fast, let alone move my eyes back and forth from puzzle to clue.
>
> I wouldn't be surprised that between editing the *New York Times* puzzles and those for other publications, you must solve a couple of dozen a day.
>
> What is your opinion on the possibility of a 4–5 minute solution of puzzles of this size and novelty?

I'm really not an authority on speedy solving. My own record is ten minutes for a simple 15-by-15 daily puzzle and twenty minutes for an easy Sunday 21-by-21 puzzle. But those are rare feats for me; it's not my nature to rush.

At any rate, my guess is that it's almost impossible to solve a 15-by-15 puzzle accurately in fewer than eight minutes. As for the large Sunday ones, I reckon that twelve minutes might be possible for a speed demon. To tell the truth, I believe that a lot of exaggeration takes place on this subject.

Unfamiliar Roles or Meanings

At a party, ask the group: "What part of speech is *head*?" Some will immediately describe the word as a noun; others will say that it's a verb. But few will think of it as an adjective, as in *head* cook.

Speaking of multiple roles played by words, here's a letter that speaks for itself. Only the name of the writer has been changed to protect the innocent.

> Pray tell, the dictionary equating "bore" with "tolerated"? I am at an absolute loss!! *Please* respond?
>
> > Yours absolutely frustratedly,
> > Jane Doe
> > Who is not a bore—and is tolerated!

A Little Latin

Once in a while when I try to be different or humorous, I cause trouble. For instance, J.J. of New London, New Hampshire, was among the fans who couldn't understand why ADAM was defined as "Costa" loser.

Costa means "rib" in Latin and has been bodily transposed into English. The problem is that the word means "coast" in Spanish (Costa Rica: "rich coast"). Also, some solvers may forget the following paragraph from Genesis.

"And the rib, which the Lord God had taken from man, made he a woman, and brought her unto the man."

Another Kind of Rib

Among the many physicians who are crossword aficionados is Dr. J.A.S. of New York City. He sent the following inquiry.

Earlier this month, in a weekday puzzle, you have the clue, "brin on a fan." A search through my dictionaries (*Webster's Unabridged* and *Oxford English*) was fruitless. Neither listed *brin.* Where did you get it?

Dr. S. was informed that the *American Heritage Dictionary of the English Language* describes *brin* as "one of the ribs of a fan."

Of course, the lexicographers were not talking about puzzle fans. It's a certainty they were not giving us a ribbing.

Word Games

Word lovers are constantly posing tricky questions to one another and, in some cases, making bets. As a result, I get besieged with inquiries. Here's one from D.B. of Wantagh, New York.

A question was given to me which I have been unable to answer. I was hoping you could think of a word, besides *hungry* and *angry*, which ends in -*gry.* A reply would be greatly appreciated.

There are several abstruse words that fit the category. My favorite is *aggry*, which appears in *Webster's Second.* The definition

is "Designating a kind of variegated glass beads of ancient manufacture, found in the Gold Coast, West Africa."

Puggry is another possibility, but it's a second spelling for *pug-
ree*. In India, people wind this light scarf around a hat or helmet
protecting them from the sun's rays.

Recondite Repeater

The verb *iterate* crops up in puzzles regularly for two reasons:

1. It begins with a vowel—an inordinate number of puzzle
   words start with *A, E, I, O,* or *U* because of the very nature
   of the beast.
2. It alternates vowels and consonants—consider this line-up:

S	E	V	E	R	A	L
I	T	E	R	A	T	E
R	O	T	A	T	E	D

Now note how each of the three-letter vertical entries makes
sense. The only one that has a shade of strangeness is ETO, but
most crossword mavens know the abbreviation for European
Theater of Operations, usually defined in puzzles as "W.W. II
post for D.D.E."

When I was a new constructor, I used the alternating technique
often, but as I gained confidence and skill, I put away my "chil-
dish" ways.

At any rate, I became tired of constantly defining ITERATE as
"Repeat" or "Say again." And so, I was delighted when I found
in *Webster's Second* a sort of synonym for the verb, namely *battologize* (which really means "to repeat needlessly").

The debut of *battologize* engendered this interesting epistle
from S.S. of Mount Sinai, New York.

> About a month ago, you had me ululating and stumped me
> with the word *battologize*. I looked in every word source I could
> lay my hands on, including practically all the unabridged lex-
> icons, and could not find it anywhere. Please rescue me and
> relay the meaning post-haste. I may even utilize it in a logograph
> I am constructing and plan to submit.

Mr. S. revived for me a word I had forgotten. Did you know
that logograph is a word puzzle, such as an anagram?

Nef Said

Dr. E.N. of Poughkeepsie, New York, was vexed by a clue in a puzzle by A.J. Santora. The good doctor sent the following message:

> Much to my chagrin, the answer to 15 Down, "Seaman's clock," is given as NEF. This sent me to my unabridged *Oxford English Dictionary*, where I could find no usage of *nef* that even vaguely approached "Seaman's clock."

Dr. N. had reason for some chagrin. As far as I know, the only dictionaries that use the clock definition are *Webster's Second* and *Webster's Third*. Moreover, they specify that the object was restricted to the sixteenth century. Editor Maleska should have changed the clue. Here's what *Random House, Second* has to say about *nef:* "A silver or gold table furnishing in the form of a ship, either for holding utensils or for ornament."

Another Homographic Pair

Earlier in this chapter, words that are spelled exactly alike but have different meanings and derivations were discussed. Here is an example that deserves special attention.

arete	Alpine crest
arete	Excellence; valor

The first of the two has come down to us via the French. The second has a Greek ancestry. For some reason, it is less used than its fraternal twin. In fact, most unabridged dictionaries do not list it. Hence, when I put it into the spotlight, I get lots of letters. A delightful one came from D.A. of Milwaukee.

> ARETE? "Excellence or valor"? In what language, please?
> I demand an answer, or I shall speak to your supervisor. (I'm a bill adjustor at Gimbel's Midwest, and this is what all the customers say to *me* when they call.)

The Portmanteau Muddle

The letter below came from Gilbert 5-10-25¢ Stores, Inc., in Glendale, California. It was signed by the office staff in 1983.

> SMOG—"Portmanteau word." A portmanteau is a trunk, valise, bag, suitcase, etc. How in the world is the word SMOG related to this?
> We are frustrated and would appreciate your reply.

In my reply to the good folks at Gilbert's, I probably pointed out that Lewis Carroll invented portmanteau words. He said, "You see, it's like a *portmanteau* . . . there are two meanings packed up in one word."

Some of Carroll's coinages are *slithy* (*slimy* blended with *lithe*) and *chortle* (*chuckle* mixed with *snort*).

Smog, of course, amalgamates *smoke* and *fog.* Other examples of portmanteau words are:

smaze	*smoke + haze*
motel	*motor + hotel*
brunch	*breakfast + lunch*
aniseed	*anise + seed*
bookmobile	*book + automobile*
guesstimate	*guess + estimate*
camporee	*camp + jamboree*

Incidentally, linguists have a term for a frowned-upon relative of portmanteau words. They call it *contamination* when people borrow the prefix from *irresponsible* and apply it to *regardless,* thus creating the tautological *irregardless.* Another example is *different than*—a blend of *different from* and *other than.*

The Greek Connection

R.M. of San Francisco inquired:

> Why do they call an electrocardiogram an EKG? How come the *K*? I can only surmise that a European inventor, whoever he was, spelled it *elektro.*

The answer is that the source of the middle of the word is the Greek *kardia,* meaning "heart."

The Latin word is *cor* (plural, *cordia*) from which we get *cordial.*

Dirty-Tricks Dept.

A.A.N., who also asked about *grognard,* was one of the flabbergasted solvers who looked for a four-letter word for "Cook book" and discovered it was COMA.

The reference was to the best-seller by Robin Cook.

A more familiar one is "Hardy girl," indicating TESS, a heroine of a novel by Thomas Hardy. Similarly, the clue for NATHAN might be "Hale Fellow" and OSCAR could be defined as "That Wilde man."

The Presence of Obsolescence

Let me conclude this chapter with a letter about one of Thomas Middleton's acrostics. It's by R.G.K. of Bellerose, New York.

> Being cognizant of the enormous difficulties attendant on the construction of an acrostic puzzle, I must preface this letter with high praise for the caliber of such puzzles which appear regularly in the *New York Times Magazine.*
>
> Such faith do I have in the skill and wisdom of the composers and editors of the *Times* puzzles that when I found the word NEFANDOUS emerging as the answer to the definition, "Unfit to speak of; execrable," I assumed that this was a word I had never heard of, but would use in the future. To reinforce my understanding of the word, I looked it up in my largest dictionary, only to find it was notable by its absence from those august pages. *Nefarious,* however, was there, and fit the definition admirably.
>
> Still enamored of the infallibility of the *Times* staff, I tried to change NEFANDOUS, but found that this created the words "agree*mert*" and "*irive*" in the text of the puzzle. I must sadly conclude that even you can make a mistake. Anything can indeed happen, and often does.

Nefandous is listed in *Webster's Second* and *Webster's Third,* but it has been dropped in three of the latest lexicons. That's a shame because it is not an exact synonym for *nefarious.* Literally, it means "Not fit to be spoken of."

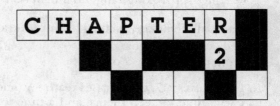

COMIC RELIEF

Yesterday and Today

In the beginning, crossword puzzling was a serious matter for the constructors and solvers. For three decades a no-nonsense approach existed. One important reason for this lack of levity was that Margaret Farrar, the foremost of the leaders in the field, was under direct orders from her *Times* bosses to keep the black-and-white squares dignified and staid.

But puzzledom's First Lady had a grand sense of humor, which could not be squelched forever; during the forties, bits of humor crept into the clues and even into the entries in the diagrams. Puns, anagrams, and other forms of wordplay gradually became welcome in the fifties and are popular today.

Although crosswords are still basically sedate and decorous, attention should be paid to the funny things that are happening on the way to the twenty-first century.

In the pages that follow, several types of crossword humor are covered. Among them are:

1. Intentional tomfoolery by the constructor or the editor, or both.
2. Inadvertent comedy by fans.
3. Deliberate drollery by fans.
4. Laugh-provoking tangential material.

Get ready for many a chuckle and several guffaws.

Fun-Loving Fans

In Ecclesiastes 3:7, the phrases read: "A time to rend and a time to sew; a time to keep silence and a time to speak."

We used "a time to sew" in the puzzle. M.K. of Long Island City couldn't keep silent. He asked if the next line was "a time to rip."

We have the feeling that he was punning on *sow* and *reap*.

J.B. of West Hartford, Connecticut, came up with this comeuppance:

My conation for completing puzzles was severely hampered last Friday by your flagitious use of obscure and difficult words. I may have to curb my esurience for puzzles, lest my head spin so fast that I become acephalous.

L.G.F. of New York City takes up where Ms. B. left off:

I cannot complain about your tactic in re-inforcing us sub-par idiots by giving us easy puzzles two or three times a week and then destroying us the other days. Perhaps this ingenious tactic is used to cut the wheat from the chaff.

But whatever reason, I must accept my minor role in your master plan of things. You, sir, control the world of "down and across."

Yet, despite my eternal lament, I admit that:
a) I don't know the name of Zeus' daughter from his third marriage to Thor's cousin on his mother's side. (In fact, I wasn't even invited to the wedding); or
b) the only Crimean War Chief I knew was the late great Sir C. Aubrey Smith who, by the way, still speaks well of you; or

c) the name of the tint used by Australian Aborigines to dye their hair during the rainy seasons on even-numbered years; or

d) the color of Wyatt Earp's third horse who threw a shoe during the "shoot-out" at the O.K. Corral; or

e) the names of the constellations and stars that I cannot see as well as "Welsh emblems," etc.

Oh, where have you gone, Will Weng?

Fear not, Mr. Maleska, I will continue to attack your puzzles because I have been accustomed to being "Maleskacized" on a daily basis. I just can't live without it.

Very truly yours,
S.G.

P.S. Strong letter to follow.

K.B.C. had a punny time calling attention to one of our directorial errors:

I'm not one to fawn on editors of your elk, but I felt I had to write in this case. Your recent diagramless puzzle, which had "deer" as its theme, had an incorrect clue at 21 Down. Michael Cimino was the director of *The Deer Hunter,* not Martin Scorsese as your clue indicated.

I know that you're probably thinking, oh, yeah, easy for you—hind sight is easier than foresight. Don't take it too much to hart; I ordinarily find your work exceptional. I just hope that this small error won't cost you any doe.

SHOTS FROM LAWMEN

Too Subtle?

In a Sunday puzzle called "Name Givers" Rudolf Diesel was called "Motorman?" and John McAdam was dubbed "Highwayman?" In keeping with the offbeat humor, the clue for Nicolas Chauvin was "Porky patriot?"

An attorney from Illinois saw no reason for the swinish adjective. He explained to me that the French word for "pig" is *cochon.* In turn, I had to jog the counselor's memory concerning the use of "male chauvinist pig" by some women.

Another Attorney

Sometimes my sense of humor confounds literal-minded people. Here are some paragraphs from a long letter written by a Virginia lawyer in response to a jocular definition:

> I am writing concerning the crossword puzzle in the October 25, 1987, magazine.
>
> In particular, I was quite surprised at the answer to 71 Down, "Fail to pass the bar." I assume that this statement refers to the most archaic and useless of tests, the Bar Exam. I have had occasion to know many fellow lawyers who failed to pass this exam. However, until I read the answer to your puzzle I would have never thought to use the word TOPE to explain this phenomenon. I freely admit my ignorance when I encountered the answer the following Sunday. My dictionary reveals the following definitions for *tope;* n., a fish of the shark family; n., a wren; n., a grove or clump of trees; n., a Buddhist shrine; and v.i., v.t., to drink to excess.
>
> While perhaps many individuals would refer to lawyers as "sharks" or would expect those of us who subject ourselves to the bar exam as having a need to "drink to excess," I do not believe that any of the four above definitions accurately answers the question of the moment.

And Still Another!

> Dear Mr. M.,
>
> I practice patent law in Pittsburgh and am a near-daily worker of your puzzles.
>
> My morning was brightened, today, by an error made by one of our inexperienced stenographers. Typing a patent specification, she referred to a "turban generator."
>
> If you do not have some index where you would enter *milliner* for "turban generator" and vice versa, I think you should have.
>
> Very truly yours,
> J.N.L.

P.S. This talented young woman has also give us "consentric" and "trunkated," which make good-enough answers, but I am in somewhat of a quandary about how they should be clued!

Off the top of my head, I'd define *consentric* as "acquiescing roguishly" and *trunkated* as "chopped off the main stem of a tree."

How's That Again?

In 1987, I defined RETRIAL as "appeals-court event." Apparently, most of the legal eagles among the solvers agreed with the clue. But an attorney from Boston took exception:

> I guess you've heard from the lawyers, but here goes: A retrial is never an appeals-court event. A trial or retrial, as an "event," can only take place in a trial court, not in an appellate court. A retrial may be an appeals-court "order," as the result of an appeal; but the retrial will take place in the trial court on remand.

Now, folks, if you don't understand the counselor's explanation, I appeal to you to give it a retrial.

JOKERS WILD

Plane Talk

A colleague at the *Times* recently gave me this crossword puzzle joke. Who makes up these stories anyway?

It seems that there were three people sitting side by side on an airplane. The man on the aisle was a lawyer, in the center was a divinity student, and at the window was a man in overalls.

After the plane took off, all three people took out the Sunday *Times Magazine* and went to work on the crossword puzzle. After about fifteen minutes, the man in overalls folded his magazine and put it away. The lawyer was astounded—how could this seemingly average person do the puzzle so quickly? He leaned over and said, "Excuse me. You didn't finish the puzzle, did you?"

The man in overalls said, "Yes, I did."

"May I ask what you do for a living?" asked the shocked lawyer.

"I'm a bricklayer," replied the man.

"This is impossible," said the lawyer. "I work with words for a living, I have a B.A. from Columbia and a law degree from Harvard, and I haven't finished yet."

"Sorry if you are having a problem," replied the bricklayer.

"Look," said the lawyer, "there are difficult words here. For example, what is a four-letter word for "woman" ending in U-N-T?"

"AUNT," replied the bricklayer.

"Excuse me," said the divinity student, "does anyone have an eraser?"

NOTE: The student had written *lady!*

Cooked-Up Humor?

Back in 1984, L.C. of Fayetteville, New York, wrote to me about his enjoyment of *A Pleasure in Words*. In the letter, he talked about the misconceptions that can arise because of a limited vocabulary. As an example, he cited an apocryphal story.

About 1902, in Syracuse, New York, there lived an old bachelor named Patrick O'Dowd. He had amassed a small fortune ($250,000). He wrote to Notre Dame University that he planned to leave it to that university when he died. The chancellor of Syracuse University heard of this and wrote Pat a letter reminding him that he had made his money in Syracuse and he *should* leave it to Syracuse University. Pat deliberated, then agreed. He wrote to Notre Dame and explained that since he had become enriched in Syracuse, he should leave his money to that university.

Monsignor O'Shaunessey of Notre Dame read the letter and grabbed the next train east. He was shown into Pat O'Dowd's parlor with all the respect and deference he was entitled to. He wasted no time after Pat had explained again why he was leaving his money to Syracuse University instead of Notre Dame.

"Did you know, Mr. O'Dowd, that the boys and girls *matriculate* together at Syracuse University?"

"The Saints presarve us," said Pat, looking heavenward.

"Furthermore," the Monsignor continued, "they use the same *curriculum*."

"Heaven help us ahll," cried Mr. O'Dowd in real pain by now.

"Not only that," the merciless prelate continued, "before they graduate, they are required to show their *theses* to the professor."

"*That* does it," wailed Pat. "I'm leavin' it ahll to Notre Dame like I said."

Irish Ire

The preceding joke reminds me of an error in judgment that I once made. Just before March 17, I published a Sunday puzzle called "Tippling to the Top." It featured the following original verses by Alfio Micci:

> There was an Irish tenor
> Who put whiskey in his tea;
> He said it was the only way
> That he could sing high C.

About a dozen letters of protest poured in from sons and daughters of Erin. Rightfully, they accused me of perpetuating an ethnic slur. Of course, I apologized abjectly and made it a point to tell my angry correspondents that my mother's maiden name was Nellie Kelly. Begorra, 'tis true!

MISUNDERSTANDINGS

Corny Correspondence

In slanguage a *ham* is an incompetent performer and *corn* is banal material. This combination caused unconscious humor to emanate from a Bible-minded solver in Newton, Massachusetts.

In the crossword puzzle for Monday, June 3, 1985, you have a definition for 11 Down, which is "Ham's trite offering." The answer to 11 Down is, as I had to conclude on the basis of crosswords, CORN.

I cannot, for the life of me, trace the origin of the idea of "Ham's trite offering" to any offering of any kind. What I do recall is the fact that in Genesis, Chapter 4, we have the story of the Divine rejection of Cain's offering, which was "of the fruit of the ground," which could certainly be "corn."

But what Ham has to do with this offering I know not. Perhaps you can enlighten me as to the source of this Ham and his "trite offering" of corn.

Up the Creek?

The Seine is a French river. *Seine* is also the word for a fisherman's net. Referring to the latter, we defined the word as "Catcher in the Rhine." That attempt at humor prompted E.S. of Princeton, New Jersey, to give us a geography lesson on the location of the river.

At the Supermarket?

R.K. of Bellerose, New York, erroneously accused us of male chauvinism in 1985. The puzzle contained a slight change in a proverb. It read: WHERE THERE'S WIFE THERE'S HOPE. But R.K.'s personal solution came out: WHERE THERE'S WIFE THERE SHOP I.

The Heat Is On

Assistant Professor P.I. of a New Jersey college was among the many solvers who were shocked when the solution for "Child's need" became OVEN. He wondered about angry parents who are so distraught that they feel like baking their brats, but he felt relieved when I explained that we were referring to Julia Child, the noted TV chef.

Naive Needler

In a humorous puzzle, A.J. Santora defined WHIPPERSNAPPER as "sadist." A woman from New Jersey obviously had never heard of S&M and the painful practices by devotees of that form of gratification.

> You or A.J. Santora do not know what a "Whippersnapper" is. It certainly is *not* a "sadist." A "Whippersnapper" is an impertinent, insolent young person. You could have used: "smart aleck; wise guy; braggart; show off." You two do not read Mr. Wm. Safire "On Language" very thoroughly. Look up *Whippersnapper* in *Webster's New World Dictionary of The American Language.* Hurry up!
>
> P.S. In the Hebrew, the word, *pishica* can also denote "Whippersnapper," a nervy, outspoken Jewish kid.

Mixed Blessing

A puzzle by Louis Sabin was called "Word Play." Some examples:

Touchdown celebration?	FAN DANCE
Genuine possessions?	REAL ESTATE
Jack's heir?	BENISON

That last bit of wit elicited a letter from an exasperated fan in New Paltz, New York:

> Maleska!
>
> How in Hell do you get BENISON as an answer to the clue "Jack's heir?"
> A benison was, and as far as I know, still is a "blessing." A son, Jack's or anyone else's, is a blessing—I'll grant you that. But, what in Hell does Jack—the explicit Jack—not just any person or thing—have to do with a blessing?
> My wife has suggested that the reference to "Jack" really means "Jacob" of the Old Testament, and that Jacob's son was a "blessing" and comfort to him. Just when in Hell did we become so familiar as to call Jacob "Jack"? is my answer to my wife's tortured reasoning.
> An explanation would be appreciated.

> Dear Mr. L:
>
> Explanation: Benison = Benny's son.

Scapegoat

D.D. of Santa Fe asks:

> Since when has *assault* become a synonym for *goat*? It's confusing and I am discombobulated and not couraged either. Do you read all the puzzles before publication?

Here's my reply:

> Dear Ms. D.
>
> Thanks for your interest in the puzzles and for taking the time to write. As for the answer to "assault," it was GO AT, not

GOAT! Now you might say that I should have told you that the answer was *two words,* but *Times* solvers don't like to be babied.

I'm reminded of the occasion when Margaret Farrar, original *Times* editor, published a clue: "Make a _____ (succeed)." The answer was GO OF. She received many letters asking her how make a GOOF could equal "succeed"!

Ripping the Quip

Most daily crossword puzzles have a serious quality even when an unusual theme is featured. To balance the scales, I have asked a few constructors to embody a joke in the diagram. One such puzzle contained the following:

THE JOB STRINGING
VIOLINS DOES TAKE
A GOOD DEAL OF GUTS

An Ivy League male student objected in the letter below:

I'm writting you this letter to complain. I am majoring in linguisticks at my school, and I enjoy the crossword very much every day. *However,* Mr. E.T. Maleska, I have take exception to this puzzle. This so called *quip* is completely *fakey.* "The job stringing violins does take a good deal of guts"? Who are you kidding? And INBRED fer "native"? What do you think this is? Russia? Are all the native Americans INBRED? I am outraged.

Yours truly,

P.S. Are you living?

It should be noted that *Random House, Second* gives *native* as a synonym for *inbred.*

Another Quip—Another Slip

In one of my puzzles a soothsayer tells Caesar to beware the Ides. The emperor replies: "But I never fish."

Here is a letter from M.P.M. of Manhasset, New York:

Please tell me what BUT I NEVER FISH has to do with BEWARE THE IDES.

I waited for today's paper to be sure that there was no mistake. What kind of answer is that? I don't get it.

I was annoyed and might not have mentioned it, if it were not for today's error—1 Across "Fisherman's barbed spear."

A gaff is a hook—not a spear.

A gaff is barbless—pointed, but barbless.

Mr. Maleska, GAFF was a gaffe.

You goofed.

Mr. M.'s *gaff-gaffe-goof* play on words deserved kudos, but unfortunately he was wrong. A gaff is indeed a hook, but by synecdoche it has also become the barbed spear itself.

By the way, *ides* are fish.

Spoonerisms

In a Simon & Schuster book, one of the puzzles featured such phrases as "kistomary to cuss the bride." It evoked an interesting letter from Persis Cope, an avid fan from Upper Montclair, New Jersey.

Dear Mr. Maleska:

The spoonerism puzzle took me back to a crowded elevator in a dormitory in Ann Arbor when, for some reason, it was suggested that everyone turn her name into a spoonerism. My reversal (Cursis Pope) brought forth a short gasp from a devout Catholic in the group, but the one who stopped the show was *Nellie Becker!*

Donne In!

ISLAND was the word in the puzzle. The clue read: "Man is one."

Solver B.B. cleverly queried: "Is John Donne undone?"

Letter Lingo

EMS	Printers' measures; German river
ENS	U.S.N.A. grad; conceptual being; printers' measure
ELS	Overhead r.r.'s; Chi transportation

The above are common clues for three-letter words that crop up often. But sometimes a change of pace occurs:

EMS	Quartet in "*Midsummer* Night's Dream"
ENS	Quartet in "*N, No, Na*nette"
ELS	Quintet in "*La La, Luci*lle" or Sextet in "*Litt*le Ne*ll*ie Ke*ll*y"

Such rather jocose deviations from the norm always cause some fans to be baffled. Even when told that there are six els in the title of the George M. Cohan production, a few still want to know what connection railroads have with music.

MORE TRICKS OF THE TRADE

As indicated earlier, sometimes I like to spice up a puzzle by using unusual clues. Here are some prime examples:

Q. Please explain how "Bill's possible future" can become ACT. What young performer are you talking about?

A. In Congress a bill that is passed becomes an act.

Q. Kindly explain "Modern art." The correct answer seems to be ARE, but I don't understand it.

A. *Art* is an old variation of the verb *are,* and is often preceded by *thou.*

Q. How do you explain "A relative" becoming THE?

A. *A* is an article. *The* is also an article.

Q. We don't understand SRIATSPUGNIKCIK ("Promoting in a way") at 10 Down and SDRAWKCAB ("Like 10 Down"). Would you please enlighten us?

A. The entry at 10 Down is *kicking upstairs* spelled in reverse.

Note that it's especially appropriate because it's a vertical entry. The other entry is the word *backwards*, also spelled in reverse.

Q. Your alphabetics really had me stumped a few days ago. Please explain!

The fan then went on to list the following:

Clue	Solution
B	BROADWAY OPENING
K	STORYBOOK ENDING
I	MEDICAL CENTER

A. The first letter of *Broadway* is *B*.

The word *storybook* ends in *K*.

The central letter of *medical* is *I*.

Similarly, note the following:

Clue	Solution
S	LAST OF THE MOHICANS
O	SECOND IN COMMAND
H	BEETHOVEN'S FIFTH
V	CENTER OF GRAVITY

Q. I don't understand your sign language. How does "HIJKLMNO" get translated into WATER?

A. It was a joke. *H-to-O*. Get it? Sorry!

Leg Puller?

Some critics have accused me of being too stodgy and out-of-date. They point out that I'm more likely to refer to silent-screen star Renee Adoree than to Roger Rabbit or to feature an old opera singer than a group like the Grateful Dead.

The faultfinders are probably right. Hence, I wonder how I should react to the following letter from a Penn student.

As a young, impressionable college student, I have always looked upon the *Times'* crossword puzzle as a symbol of literary wit and intellectual trivia. How the mighty have fallen. On Tuesday, February 25, I found myself stumped by 31 Across. I was utterly dismayed to realize that the answer referred to, of all people, Aimee Mann, the lead singer of the pop group "til tuesday." Hardly a literary allusion. The next day I hoped to restore my faith in this perennial institution, but after reading 1 Across, I suddenly felt weak. This couldn't be happening. The crossword puzzle that I have held in such awe had included, as its first answer, the word RAMBO. My world will never be the same.

Sincerely,
S.E.S.

The Callipygian Quest

Here's a recent letter from a fan from the state of Washington.

I am desperate. A couple of years ago, I received your book on the world of words as a gift. After reading it with great interest, I gave it to a friend who was just then getting into crosswords.

In that book, you introduced me to the word *callipygian,* and stated that it referred to a statue of Aphrodite located in a museum somewhere in Italy.

My wife and I are leaving in three weeks for an extended visit to Italy, and I would very much like to photograph this statue.

I cannot locate a copy of your book in our small library. Would you be good enough to write and tell me in which museum the statue is located?

Parenthetically, three of my scuba diving friends and I have formed the "Cayman Islands Callipygian Appreciation, Cribbage, and Diving Society." I would like to create a logo for our society, based upon a photo of Aphrodite of Callipygius, which I could take during our upcoming trip (if I can find the museum).

If you will grant my request, I will send you a copy of the logo, with our thanks.

In my reply I told Mr. R. to be sure to stand behind the statue, which is located in Naples. *Callipygian,* you see, means "having shapely buttocks."

I'm So Happified

Elate is a verb that appears time after time in puzzles. Since I am always on the lookout for new definitions, I was pleased to find *happify* in *Webster's Third*. A few days later, I was even more delighted to receive the following letter from a clever Gothamite:

> I was thoroughly enchanted with HAPPIFY (5 Down, 10/31/85). That's a wonderful word, man, a real killer, and it couldn't have come at a better time. I was beginning to feel stifled by the narrow confines of the English language. A new word—just what was needed.
>
> Just think of the vistas it opens up—now we can look forward to neologisms like *easify* ("Make easy"), *emptify* ("Make empty"), *peachify* ("Make peachy") or *merrify* ("Have a good time"). Maybe even *skinnify* or *healthify* or even *richify*. Hosanna!
>
> I trust this finds you hale and hearty and never at a loss for words.
>
> Sincerely,
> B.B.

Cartoons

People often send me cartoons about crosswords. My favorite is one by J.E.F. It depicts a drunk emerging from the Esne Tavern run by Eugene T. Maleska. The fellow has a glass of spirits in his right hand. His left hand is raised in joy, his eyes are crossed; and he is shouting, "Evoe!"

Another goodie shows an animal in a cage at the zoo. A sign reveals that it's a gnu. The entire wall behind the beast is a crossword puzzle. Gazing at this scene, one visitor says to another, "I'm glad to see every animal is kept in its natural habitat." The artist's name is harder to decipher. It looks like Sal Wadron.

What else is gnu? Well, there's a scene in Heaven, where an angel is apparently creating a gigantic crossword puzzle. Behind him is a drowsy, bearded oldster looking very much like a king.

The angel points to a blank space in the diagram and says: "We need another 3-letter antelope in Africa, boss."

The cartoon is signed "DH."

An unsigned drawing depicts Sidney Sneath, Crossword Puzzle Editor, standing at the entrance to his office and staring with satisfaction at a workman who is kneeling on the floor and laying black tiles along with numbered white ones.

The workman's pattern, by the way, is asymmetrical!

In one of Tom Wilson's "Ziggy" cartoons we see a magazine stand. Outside it are two stacks. The sign atop one reads: "Newspapers 25¢." On the other pile the sign says: "Newspapers with Puzzles Already Done 15¢."

Is there a cartoonist named Doog Goag? That's the best I can do in trying to interpret his signature. At any rate, in one of his drawings two women are standing before a tombstone that is inscribed: "Here lies Warren X. Brown—2 Across, 6 Down."

The tearful widow says to her friend, "It seemed only fitting. Crossword puzzles were his whole life."

Incidentally, in *New York Magazine,* one of Mary Ann Madden's contests in the early seventies asked for fitting epitaphs for well-known people. At that time, Will Weng was the crossword puzzles editor of the *Times.* A winning entry gave his name along with "2 Across, 6 Down."

A cartoon by O'Neill shows a woman sitting on a couch. All around her are tomes and papers. On her lap is a crossword puzzle and she is holding a pencil. Her head is turned toward her husband who is slinking away. She yells at him: "You don't care about 21 across! You don't care about 48 down! What do you care about?"

B. Brown published a cute cartoon in *Modern Maturity* during 1987. A caged parrot's talon is grasping a pencil and the bird is gazing down at some black and white squares. Nearby a woman says to her husband: "I put a crossword puzzle in his cage and he hasn't said a word all day."

Another avian cartoon is by F. Folkes. One bird is introducing itself to what looks like an ostrich. The bird says: "I'm a smee and the odd thing is I frequently crop up in crossword puzzles."

Probably the best of my collection is an unsigned cartoon showing a display case in a museum. At the top in large letters the following message is proclaimed: "Great Puzzles of the World: Brain Teasers That Have Baffled Mankind."

The Riddle of the Sphinx and the Gordian Knot are at the left. Rubik's Cube and a W-4 Form appear on the right. The middle is occupied by the "NY TIMES CROSSWORD PUZZLE."

A cartoon by Eli shows a man standing before two elevators. The one at the left is ordinary and its buttons read "UP-DOWN." However, the buttons for the one at the right read "ACROSS-DOWN." The doors are open and on the three walls inside we see an enormous crossword puzzle. Moreover, a large pencil leans against one of the walls.

Comics

I am also the recipient of comic strips mailed by thoughtful solvers all over the country. Here are some of them.

Artist Thaves has created two characters named Frank and Ernest. In one strip Ernest is trying to solve a crossword and Frank offers his assistance.

E. Okay . . . a 4-letter word for "heavenly body."
F. CHER
E. An 11-letter word for "a messed-up kiss."
F. BLUNDERBUSS
E. And here's a toughie . . . 3 letters for "a U.S. terrorist organization."
F. That's easy . . . I.R.S.
E. Gee, it's great watching a real pro at work.
F. It's a gift, Ernie. A gift.

In a comic strip called "Motley's Crew," an irate man on the phone says: "An' tell your editor an' publisher *this* for me . . . if I see somethin' like this *again*, I'm gonna cancel my subscription."

A woman within earshot asks the son of the angry fellow: "Did your father find an editorial he didn't agree with?"

"Worse," says the son. "A mistake in the crossword puzzle."

(I can personally attest to the truth of that type of episode.)

Mell Lazarus has created a popular comic strip called "Miss Peach." In one of the incidents the children have published the *Kelly School Clarion*. A character named Arthur is asked why he printed the wrong solution to the crossword puzzle.

Arthur replies: "Because the folks who aren't good at it deserve a little consideration, too."

In a strip called "Shoe," Mr. Shoemaker (who apparently published a newspaper) is asked by his secretary why some of the letters from readers are addressed to the Marquis de Sade.

His answer: "That's just fan mail for the crossword puzzle editor."

"Blondie" is a strip by Raymond Young. In one episode she asks Dagwood for a four-letter word for something unattached. Then she says, "Never mind . . . it's LOOSE."

When Dagwood points out that LOOSE has five letters, she replies, "Not if you put two little O's in one square."

Caricatures

It has been said that you aren't really famous until:

A. Your name appears in a *New York Times* crossword puzzle.
B. Your features are distorted by a professional caricaturist and placed on display for the delight of the public.

Well, it so happens that I can lay claim to fame under Category B at least twice.

In a publication called *The Oregonian,* I'm waving a crossword

and am surrounded by dictionaries. Three sharpened pencils
project from the crease behind the top of my left ear. They look
like spears ready to pierce an unwary puzzles addict. My jacket
is full of black and white squares. This pen-and-ink "portrait"
is by Ted Reeves.

My mug is also featured on the colorful cover of a weekly
magazine published by the Rochester *Times-Union* newspaper.
Once again, I'm in a checkered jacket. My tie and even my cuff
links adhere to the same motif. Artist Joseph A. Iula has drawn
the following next to my funny face:

```
                M
                A
                L
    E  U  G  E  N  E
                S
                K
    A     M  A  N        O  F
                A
    M  E  A  N  I  N  G  S
                Y
```

Needless to say, I'm thrilled to have my likeness distorted. It's
a strange kind of compliment, I admit, but it pleases my wife so
much that she has framed both caricatures and has hung them
on one of the walls in our house.

Before leaving this subject, I must tell you about a cartoon
sent to me by a fan in Pennsylvania. It shows two tramps shiv-
ering in a garbage dump.

As the snowflakes glide down all about them, one hobo says
to the other: "I did it my way, but if I had to do it over again
I'd do it Frank Sinatra's way."

I sent the cartoon to F.A.S. and a week later his secretary told
me that he got a good laugh out of it.

The incident is mentioned because Ole Blue Eyes is one of
my most avid puzzle mavens.

CHAPTER 3

FAN-ANTICS

One of the pleasures afforded to a crossword puzzle editor is the opportunity to correspond with articulate, creative people who love words and have a sense of humor.

Sometimes they break out into verse, especially on the subject of crosswordese. The meter may limp somewhat; the rhymes are not always on the mark; the facts may be twisted here and there—but it's easy to discern that they are having lots of fun writing about their favorite pastime. Here's an example, sent to me by C.H.K. in Sepulveda, California:

CROSSWORD DOGGEREL

A nene alit in a haha;
Nearby sat an erne from St. Lo.
"The oast is awry,"
Elia did cry—
Anoa, Aloha, aloe.

– O – O – O –
The Elbe and the Aare and the Ebro
Are rios I ne'er have espied:
But the proa's asea
With a Bora alee,
And Aida is Radames' bride.
(I think.)*
– O – O – O –
Waner was a winner, but a oner he was not;
The same is often rumored re the diamond hero
   Ott.
No losers were the three Alous (Jose, Felipe, Matty),
And Roses are abloom both in Tralee and Cincinnati.
– O – O – O –
(Aside to NYT epic verse committee):
Oh, New York *Times*, please print this bumf,
And send me some champagne;
There's no quaff here in Lotus Land
That's worthy of the nagne.
But we'll have subways soon, like you,
Or so smart money bets—
For what L.A.'s big guns request,
They almost always Goetz.

May 15, 1985

*Wrong! Radames never married Aida.

C.G.S. of Dedham, Massachusetts, decided not to roam from
one topic to another, but to dwell on a single topic—the emu.
Her verses feature a before-and-after idea that makes me want
to ask for a raise.

THOUGHTS WAY BACK WHEN—

You think I'm a nerd
Not knowing the word
For a flightless bird
"Three letters"—I've heard.
If you only knew
What I'm going through.
I haven't a clue.
Could it be a gnu?

Oh no! That won't do—
Though it ends with *U*.
I know—and you too—
It lives in a zoo.
So what is the bird
Of which I've not heard?
With an *E*—absurd!
My mind's getting blurred
It's gathering moss
And I'm getting cross
Now I know, why, Boss,
Your puzzle's named "cross."

1984

But no more do I
Get cross when I try.
Your humor's so wry!
That that's why I buy
The *Times* on Sunday—
That's my big funday.

Now, just for a change let me share with you a piece of prose by B.R. of Rumson, New Jersey. Readers who are not veteran solvers will be glad that the author has appended a translation.

A FABLE IN CROSSWORDESE

When the salse erupted o'er the arete for the first time in eons, the sere wind was as feral as an oe. Nenes and anis aviated from an arar, and e'en an ai was astir, and eely enow, to ope an orb. In a lea anear, anoas and arnas ran amok, and in the redan, a powwow of an octad that included a bey, a dey, an emir, an emeer, an ameer, a shah, a tsar and a rey, agape at the eerie vista, had to decamp to the orlop of an aviso for egis. Before the nef showed time for sunup, however, a horde of esnes, peons, helots and thralls, wielding besoms, had exerted ergs amain in mopup so that Selene radiated on a scape that was irenic anew.

TRANSLATION

When the mud volcano erupted above the mountain crest for the first time in ages, the dry wind was as wild as a Faroe whirlwind. Hawaiian geese and cuckoos flew from a sandarac tree, and even a two-toed sloth was roused and wriggling enough to open an eye. In a nearby meadow, wild oxen and water buffalo went crazy, and in the fort, a meeting of a group of eight potentates, staring at the wild scene, had to flee to the lowest deck of a dispatch boat for protection. Before the ship-shaped clock showed time for dawn, however, a crowd of menial laborers wielding brooms had exerted effort strongly so that the moon goddess could shine on a landscape that was again peaceful.

A few years ago, the *New York Times* carried the following conversation in its *Book Review* section. The spoof on crosswordese was first published in 1925 in *The Bookman* magazine. It's interesting to note that crosswords were only twelve years old at that time.

MRS. W.   What is it that you are working at, my dear?

MRS. F.   I'm tatting Joe's initials on his morreen vest. Are you making that ebon garment for yourself?

MRS. W.   Yeah. Just a black dress for everyday. Henry says I look rather naif in black.

MRS. F.   Well, perhaps; but it's a bit too anile for me. Give me something in indigo, or, say, ecru.

MRS. W.   Quite right. There is really no neb in such solemn vestments.

MRS. F.   Stet.

MRS. W.   By the way, didn't I hear that your little Junior met with an accident?

MRS. F.   Yes, the little oaf fell from an apse and fractured his artus.

MRS. W.   Egad.

Similarly, the early puzzles took a ribbing from a well-known light-verse writer who died in 1927. A fan sent me "The Destiny That Shapes Our Ends" by Keith Preston. It appeared in the thirteenth edition of Bartlett's *Familiar Quotations*, no less.

> Imperial Caesar dead and turned to clay
> Estopped a hole to keep the wind away;
> The great god Ra whose shrine once covered acres
> Is filler now for cross-word puzzle makers.

What intrigues me most about those four lines is the reference to Ra. In the twenties and thirties, most puzzle editors allowed two-letter words. Hence, it was RA, RA, RA in crossword after crossword. People who had never heard of that Egyptian sun god now were getting their fill of him.

But under the leadership of Margaret Farrar in the forties, constructors were required to eschew two-letter entries in most puzzles. And so, the hero of Heliopolis lapsed into obsolescence in Puzzledom and the fans cried: *"Rah! Rah! Rah!"*

Sometimes it's a two-way street. The fans send me verses and I reply in kind. One such exchange occurred when I let a misspelling of Dr. Seuss's name creep into print in 1988. L.M. of Kew Gardens, New York, razzed me in rhyme.

> On Monday, December twenty-eight,
> While doing the puzzle rather late
> And filling in on Thirteen Down
> My forehead suddenly starts to frown:
> ABOU and SOIE, it all fits well,
> But Author SUESS, that rings no bell,
> The *E* is preceded by the *U*,
> While just the opposite is true:
> It's Dr. SEUSS not SUESS, you know,
> Oh, *Times,* how could you blunder so!!

My reply:

> Oh Dr. Seuss, you cooked my geuss.
> But what the deuss,

> A rare mistake was deu me;
> So seu me!

In 1985, a nonagenarian O.W.G. of Fairhope, Alabama, modestly declared:

> My wits are not as sharp as they were . . . once—
> At times I feel that I've become a dunce—
> Your puzzles are so clever—so unique—
> Sometimes I think you have me up the creek.
> But I'll hang in there, come hell or high water—
> Past 90 now and just begun to fight—
> Your puzzles haven't got me down—not yet—
> But make them any harder and they might!

Thank you for many hours of pleasure even if it is hard work at times. I'm glad too that piano is my forte—not writing. (No pun intended.)

Ms. G.'s verses inspired me so much that I sent her a pair of couplets.

> Thanks for your delightful verses;
> I'm glad you didn't send me curses!
> I hope that when I reach your age
> I'll be so witty, sharp, and sage!

Occasionally, the roles will be reversed: the fan's communication will be in prose and my answer will be a rhymer. For instance, in 1986 a *Times* daily puzzle featured all the boroughs of New York City except Staten Island. That glaring gaffe generated a delightfully written objection from the pastor of Staten Island's Trinity Lutheran Church.

> Allow me to protest the unconscionable omission of Monday's puzzle (10/6) regarding the borough four thousand New Yorkers call home.
> Admittedly, there are too many cocktails consumed in Manhattan, too few trees in Brooklyn and not much to cheer about in the Bronx. In addition if recent scandals are any indication, the people of Queens are not abiding by any rules at all.

However many of us are sensitive about our forgotten borough and we resent the fact that it is ever left out of the *New York Times* puzzle.

Moreover, you should know that ours is the first of the five boroughs to be named. It is reported that a German sailor on the *Half Moon,* upon entering the lower harbor in 1609, was heard to ask, "Ist zat ein Island?"

In reply, I inflicted some apologetic verses upon my ecclesiastical correspondent.

> I'm sorry we caused your brows to furrow
> When we omitted your wonderful borough.
> And here and now I pledge to you
> That your isle will receive its due.
> In puzzles I will feature STATEN—
> And now let me resort to Latin.
> > *Pax, amor et felicitas*

One of the primary commandments for puzzle solvers is: Thou shalt not be inflexible. In other words, when you enter an answer, do not act as if it's engraved in gold. K.C. of Jennerstown, Pennsylvania, either made that mistake or decided to pull my leg. In a *Times* puzzle the clue for 6 Across was "Traffic-light item." He wrote in JAM. And so, when he came to "Item for Ansel Adams" at 6 Down, his solution evolved as JAMERA.

Here's his letter to me:

While sitting in a traffic *cam*, with nothing better to do, I reached for your recent diagramless puzzle (Sunday, Oct. 12) and attempted to thus pass the time. I became so absorbed in trying to solve its Columbus Day theme, that I didn't notice the light had finally changed. Further, when I attempted to complete 6 Across or 6 Down, I became so enraged at the incongruous answers I was getting (not to mention the blaring horns behind me) that I got out of my stalled (34A) car and caused a row (54D). Needless to say, the police soon came, followed by a TV crew with their *jamera.*

I am now in a penal (18D) institution with lots of time to spend doing puzzles. One thing still bothers me, however. Was I correct? Was there a mistake at 6A/6D in the puzzle?

Such a creative canard deserved more than a pedestrian reply (pun intended). I wrote:

> My puzzle made you a traffic jammer,
> And so you landed in the slammer?
> I really don't believe your tale
> And so I'll let some prose prevail.

A cam is a little mechanical device that helps to set gears in motion and is present in every traffic light. When the tiny cam jams it causes "damns!" People get red-faced while looking at a red light for eons, and they are green with envy as the cars at the left or right keep speeding by.

> Now as you sit in your lonely cell,
> Please remember *all is well.*
> No blaring horns, no angry cries
> From all those other cammed-up guys.
> Your only problem's you're at a loss
> To figure out that 6 Across!

In the "Gotchas" chapter, the reader will see how many times the solvers correct my mistakes and expand my knowledge. What follows here is another example. The tone of the letter from G.H. of Scarsdale is not gotcha-like. Also, my reply is another rhymer. Hence, it belongs in this section. Mr. H., in his first paragraph, is referring to an article on crosswords that I published in the Sunday *Times Magazine.*

In your most amusing piece not-so-recently, you commented that you learned many a fact from your readers. Here's one out of personal experience.

In the 7/10 puzzle, tongas are defined as "carriages drawn by bullocks." I wish I had a rupee for every tonga I rode in during 1944–46, and all were drawn by *horses.* They are the local taxis, and if they had been drawn by bullocks, we would have spent our lives going a few blocks.

Even Webster agrees that they are "2-wheeled vehicles for two to four persons drawn by one horse and common in India." Though I did not speak Hindi, I do not believe that the same word was used for the peasant carts drawn by bullocks.

This letter is strictly for fact-finding purposes and should not be interpreted as prosecutorial. No response is necessary.

My reply was a three-liner:

> Ah, the bullock no longa
> Is drawing the tonga—
> I guess I was wronga!

The interesting part of the above correspondence is that my source was *Webster's Second.* The bullocks were spoken of in that vintage dictionary. No mention of the beasts was made in *Webster's Third,* which was published three decades later. The old order really doth change, yielding unto new. That's no bullock!

H.T.I. of Ardmore, Pennsylvania, sent me this unusual verse in 1985 after I had described *gam* as a "school of whales."

MEMO FROM
HERMAN MELVILLE TO
EUGENE T. MALESKA

> A gam
> Is a dialogue at sea,
> By damn.
> A pod
> Is a bunch of whales,
> By God.

Both stanzas of Mr. I.'s poetic effort are correct, but *gam* refers not only to seamen's conversations on the water but is also a synonym for *pod* (and, in slanguage, for *leg*). When looking up the word, I discovered that it can also be used as a verb. *Webster's Third* quotes A.B.C. Whipple: "Whalers *gammed* in midocean on a hot tropical day." Would it be correct to say that they had a *gam* session?

In July 1988 the people in charge of layouts for the *Times* made a grievous goof: They printed the wrong answer for the previous day's puzzle. That error generated a spate of letters. Among them was the following bit of delicious doggerel from a Melville, New York, woman:

> 'Twas July the fifteenth in '88.
> How could I ever forget that date?

I turned to a page in section C
Of *The New York Times,* just delivered to me,
To do the day's crossword and check the solution
Of July 14th's puzzle sans circumvolution.
But something's awry, an event unforseen,
July 15's crossword, dated 7/16!
The "previous puzzle's solution" not right?
How could I recover from such an affright?
Then I thought of the headlines, the world's disarray.
In its proper perspective this goof was O.K.
In fourteen letters, the crossword world's king.
Eugene T. Maleska, your praises we sing!

The writer of those rhymes appended a letter in which she told me that the puzzles had been her salvation during recovery from brain surgery.

It often seems that the solvers are trying to outdo one another in cleverness. I once received a delightful New Year's present from K.L.H. of New York City. It was preceded by an interesting explanatory letter.

Dear Mr. Maleska:

First of all, let me say that, as far as I'm concerned, a morning without the *Times* crossword puzzle is like a morning without coffee! My brain absolutely refuses to turn to its job of writing ad copy until the puzzle is done, in pen, with as few mistakes as possible. And I'm convinced that Sunday would not be a legitimate part of the week without the Sunday puzzle!

So much for my idiosyncrasies. The reason I'm writing to you is that your puzzles have presented me with a problem, and I thought you might enjoy the solution. I've always known that there were nine Greek Muses, but I never knew who they were or what they mused about. So I did a bit of research, and, voilà! Rather than rest on my newly acquired knowledge, I incorporated it into my annual New Year's Poem (for family and friends, English teachers and puzzle fanatics all) and made it a test to see who could correctly pronounce all nine Muses using rhyme and scansion as a guide.

It was quite a bit of fun, from research to writing to hearing people stumble over Terpsichore, Erato and Thalia!

In appreciation of many happy mornings of puzzlement, I'm

passing along my "Amusing Little Ditty." I hope it gives you a few New Year's chuckles!

Happy Holidays!

And now, I proudly present Mr. H.'s poem. Note how the rhythm is reminiscent of Clement Moore's famous Christmas verse.

AN AMUSING LITTLE DITTY

It was late in December, a magical time,
When everyone's spirits were soaring.
I was trying to pencil a holiday rhyme;
The results, sad to say, were deploring.
But as midnight was tolling, a Greek delegation
(Nine elegant ladies Pierian)
Descended upon me with some agitation!
My poems, they said, were barbarian!
"Yet, you're mortal," they said as I cowered in fright,
"And you're prone to creative abysses.
"So we've come from Olympus, our aim to enlighten.
"You know that a myth never misses!"
"There's comedy lacking, I think," said Thalia.
For Clio, historic exotica.
"By Zeus! By Apollo! That's not the idea!"
Said Erato, touting erotica.
Two of the Muses ignored my distress
And created a bit of a stir.
Euterpe refused us her music unless
Polyhymnia's hymns could be hers.
Calliope's epical highs were inspiring.
Urania's high was astronomy.
Terpsichore's dancing was simply too tiring;
I sagged like the tragic Melpomene.
It was long after midnight (in fact, it was dawn)
When they finally shimmered away.
So, inspired and be-Mused, I collapsed with a yawn . . .
And a pencil . . . and something to say!
Now the rhyme is on paper. I hope it amuses!
If not, there is one consolation.
'82 is the year that we'll know all the Muses
For each damned Maleska creation!

Isn't that a beauty? I loved the punny title. It "inspired" me to make this comment about Line 12: "A myth is as good as a smile."

On the subject of mythology, I must tell you once again about one of the worst errors that I have made in all of my years as a crossword puzzle editor.

Will Weng, my predecessor at the *Times*, had given me two pieces of advice with regard to maintaining accuracy:

1. Never work late at night.
2. Never trust your memory.

Unfortunately, I disregarded both precepts upon a winter midnight not so clear. TRAFALGAR SQUARE was the fifteen-letter entry in a daily puzzle by Herb Risteen. Like the cat in the old rhyme, I'd been to London—not once but twice. With a yawn, I crossed off Mr. Risteen's generalized clue and zeroed in with "Where to see Eros."

The Gotcha crowd had a heyday with that blooper. Inundated by scores of letters, I resorted to a collective communication.

Dear Friends,

Oops! Mea culpa! Sorry! Etc., etc. My egregious error on January 11 has engendered so many letters that I have resorted to this general reply.

Yes, you are right. Eros is in London's Piccadilly Circus and *not* in Trafalgar Square.

Among the letters were at least two sets of verses. E.R. wrote:

> Your puzzle did not little to irk us—
> If Eros dwelleth anywhere,
> It is in Piccadilly Circus
> And hardly in Trafalgar Square.

From A.G.L. came the following:

> Though you may find the notion silly,
> Eros' cirque is Piccadilly.
> Most Londoners are quite unaware
> That Nelson owns Trafalgar Square.

Some letters were triumphant, others were gleeful, and a few had an angry tone. Several solvers, opining that I am infallible, asked if Nelson and Eros had recently been relocated. One or two, suspecting trickery, wondered if Eros could be viewed from Nelson's perch.

At any rate, I am now enrolling you in my exclusive Gotcha Club. Congratulations!

Pax, amor et felicitas

When fans tell me that the puzzles have expanded their knowledge, I am pleased. But when they tell me in rhyme I'm superdelighted. Here's an example of well-formed verse. The author is F.F.S. of Levittown, New York.

Doing the crossword puzzle of April 16
in *The New York Times Magazine,*
I discovered that an OUNCE
is not only a UNIT OF WEIGHT;
it is also a cat that can pounce
and serious havoc create
to the dismay of many a shepherd,
for a pounce ounce is a SNOW LEOPARD.

If brevity is the soul of wit, then J.S. of Brooklyn, New York, wins the prize for sapience. He (or she) wrote:

You deserve to get a lot of flaq
About the crossword spelling of Irak.

With regard to concise criticism, here's an amusing anecdote. In 1990, I published "Upward Bound" by John Russell. As the title hinted, the trick was to spell the vertical entries backward. In disgust, an Israeli fan sent the message that follows on page 67:

```
       s
       k
       n
       i
       t
       s

       t
       I
```

PS: I spent 30 *shekel* ($15) every Tuesday to buy the previous Sunday *Times*. This week I feel it was a total waste. The least you might do is airmail me a free copy . . . *Shalom*.

Coming back to verses about crosswordese, here's another excellent one whose author originally wrote it for a creative writing class. What's really special about this poem is that the translation also rhymes.

MATERNAL LEXICON

Mater, amah, doting esne
In eria's seine has love enmeshed thee.
Shepherd abroad your brood of tyros
Offspring of the dart of Eros.
Take them now to see the raree;
Now to seek aquila's aerie.
In summer purling ria greet;
In winter scale snowcapped arete.
Soiled fire visages you lave
Contused genu bind to save.
Stave off the feral Philistine,
For their angst be anodyne.
When they at last, in life's aurora
Embark alone to the agora
Image ana from days of yore
Escudo be against dolor.

TRANSLATION

Mother, nurse and loving slave
Caught by love in silken net

Guide your children, the beginners
Whom Cupid's arrow did beget.
Take them to the street show now;
Now to find the eagle's nest.
In summer play in the rippling river;
In winter on snowy mountain crest.
Wash their dirty, laughing faces.
Bandage bruised and bleeding knee.
Keep off wild and vicious foe,
To anxious fears a soother be.
When daybreak of their manhood comes
And they leave for the market place
Photo albums of yesterday
Shield you from sorrow's lonely face.

One of my favorite people is Hope Atkinson of South Dartmouth, Massachusetts. Each year, ever since 1982, Hope conducts a cozy crossword puzzle contest for the benefit of her local library. I supply the puzzles and sometimes attend as the guest speaker.

Hope likes all kinds of word games. Recently she called my attention to the game of heteronyms. In case you need an explanation, a heteronym is a word spelled the same as another but having a different sound and meaning. The object of the game is to compose sentences that contain such words. Here are some examples.

"*Lead* me to that mine full of *lead*," declared the prospector.
When people go on *tears*, their sprees may end in *tears*.
After you *wind* up a top, you should throw it away from the *wind*.

The criteria for judging the winner of the game are twofold:

1. The person who comes up with the most sentences.
2. The one who composes a sentence considered to be best.

I never know what to expect next from my wild and crazy fanatics. Every February brings Valentines from some of the female solvers. The one that I like most is a rhymed message from Alice

S. of Ridgefield, Connecticut. When it arrived, I was pleased to note how its tone changed from sadistic to eulogistic—all because a few puzzles in a row had apparently been less difficult to solve.

A BELATED VALENTINE GREETING

violets are blue
roses are red
many's the sunday
i wished you were—
well—maybe not dead
but dropped on your head
or very sick in bed.
sundays were bad.
i was down and a-cross.
the many blank spaces
left me at a loss.
but two in a row
i've been able to complete
for me—absolutely an incredible feat.
you've obviously lost your touch
but *thank you so much.*

Speaking of reaction to puzzles on a *personal* basis, B.W. of Riverside, Connecticut, comes to mind. In response to a Sunday puzzle, he submitted the following:

Clue: Puzzle editor seeking internal irrigation
Answer: EUGLESKA.

The puzzle that triggered Mr. W.'s humor was "Missing Links" by Peter Swift. Here are some examples of Swiftian high jinks:

Clue	*Answer*
Mime in search of a shade tree?	MARCARCEAU
Actress lacking applause?	JUDITERSON
Violinist coinless in a phone booth?	YEHNUHIN
Admiral longing for a pet sea bird?	CHESIMITZ
Mystery writer without clues?	MICPILLANE
Novelist not dealt winning cards?	WALLTEGNER

What are the *missing links*? ELM, HAND, DIME, TERN, KEYS, ACES.

• • •

Because of Shakespeare's account of the assassination of Caesar on March 15, many people know that the date is called the Ides of March. Therefore, some individuals may assume that the Ides fall on the fifteenth of every month. Not so. In a 1986 puzzle by A.J. Santora, IDES was defined as "Nov. 13, e.g."

Mrs. C.M.K. of Melvin Village, New Hampshire, was not fooled. She sent the following message:

> In March, July, October, May
> The Ides are on the fifteenth day,
> The Nones the seventh; all else besides
> Have two days less for Nones and Ides.

Alice Parker Tallmadge, the professor of Latin and Greek at Cedar Crest College, Allentown, Pennsylvania, in the 30's and 40's, insisted we memorize that verse. Mrs. Tallmadge was an exciting teacher; even her tests were fun. It is too bad you and Mr. Santora could not have attended her classes. Cedar Crest is a women's college.

If you're a doubting Thomas, let me assure you that Mrs. Tallmadge's rhyming mnemonic is correct. Incidentally, *Ides* means "division" in Latin. Apparently the period at the middle of the month was a kind of dividing line for Romans.

Nones means "ninths." The date was the ninth day before the Ides, both days included. Thus, Nones fall on March 7, November 5, etc.

Another important Roman date was the first day of the month from which the days were counted back to the Ides. It was called Calends or Kalends. From it, we get our word *calendar*.

As I've intimated before, puzzle solvers are a *fan*-tastic group. Another example stems from a mistake I made when I erroneously defined *lisp* as "Talk like Elmer Fudd."

Novembew 23, 1982

Eugene Maweska, Editow
Puzzews Page
New Yowk Times Company
229 West 43 Stweet

New Yowk, New Yowk 10036

Deaw Mw. Maweska:

In aw my yeaws of doing the Sunday *Times* cwosswowd puz-zews, I have not been upset by any cwues the way I was wast week (Novembew 21, 1982).

This wettew may seem humowous to you, but as a speech pathowogist, I was howwified at the cwue fow 38 Down ("Talk like Fudd"). Ewmew Fudd does not *wisp*—Daffy duck wisps! Fudd *wawws* ("lalls"), as does Baba Wawa in Giwda Wadnew's impewsonation. In this pawticulaw disowdew of awticuwation, a "w" is substituted fow the sounds of aw ("r") and ew ("l").

Pwease watch this ewwow in the futuwe. If you need any fuwthew cwawification, pwease contact me.

> Vewy twuly youws,
> G.S., CCC-SP
> Cewtified Speech Pathowogist

Needless to say, I told my cowwespondent that I was sowwy.

Tom Swifties are punny sentences mocking the use of adverbs in the popular Tom Swift series of books by Edward Stratemeyer. Here are a few examples in which the adverb playfully mocks Tom's message:

"I never sent the package to the poor," said Tom *carelessly*.
"I won the cup," said Tom *lovingly*.
"It's an amulet," said Tom *charmingly*.

In 1986, a Tom Swifties crossword puzzle was published in the Sunday *Times*. A solver named H.H. sent me a handwritten letter objecting to the use of the adverb *cautiously* in one of the main entries involving "The Raven" by Edgar Allen Poe.

In reply I wrote:

> "Cautiously was wrong;
> It didn't belong," said Gene *Poe*tically.

Oh, yes, let me not forget that Mr. H. concluded his letter as follows: "P.S. Please excuse my penmanship. Mr. Typewriter went ka-blooey . . . he said explosively."

•   •   •

One of my most ingenious constructors is Dr. Ernst Theimer. One Sunday he really gave the fans an unusual challenge. At 60 Across, his crossword featured the motto of the Three Musketeers: "All for one and one for all." The puzzle was entitled "Taking 60 Across Literally."

The result was that the fans found themselves writing crazy words into the boxes. For example, if the clue for a five-letter word was "Tiny," the answer was SMONE instead of SMALL. And if the definition was "Lying face down," PRALL was substituted for PRONE.

J.S. of Great Neck, New York, was among the solvers who just couldn't resist giving Dr. Theimer a dose of his own medicine.

> Prall as all is to coneing up all's resources so that all can say "dall" after completing the Sunday puzzle, all was really unall after last week's choneenge. "Apponeing," I thought. "Allrous!"
>
> Finoney, all soneied forth and, alall, at all a.m., all was dall even soallr than all thought all would be.
>
> No longer apponeed or goneed, all felt quite enthroneed, especioney because all had exerted such an hallst effort and hadn't roneied any help.
>
> Every compallnt was infoneibly brilliant. I wish that the constructor could be clalld!

I relayed the hilarious letter to Dr. Theimer and he replied to Ms. S. as follows:

> Dr. Maleska had passed along one the nice complimentary letters on my Nov. 4 puzzle. Answering has kept me from being lallly but leaves no time to reply in kind. However, many thanks for the take-off, though if you will forgive a bit of nit-picking, *really unall* should have been *reoney undall*. (You see, I read it carefully.)

I'm a big fan of cryptic puzzles, such as those published by *The Times* of London. In January 1987 the large Sunday puzzle that I had edited contained the kind of word play that the British use. E.K. of Totowa, New Jersey, was wise to my game. She wrote:

Do I detect an effort on your part to wean us *Times* Puzzlers to the pun/anagram English-style puzzles? If so, I *do* hope you'll abandon your nefarious scheme! I *hate* the English puzzles; I *hated* yesterday's puzzle. Even now, when I've finished it, I don't understand some of the solutions . . . i.e., financier and retailer etc.

Please reconsider!

However, Ms. K's postscript is even more interesting.

PS: You may enjoy a story that's a favorite among my puzzling friends: a friend who always worked on the *Times* puzzle each Sunday afternoon, stopped to visit an acquaintance early on Sunday morning and happened to see that day's *Times* puzzle completed and lying on the coffee table. She didn't know that her acquaintance did the crosswords and was mightily impressed that the puzzle was completed—and so early on Sunday morning.

But she also saw that 1 Down was entered as:

$$J$$
$$R$$
$$W$$
$$E$$

—or something similar, and when she asked what JRWE spelled, her friend replied, "Oh I don't do the Downs; I just do the Acrosses!"

That anecdote reminds me of one concerning playwright George S. Kaufman. It's probably apocryphal but I think it's worth repeating.

The story goes that Mr. Kaufman boarded his commuter train every morning, opened his *New York Times*, pulled out his pen, and proceeded to solve the daily puzzle in less than a minute. Fellow passengers across the aisle were amazed. They knew Mr. K. was brilliant, but this feat with the puzzles seemed almost impossible. They longed to see if perhaps the playwright had made a mistake or two. But when the train arrived in New York City, he always folded the newspaper neatly under his arm and walked off with his nose in the air.

Ah, but one rainy day while George was adjusting his umbrella, he forgot to carry off his *Times*. Eagerly his fellow puzzle fans grabbed the newspaper and sought out the crossword. Every white box had been filled in with an *X!*

Solving crosswords can be an addiction, albeit less harmful than taking drugs or smoking. To some people, the puzzles can be as important as the security blanket is to Linus in "Peanuts."

I found out how serious the matter is when a strike closed down the *Times* for several weeks early in my tenure as editor of the puzzles. Mournful pleas poured in from fans who needed a fix. "Where can I find crosswords of the same caliber as yours?" was the typical appeal.

During another newspaper strike in Kansas City, the top brass was taught a lesson. They decided to publish limited editions omitting all the frills. But when readers discovered that the puzzle was missing, the editors were swamped by a flood of angry letters and phone calls. They surrendered immediately to the addicts, and peace was restored.

M.L.B. of Little Ferry, New Jersey, is an aficionado of the *Simon & Schuster Crossword Puzzle Book*. She avers that solving those puzzles has a salutary side effect.

> I find doing puzzles the perfect "diet aid." To help allay hunger pangs and keep me from nibbling goodies between meals, I do puzzles!

Addiction can be a problem for constructors, too. At one time in my life, I put together four large crosswords each month for the Dell puzzle magazines and also contributed regularly to the *Times* and other publications. While others were playing around on weekends, I was trying to make the Down words fit with the ones going Across.

But after reading the following article in the Newark *Star-Ledger* on March 29, 1988, I feel like a dilettante.

> Rjoger Bouckaert has spent almost four years compiling a 50,400-word giant crossword puzzle to smash his own world record—but he said yesterday he's fed up now. Bouckaert, a

56-year-old prison guard from Bruges, Belgium, has spent five hours a day and every single holiday since July 1984 looking up Dutch words for a puzzle 98.5 feet long and 21 inches high. "I'm absolutely fed up with it now," he said. Bouckaert completed his previous record puzzle of 25,283 words in February 1984. "But all the people I met asked me when I would start a new one. I took a few months off and started again," he said. The new crossword contains 26,053 vertical and 24,347 horizontal words.

When I was a young educator, the most fearsome group in the New York City school system was the Board of Examiners. That formidable body stood like Cerberus at the gates, gleefully (it seemed) turning away any pretenders who wished to teach in the Big Apple or rise to higher positions.

Candidates were confronted with a battery of hurdles including short-answer, essay, physical, oral, interview, and field tests. Failure in any one of the examinations meant elimination. Many candidates were immediately rejected because of the dreaded vocabulary test, which usually came first.

One of my fellow survivors of successive ordeals concocted by the Examiners is Mr. R. Like me, he gave some credit to crossword-solving for his ability to surmount the initial stumbling block.

Mr. R. got so absorbed in the lexiconic field that he wrote some verses on the subject. I think you'll enjoy this sample of his work.

TYRANNY OF WORDS

(An epoptic semasiologic diagnosis, followed to its logical conclusion, of any candidate for the high school English examination.)

> Trucidation, colophon,
> Subornation, gonfalon,
> Maceration, reliquary;
> Does crinigerous mean hairy?
> Ecumenical and sib,
> Words nobody can ad lib.
> Crepitate and crapulent,
> Crepuscular and flatulent;
> Is a martinet draconic?

Is a pasquinade sardonic?
Ferruginous, farraginous;
You can imagine us.
Missal, anchorite, and kine,
Mistral, sybarite, and tine;
If it's costive, it's not sleazy;
If it's ordure, then it's queasy.
Mendacity, mendicity,
Antiphonal lubricity.
Inspissated, imbricated,
Tessellated, marinated;
Venous, venal, venial, vernal,
Ebullition that's internal.

While we are still on the subject of words and meanings, K.A.P. of Satellite Beach, Florida, has sent out a witty list called "Medical Terminology for the Layman." The definitions should be good for what ails you.

Artery	The study of fine paintings
Barium	What you do when CPR fails
Cesarean section	A district in Rome
Colic	A sheep dog
Coma	A punctuation mark
Congenital	Friendly
Dilate	To live long
Fester	Quicker
G.I. series	Baseball games between teams of soldiers
Grippe	A suitcase
Hangnail	A coat hook
Medical staff	A doctor's cane
Minor operation	Coal digging
Morbid	A higher offer
Nitrate	Lower than the day rate
Node	Was aware of
Organic	Musical
Outpatient	A person who has fainted
Post-operative	A letter carrier
Protein	In favor of young people
Secretion	Hiding anything

Serology	Study of English knighthood
Tablet	A small table
Urine	Opposite of you're out
Varicose veins	Veins which are very close together

L.M.K. one of my loyal fans, popped up with her husband in Ron Alexander's "Metropolitan Diary" column in the *New York Times* on February 4, 1987.

They're not using cards, dice or boards for their at-home games in Fair Lawn, New Jersey, this winter. Not in the home of [J.] and [L.M.K.], anyway, where a new game was born on a recent night. It began when, after having viewed an episode of "Cagney and Lacey," Mrs. [K.] remarked to her husband, "Tyne Daly has an arresting face."

"And Madame Curie had a radiant face," her husband shot back. Millions of bucks have been made on such comebacks. The [K.'s] have come up with, among others, Diana Ross has a supreme face, Sally Ride has a cosmic face.

They call their game "About Face." Readers are invited to join in. The first prize may be a trip to Fair Lawn.

My contributions to the above are:

1. Jerry Stiller has a more quiescent face.
2. Anne Meara has a reflective face.

Some members of the so-called New Wave of puzzle constructors have criticized me and other older editors for references to silent screen stars and other people like Tokyo Rose, Harold Teen of comics, et al. They claim that it isn't fair to young solvers.

S.M. of Baltimore objects to their objections. Her letter to me concluded:

And if my kids, at 27 and 23, don't know about Rosie the Riveter, Pola Negri, and silent films, shame on them! Puzzles are sort of a continuum of our culture. Judging from the lousy writing in newspapers and books, they may soon be our only erudite link to the past.

• • •

Constructor Jeanette Brill of Lauderhill, Florida, has sent me "proof" that Leona Helmsley is an aficionado of crosswords. A newspaper article listed Mrs. Helmsley's account of her personal expenses. It included "a yearly membership to a crossword puzzle club—$21." Well, she has had a nice hobby to help her to while away the lonely hours in her cell.

The winner of the annual National Spelling Bee in 1990 correctly spelled *Fibranne,* which is a new trademark and is not listed in any dictionary published before 1988. Any youngster who previously misspelled that name for a fabric of spun rayon should claim a foul. I was rooting for the lad who had correctly reeled off, in sequence, the twelve letters of the word that means "the act of listening, either directly or through a stethoscope or other instrument, to sounds within the body as a method of diagnosis." The word is *auscultation.*

Once in a while, a fan asks that all foreign words be banned from the puzzles. Such requests are not only unrealistic but also narrow-minded. Let me get personal. In high school or college, I never studied French or German, but the appearance of words from those languages in puzzles has served as a spur for me to study both tongues at home and develop more than a mere acquaintance with Gallicicisms and Teutonicisms.

Sometimes we try to coordinate the publication of a puzzle with a noteworthy event like Irving Berlin's hundredth birthday or the bicentennial of Bastille Day in July 1989. But coincidences occasionally occur. More than a decade ago, a daily *Times* puzzle happened to contain the name of a scientist who had pioneered in the development of television. On the day when the crossword appeared, a drunken driver crashed into the scientist's car and killed him. A fan from New Jersey seriously asked if I had psychic powers!

More recently, R.L. of Hanover, New Hampshire, called my attention to a pleasant coincidence. In the third week of May

1990, a *New Yorker* magazine artist and I featured that fabulous bird called the roc. The cartoon showed a garrulous Arab pestering the occupant of the seat next to him. The Arab is saying, "Finding myself between a roc and a hard place . . ." My clue for the bird was "Sinbad's transportation."

On the subject of artwork, some solvers like to send me cartoons of themselves triumphantly yelling "Gotcha!" or shedding tears because of inability to complete a difficult puzzle.

I'll never forget the time I had the word *hanger* in a puzzle. I misread it as *hangar,* and the definition read: "Place for the Spruce Goose"—a neat reference to Howard Hughes' gigantic airplane. Several fans, including G.L.P. of Houston, sent me drawings of a plane being held up by a coat hanger.

Every year at least one message from a solver is embodied in a diagram that looks very much like an acrostic. The latest has come from M.G. of Scottsdale, Arizona.

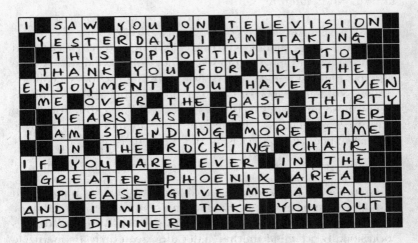

And now, let me close this chapter with some of the most creative and challenging material I have ever received in letters from a fan. What precipitated the correspondence was an invention of mine called Scanagrams. It consists of couplets in which one of the words is an anagram for another that must be filled in. Some examples follow on page 80.

CAUTION, HIAWATHA!

Your frail canoe may quickly tip
If you should take that *(ocean)* trip!

UNTIL THE FUR FLIES

A girl who wears a *(sable)* may
Attempt to look a bit blase.

BEWARE THE IDES

March has a certain *(charm)* about it,
Though Caesar's ghost will surely doubt it.

H.H. of Victoria in British Columbia enjoyed these and the seven other Scanagrams that followed in *A Pleasure in Words*. In his letter he described the delight that the book had brought to him and his wife. Then he said:

We have different ways of reading books like yours. My wife begins at the beginning and reads every word through to the end. I tend to dip in at random, picking out gems here and there. Though I think my method is more fun, it does mean that I miss things. Thus it was only the other day that I came across your little couplets called "Scanagrams," and went to work on them. They reminded me of a different sort of scan-agram which I first came across about forty years ago. An old friend of mine, a British cryptanalyst (now dead, I'm afraid) wrote a set of verses of which I'm enclosing copies—I think you'll enjoy them. In each verse, the blanks represent words which are all anagrams of one another. (Maybe I should call them "Blank Verses.") . . .

Once you guess a word from the context, the rest is not too difficult, but I think they're fun. To put you on your mettle I've enclosed the answers in a sealed envelope.

Good solving!

Here's the word game by Mr. H.'s late friend.

BLANK VERSES

by K.O.

Drinking Song

Come, landlord, fill the flowing *(post)*
Until the *(tops)* run over;
Tonight we *(stop)* upon this *(spot)*,
Tomorrow *(post)* to Dover.

Spanish Love

A *(grandee)* of Ciudad Rodrigo
(Enraged) his betrothed in Oswego.
To *(derange)* him she chucked
A *(grenade)* which he ducked,
But it *(angered)* her erstwhile amigo.

The Restless Lover

Dear lady, grant your *(slave)* his whim,
And let the next *(valse)* be with him.
The way to *(salve)* his burning heart
Is through this sweet and gentle art.
Rebuffed, he *(laves)* his hands of you,
To seek fresh *(vales)* and pastures new.

The following verses are my attempts to add to the literature of "blank verses."

The Seasons

When *(Eros)* stirs the blood in May,
And *(roes)* begin to prance,
(Though bears wake, *(sore)* from winter's stay,
Indifferent to romance),
Then we foresee the summer's *(rose)* unfold,
While nature mines the *(ores)* for autumn's gold.

The Play's the Thing

"Oh *(Deus)*!" cried Irving, "I fear
That *(Duse)* will refuse to appear;
For I've *(used)* my last cent,
And they've *(sued)* for the rent,
And the theatre *(dues)* are too dear."

Several weeks later, Mr. H. sent me another letter.

Since I wrote you last, I've been rooting around in my old papers trying to dig up some more of [K's] rhymes. I know there are several more, but so far I've only found the following one:

Winter Sports

St. Moritz, *caster* of a spell of sun,
Displays for us the tricky "*Cresta*" run,
Which *traces* icy curves to form a maze,
Where madmen fly on flimsy *crates* called sleighs.
(She *caters* not to him who counts the cost,
Whose heart *reacts* to fear lest life be lost.)
O thou who *racest* down the slope on skis,
Rounding the slalom poles with bended knees,
Carest thou not for instant forms of death.

CHAPTER 4

LEAPERS

Almost half the fan mail that I receive comes from a group that I call the Leapers. These are the cocksure people who grab their pens or rush to their typewriters to chide me for a mistake that I have not made. In other words, they leap before they look up the item in question.

An impetuous letter from an occasional misguided solver is to be expected, but I continue to be mystified by the multitude of erroneous accusations. Perhaps it's an American quirk to shoot from the hip or maybe it's human nature to assume that what one believes to be right must be correct. Oftentimes it's a case of believing there is only one answer.

Also, as has been explicated elsewhere in this book, people who own very old and outmoded dictionaries or who stubbornly hold on to what they learned in school fail to take into account the effects of folk usage. A case in point is a letter from D.T. of New York City. Not long ago she reminded me that *beside* should not be confused with *besides*. Her claim was valid once, but so many educated people have confused the two words that lexi-cographers have labeled them as interchangeable.

Perhaps the best way to deal with the letters from Leapers is to divide them into categories. Let's begin with the ones that relate to Geography.

Here's an example of how two places having the same name can cause a solver to leap to the typewriter. The clue in a puzzle read: "One of the Pennines," referring to the Pennine Alps. A.P.G. of California wrote:

> As I completed today's crossword puzzle in the *New York Times*, I was incredulous to see that clue 18 Across must read MATTERHORN. The Matterhorn is in the Swiss Alps, just outside Zermatt; I have climbed it and know it well. The Pennine Chain is the "backbone of England"; I know the Pennines well also, since I was born in the north of England. So how can the Matterhorn be a Pennine peak? Has Yorkshire annexed Swit-zerland? If so, your newspaper didn't print the news (not fit?).

S.F. of New York City is one of scores of fans who believe that you must travel westward to get to Los Angeles from Reno. Several years ago he wrote:

> Re: crossword puzzle, Sunday, January 25, 1987. 113D: Reno to LA direction SSE? That's the long way to get there!

The fact is that the shoreline in Southern California bends so far to the east that Los Angeles lies just a bit southeast of Reno— hence SSE. Skeptical readers should take a ruler and hold it perpendicularly from Reno to the south. You can win bets on this one!

Arguably, the following is not a geographical error, but it does involve a state in the U.S.A. My definition for IOWA was "Hawk-eye's home" with reference to the fact that Iowans are nicknamed Hawkeyes. A.P. of New Jersey is obviously a fan of the television show "M*A*S*H."

> I am writing to you concerning your crossword puzzle from 5-1-85. There was an error in your number 54 Down. Hawk-

eye's home is not Iowa, as you stated in your next day's answers, but rather, Crab Apple Cove, Maine. It is Radar O'Reilley who lives in Iowa.

I understand how difficult it must be to edit these puzzles and to check all answers, as it is difficult enough to do them!

Thank you for your time.

Here is one of those "we're both right" situations. In 1988 H.S.S. of Florida thought a mistake had occurred.

I do your puzzle in the Miami [newspaper] every day and today I found an error. 54 Down's clue is "Ill city." It works out to PERU, which is in Indiana; Cole Porter's birthplace is on a farm near *Peru.*

The truth is that there are two neighboring municipalities named Peru—one in Indiana, the other in Illinois. I wonder if the duplication causes headaches for the postmen and the residents.

In 1989 Bill Lutwiniak, one of my best constructors, had BOOMER STATE in a Sunday puzzle and defined it as "Nickname for Oklahoma." Once again, a host of Leapers took up the cudgels. They had inserted SOONER STATE, but the crossings had caused a snafu. I was forced to write a general letter.

Thanks for your interest in the puzzles. The correct answer to 67A was BOOMER STATE. Among other sources, you can find it in *Random House Dictionary—Second Edition.*

I guess you forgot that many of the states have more than one nickname. *Boomer* evolved because of the land *boom* opened up by Congress. As for *Sooner,* that nickname came about because the settlers got there "fastest with the mostest"—i.e., sooner than others.

And now let's turn to History and Current Events.

In 1987, C.B. of New York was sure he had caught me in an error.

I would like to point out an error in one of your clues in the puzzle of Sept. 17th. I am referring to 50 Across, ("Virginia of Va."). The answer came out to DARE. If the clue had been "Virginia of N.C.," it would have been correct. Virginia Dare was born to one of the English settlers that landed on Roanoke Island between Pamlico Sound and Albemarle Sound in 1584. Present day Nags Head is closest to Roanoke Island. In 1587, the English ship returned to Roanoke Island, but no one could be found. The settlers are referred to as the "Lost Colony." It is thought they may have been massacred by the Indians. I hope my information has been helpful.

Most of Mr. B.'s information is correct but he forgot that Virginia Dare was born in 1587 when Virginia was a colony— not a state.

Several years ago, when CHARTA appeared in a daily puzzle, the clue read "Magna _____." B.L. of New London, Connecticut, objected.

Sheesh! Even the crossword puzzles are screwed up! Back in Brooklyn we learned it was Magna Carta . . . not charter or charta . . .

Most reliable reference books list both spellings. *Webster's Second* places *charta* first.

O.L. of New York thought my arithmetic was faulty. Here's his letter.

About a week ago, the *New York Times* crossword puzzle called for a three-letter word representing the fifth word of the Gettysburg Address. The following day the answer to that puzzle showed the word as *ago*. The Gettysburg Address starts as follows, "Four score and seven years ago." As you will note, the fifth word is *years* and the sixth word is *ago*.

If O.L. had gone to his dictionary instead of his typewriter, he would have discovered that *fourscore* is one word—not two.

• • •

Next, let's direct our attention to the Leapers in the area of Flora and Fauna.

Back in 1983, a puzzle by Mary Virginia Orna defined ELM as "Jersey or Guernsey." N.J.R. of New Jersey demurred.

> A Jersey or a Guernsey is a *cow* or perhaps a *dam*. Webster says an *elm* is a tree. Where does Orna get to call a Jersey or Guernsey an ELM? And if her rationale is that elm trees grow on the Channel Islands—that's an unfair definition.

Yes, it was a tricky clue, but Mary Virginia was not the culprit. Instead it was Maleska the Malevolent, whose sources were *Webster's Second* and *Webster's Third*. It should be noted that the Jersey elm and the Guernsey elm are one and the same.

What I call "The Panda Problem" erupted in 1988 when the clue for PANDA was "Asian carnivore." About a dozen Leapers stormed the gates. The most thoughtful among them was M.W. of New York City. Part of his letter reads:

> I was under the impression that *pandas* only ate bamboo shoots and not the flesh of other animals. . . .
> My own experience with *pandas* comes from a visit to the Bronx Zoo where I was told *pandas* were no more interested in meat eating than they were in taking a bite out of a large red apple offered to them by Mayor Koch.

The confusion arose partly because there are two pandas. One of them is not cute at all and is not familiar to most Americans. It looks somewhat like a cross between a fox and a raccoon and is actually related to the latter. This bushy-tailed, carnivorous mammal lives in the Himalayan heights.

The so-called giant panda of China is the one that looks like a black-and-white bear. It, too, is carnivorous but normally feeds on bamboo.

Solvers of the Simon & Schuster puzzles that John Samson and I have been editing for many years usually refrain from leaping

or squawking. H.F. of Little Neck, New York, is a rara avis. He
sent us an objection in 1987.

> Re Series 142—Puzzle 32, 86 Down, "Scoters" = COOTS????
> *Coot*—a wading bird of the order "Gruiformes"
> *Scoter*—a waterfowl of the order "Anseriformes"
> True, they are both birds—but then cats and dogs are both
> four-footed mammals. Given "cat" would you reply with "dog"?

Our source was *Webster's Second* or *Webster's Third*. Here's what
Webster's Second says under *scoter:* "The species, usually called
Coots in America, but not to be confounded with the true coots
(genus Fulica) have the plumage chiefly black in the adult
male. . . ."
Once again, the clue was correct but the fan couldn't really be
blamed for questioning it.

From San Francisco came a letter written by A.H.D.

> A week ago this past Sunday your weekly torture defined a
> sea bird as a STORMY PETREL. A correct answer apparently
> should have been "storm petrel." A "stormy petrel" is a guy
> fond of strife, according to big Webster. I know the latter to
> be true also by way of the sports pages. The temperamental
> bad boys are always labeled "stormy petrels."
> Let me hear from you. In the meantime, thanks for all the
> fun you have provided over many years.

All my dictionaries declare that the long-winged sea bird is
called by either name. *Webster's Second* adds that a *stormy petrel* is
"figuratively, one fond of strife; a harbinger of trouble—from
the belief that the petrel is active before a storm."
How interesting! But even more fascinating is the fact that
New World, Third omits any reference to people. Perhaps that
expression for belligerent or ominous people has become ob-
solete. If so, more's the pity. Come on, you sports writers! Think
of all those *stormy petrels* high-sticking one another in the N.H.L.

In 1986 June G. (address unknown) took issue with an entry
and clue in a daily puzzle: to wit, AUSTRALIAN BEARS defined as
"Koalas."

No offense to you, Mr. Maleska, but Koalas are *not* bears, they are marsupials—(I know, you didn't make up the puzzle) and there are no Canadien geese—they are Canada geese—and Dashhounds (as heard very often) are really *Dachshunds* (*Docks*———).

Heaven help our school children!

First of all, the item and the definition are taken directly from *Webster's Second* and *Webster's Third*. Even though those cute little animals are marsupials, in folk usage they are Australian bears.

Miss G.'s reference to Canada geese is an *obiter dictum*: we have never used "Canadian (or Canadien!) geese" in a puzzle. Along with the schoolchildren, we thank her for her thoughts on dachshunds, and again we plead not guilty.

Ask any urban dweller to define *mast* and you'll probably be told that it's a pole on a schooner, or something like that. But a farmer may give a different reply. At any rate, R.S. (address unknown) is probably a city slicker.

You screwed up on this one. No way you'll convince me that "food for hogs" (55 Down) is MAST. It should be *mash*. Whatsa matta you gettin old? *Gotcha!*

We're all getting older, R.S., and in the process we're supposed to get wiser. As an urbanite myself, I recently learned that *mast* is a collective noun for *nuts*. Farmers feed acorns, beechnuts, chestnuts, etc. to their hogs.

In 1989, a seemingly learned letter from J.B.A. gave me a scare.

I believe there is an error in the crossword puzzle which appeared in the magazine section of Sunday, January 29th.

The clue for 49 Across is "asps," with the appropriate response, as per your puzzle, VIPERS. Asps are not vipers; they are elapids, the same general grouping of snakes in which cobras belong. Save for the fact that they are both snakes and poisonous, asps and vipers have little in common. To lump them in the same category is inappropriate. To my mind it would be as if *coyote* and *wolf* were used interchangeably simply because both belong to the genus *Canis*.

Was I wrong? I rushed to my dictionaries. Whew! *Webster's Third* averred that an asp was "any venomous snake." But my favorite vindication came from *New World, Third:* "any of several small, poisonous snakes of Africa, Arabia and Europe, as the horned viper, common European viper, or Egyptian cobra."

A lecture was given to me in 1987 when I described IOS as "certain butterflies." My "professor" was a former Gotcha Club member from Kingsborough Community College in Brooklyn.

> *Ios* refers not to butterflies, but rather to a group of moths belonging to the genus *Io*.
> Although butterflies and moths form a closely related group of insects (both belong to the order Lepidoptera), there are differences between them. For the most part (there are exceptions), butterflies are active during the day while moths are largely nocturnal. When butterflies come to rest, they fold their wings together so that they stand in a plane more or less vertically of the body. Moths, on the other hand, rest with the wings flattened like a roof over the body. Finally, the antennae of butterflies are simple, filament-like structures with a knob at the end, while moth antennae lack the knob and have a feathering appearance.

When I read the above letter I thought of the little girl whose book report announced that the pages contained more information about penguins than she cared to know. In any case, my source was *Webster's Second*.

However, here's a late bulletin. *New World, Third* does not list the Io butterfly but does include the Io moth!

The above "Who's right?" problem reminds me of a letter I received in 1984 from M.R. of the New York Zoological Society. In a daily puzzle, I defined APE as "a gelada." She wrote: "A Gelada is a baboon, which is an Old World Monkey. . . ." Her letter humorously concluded: "For your error, *Homo sapien,* I banish thee to the Audubon Penal Colony."

Is a baboon an ape or a monkey? *Webster's Second* and *Webster's Third* vote for the former, but *New World, Third* takes a shine toward the monkey. Dear reader, you're invited to cast your ballot.

• • •

Let's move on to Science and Arithmetic.

On a Saturday in 1989, while in quest of an unusual clue for SWEET, I finally decided upon "containing aspartame." That substance is listed in *Random House, Second* and *New World, Third*, but it does not appear in the dictionaries at the disposal of W.G.S. of New York City.

> 48-Across in today's Crossword should not give "aspartame" as the clue; it appears to be unknown to Webster and other standard dictionaries of the English language. Hawley's *Condensed Chemical Dictionary* (10th ed.) says it is a trademark for a synthetic sweetener produced by Searle. Be this as it may, I did not know that *sweet* is a noun!

Mr. S.'s letter taught me something. Apparently, like several other products, *aspartame* has made the jump from being a mere trademark to becoming part of our language. The definition in *New World, Third* reads partially: "an artificial low-calorie sweetener, . . . about 200 times sweeter than sucrose, used in the manufacture of soft drinks, packaged cereals, etc."

In 1984, R.S.G. of Baldwin Harbor, New York, did some stargazing and got confused.

> There appears to be an error in the Sunday Crossword puzzle of Feb. 5, 1984.
>
> The clue for 64 Across is "Bright star in Cygnus." The puzzle lists the answer as DENEB. I thought the brightest star in Cygnus was Sadr and that Deneb was the brightest star in Aquila.
>
> My curiosity is aroused! Please be so kind as to let me know if I am right. Thank you.

Mr. G. had a right to become bewildered. According to *Webster's Second* there are seven stars named Deneb! Two of them are in Aquila and one is in Cygnus. Sadr is also in Cygnus, but it lacks the luster of Deneb.

Let me quote *New World, Third* re *Deneb:* "A supergiant star, the brightest star in the constellation Cygnus, with a magnitude of 1.25."

For those who are curious about the meanings of the above names, this time my source is *Webster's Second*.

Aquila	Eagle (from Latin)
Cygnus	Swan (from Greek)
Deneb	Tail of the hen (from Arabian)
Sadr	Breast of the hen (from Arabian)

(Note that all four have reference to winged creatures.)

Finally, I have a scenario in mind. On a starry night in Arabia, seven astronomers are pointing upward to seven different celestial spots and each is proclaiming, "That's Deneb!"

D.K. of Rome, New York, sent me the following "Breezy" missive in 1988:

Today's (Sunday) puzzle contains a "boo-boo." Number 56 Down's clue asks for "Fresh ____ (8 on the Beaufort Scale)." Well enough, but my trusty reference book H.M. Bau's *The Master Crossword Puzzle Dict.* lists Sir Francis Beaufort's scale as:

8	moderate gale
11	*fresh gale*

Is this an error on your part? The rest of the puzzle was good and interesting—keep up the good work.

Personally, I wonder how "trusty" Ms. K.'s reference book is; I've never heard of it. At any rate, the *Columbia Encyclopedia* and *New World, Third* are among my many reputable sources. Here's the scale.

Beaufort Number	Description	Wind speed: km/h (mph)
0	Calm	0–1
1	Light air	2–5 (1–3)
2	Light breeze	6–11 (4–7)
3	Gentle breeze	12–19 (8–12)
4	Moderate breeze	20–28 (13–18)
5	Fresh breeze	29–38 (19–24)

6	Strong breeze	39–49 (25–31)
7	Moderate gale	50–61 (32–38)
8	Fresh gale	62–74 (39–46)
9	Strong gale	75–88 (47–54)
10	Whole gale	89–102 (55–63)
11	Storm	103–117 (64–72)
12–17	Hurricane	above 117 (above 72)

P.S. of Trenton, New Jersey, communicated as follows:

In the Crossword of November 29, the correct answer to Number 10, Down, is *daylight saving*, not DAYLIGHT SAVINGS.

A possible clue for *daylight savings* would be money deposited in the bank between sunrise and sunset.

About two years ago, Russell Baker wrote an amusing column on the daylight savings problem, which you might enjoy.

As is so often the case, folk usage has prevailed! So many literate citizens of the U.S.A. have added a final *s* to *saving* that the editors of new dictionaries such as *Random House, Second* and *New World, Third* have grudgingly acquiesced. I wonder how Mr. Baker is taking this blow.

Most Leapers are gleeful but pleasant and courteous. A few, however, are arrogant and abusive. E.S.D. of New York City belongs in the second category. Witness this letter.

In the ridiculous crossword of Sat. Feb. 21, words and definitions occur that are *not* in common usage—but even worse, the Nobel physics winner in 1911 was not WIEN, but *Wein,* thus making the entire comedy a nonsense.

Both *Webster's Biographical Dictionary* and the *World Almanac* state that the Nobelist's name is *Wien.* Incidentally, that spelling is also the German name for Vienna.

Early in 1990, a daily puzzle carried the word PHOT and defined it as a "Unit of illumination." W.M. of Santa Monica, California, didn't exactly accuse me of coining the word, but he did express disbelief because he had worked as an electrician all his adult life but had never heard of phots. When I gave him my sources, he sent me a second letter revealing his sense of humor.

> Thanks for the reply to my note re *phot*. Just shows, despite years of experience, how wrong one can be. The good news is, my partner (in the lighting business) is winning all sorts of bar bets among our colleagues using *phot*. So far we have not lost— except our success is taking a toll on our health.
> Thanks for supplying so much entertainment.

Possible conversation between W.M. and a colleague at the bar:

> W.   What's a phot?
> C.   What's a what?
> W.   No, that's a unit of electrical power. Now what's a phot?
> C.   You're an old one!

As a change of pace, let's turn to such subjects as Movies, Celebrities, and Proper Names. We'll start with a leap taken by K.U., Jr., of Fairfax, Virginia.

> Yesterday's crossword puzzle had a clue which appears to have been in error—the character ASTA was a *wire-haired* terrier, not a *fox* terrier—Maybe it was the *Fatman's* dog, rather than that of the *Thinman!!*

My source for Asta's breed is Halliwell's *Filmgoer's Companion*. In any case, Mr. U. forgot that *fox terrier* is synonymous with *wire-haired terrier*.

It should also be noted that the clue did not refer to the Thin Man. In some of my rivals' puzzles, Asta is erroneously called "The Thin Man's dog."

M.L. of Syracuse, New York, had a hard time trying to fit a four-letter name into five boxes in a 1989 puzzle.

> I will not say "gotcha" this time because I am not certain about an answer in today's puzzle.

Clue 46 Down reads "Jack ____ memorable actor."

The answer appears to be Jack PAAR. The Jack Paar I know is a radio announcer and T.V. host.

Please grade this as a "think-I-gotcha!" as they say in the Big Apple.

My sympathy went out to the solvers who chose *Oakie* as their answer. The proper one was LARUE. Remember him?

R.L.L. caught me when I erroneously attributed the novel *Brass* to Frank Norris instead of to its actual author, Charles Norris. A month later R.L.L. sought to correct me again.

Thank you for your recent reply regarding my correction on the Norris novel.

I noted another inaccuracy (I think) in yesterday's puzzle. Item 20 Across: Part of Presley's signature—if *Presley* referred to Elvis Aaron Presley. "The King's" middle name was spelled with two *A*'s—the traditional spelling—and is listed as such in Priscilla Beaulieu Presley's book, *Elvis and Me,* published by G. P. Putnam's Sons.

Because there was so much confusion concerning Presley's middle name, I wrote to the people at Graceland and received a gracious reply. It seems that the singer was baptized Elvis *Aaron* Presley but throughout his life he spelled the middle name *Aron*.

Puzzle constructors and editors are grateful for Elvis's alteration. Previously, our principal clue for *Aron* had been "Steinbeck character in *East of Eden.*"

D.B., M.L., and J.R. of Stormville, New York, took a triple trip when they leaped in 1989. Here's their letter.

We think you have a three-T-shirt error (there are three of us in the club) in today's puzzle. In 51 Down, "Conrad or Anne of films." Conrad is O.K. Nagel is right. But Anne's last name is Neagle. (We think.) No, we're sure. Inasmuch as we are the only ones who will have spotted this egregious error, three T-shirts are a small price to pay for our silence.

Ms. Neagle's first name was *Anna*. Admittedly, Anne Nagel was not a major movie star, but the Stormville trio were not entitled to a certificate. As for T-shirts, maybe I'll use that idea when I run out of certificates.

B.K. of Wheaton, Maryland, got mixed up concerning Irving Berlin's real first name at birth.

> I'm afraid there was a "false clue" in today's crossword puzzle.
> Evidently, 48 Down needed the word ISRAEL, but the clue sought Irving Berlin's name which was *Isidore* Baline. This made the puzzle a little more difficult—and perhaps a wee bit more enjoyable.

I don't know where B.K. found his *Isidore* but my sources are the *Cyclopedia of Names* and the *Book of Who*. Both state that Irving Berlin was born Israel Baline.

In February 1989 my clue for LENO was "Comedian from New Rochelle." H.T. wrote: "Sorry, Jay comes from Andover, MA."

Mr. T. couldn't be blamed for his misunderstanding because Leno's family moved to the Bay State shortly after he was born in New Rochelle. Reference books always give the place of birth as a person's home even though the individual lived there only briefly. Thus, Audrey Meadows is from China and Johnny Carson is from Iowa.

Occasionally, a puzzle will feature puns on names—especially the surnames of celebrities. Whenever such attempts at humor are used, or other forms of trickery are employed, a question mark is appended to the clue. Thus, in 1989 the definition for a nine-letter word in a punny puzzle was "Hot actress of yore?"

H.L. of Louisville, Kentucky, either was unaware of our code or failed to notice the question mark.

> Hey, you fudged on yesterday's crossword. All of us old fogies know that *Sarah Bernhardt* was spelled with an *e* and not with a *u*. I can even quote the *Columbia Encyclopedia*.

• • •

John Hancock's signature on the Declaration of Independence was so large and bold that his name became colloquially equated with any individual's autograph.

So far so good; one's signature is one's John Hancock. But wait a second! It's also one's John Henry, according to sources like *New World, Third.* As the reader may know, the other J.H. was a folklore hero who died after a contest in which he pitted his strength against the power of a steam drill.

How did Mr. Henry's name become associated with autographs? One theory is that a lot of folks merely opted for the shorter surname.

What's the relevance to puzzles? Well, in 1987 the folk hero caused G.G. of New York City to become a Leaper.

> I believe I have detected an error in today's *New York Times* crossword puzzle. Surely the clue for 47 Down (SIGNS) should be "Puts one's John *Hancock* on" rather than "John *Henry*."
>
> Yours for accuracy,

M.P. of Peekskill, New York, thought he had caught me napping in 1989. He wrote:

> In the puzzle of September 30, the definition for 47 Down was incorrect. The answer was ENOLA, which was the name of Col. Tibbets's hometown in Pennsylvania; the definition called for his mother's name, which was Gay. I am familiar with the story of the *Enola Gay,* as are so many of us who lived through WW II.

My sources state that the B-29 which dropped the atomic bomb on Hiroshima was named for Colonel Tibbets's mother, Enola Gay Haggard.

But maybe there's a connection with M.P.'s assertion. Enola is a town near Harrisburg, Pennsylvania. Is it possible that the colonel's mother was named for that place? Any reader with inside information is welcome to come forth.

A daily puzzle in 1987 carried the word PAISA and the clue was "Rossellini classic: 1946." *Paisa* was the original Italian title of the movie, but Dan C. apparently was familiar with only its English appellation—*Paisan*. He sent a clever note.

> Rossellini's PAISA certainly was a classic—I liked it even better than I did *Open Cit* or *Strombol*.

M.G.B. of Hartsdale, New York, doesn't really belong to the impetuous crowd of fans. Instead M.G.B. is a person with an inquiring mind and a scintillating style of writing.

> I am really stumped. I was delighted when I read your clue for 61 Across in today's crossword puzzle. "Felix Adler, e.g." Easy. Educator, philosopher, social reformer. Oops. Only five letters. Imagine my surprise when I discovered that the five letters were *c-l-o-w-n*. I called the American Ethical Union. Did our Felix Adler have a double life? Did he wear baggy pants and floppy shoes and a big red nose when he wasn't being a professor at Cornell University or Columbia College? "No," said the A.E.U., "Our Felix Adler was too busy writing books and founding the Ethical Culture movement. There must be another Felix Adler." I checked the *Encyclopedia Brittanica*. Only one Felix Adler. No famous clown. The library was next. Nothing. I've read that our Felix Adler had a great sense of humor and loved word games and puns, but "clown"? No, the man who founded the Workingman's School and served on the Tenement House Commission has a namesake, and I must know more about him. Was he a contemporary of Emmett Kelly and Lou Jacobs? What circus was he with? What was his specialty? *Why don't I know about him?*
>
> Please, Mr. Maleska, tell me about this man. I can't bear that everyone in New York read "Felix Adler, e.g." and knew about your clown and I only know about Felix Adler, the Humanist and humanitarian.

My source for the Felix Adler who cavorted in P. T. Barnum's rings is *Pictorial History of the American Circus* by John and Alice Durant. The authors call him "King of Clowns" and add that he was noted for his mirth-provoking antics with his pet pig.

It does make one wonder how the founder of the Ethical Culture movement felt when he discovered that a clown was his "nominal" clone.

Margaret Farrar's decision not to indicate the number of words in an entry was a good one, and I adhere to it religiously. But the practice can lead to misunderstandings.

An instance of confusion arose when the clue was "Actor Carroll: 1982–1972" and the answer occupied four boxes.

C.L. of New York City did not perceive that the answer was the actor's first name plus his middle initial. Here's her note.

> I may be wrong but I don't believe Mr. Carroll's first name is spelled LEOG as seems the case in last Sunday's Crossword. Is it?

And now we turn to Clothes and Fabrics. A few years ago Lola C. of New York City objected when I defined A-LINE as "Type of skirt." She maintained that the style applies only to dresses.

I took the case to the *Times* fashion editors and received a not-guilty verdict.

Recently, a solver wrote as follows:

> At long last I believe I have caught you in an error. The puzzle for Wed., October 29, 1986, contains: 36 Across—"Sheer fabric"; for which the answer is TOILE.
>
> Please be advised a *toile* is not a sheer fabric, but a printed one, either Oriental or Early American patterns. What you meant is *tulle*.

I quote *New World, Third* under *toile*—"a sheer linen or cotton fabric." As for *tulle,* that dictionary says: "a thin, fine netting of silk, rayon, nylon, etc. used as for veils and scarves."

A storm of letters in the clothes department arrived when TREWS appeared in a Sunday puzzle by Kay Sullivan. After consulting *Webster's Third*, I defined the entry as "What a Scotsman wears under his kilt."

S.H. of New York City led the legion of demurrers. She was so upset that she chose to go over my head and send her objection to the Letters to the Editor staff.

As a British addict of the Sunday *New York Times* Crossword Puzzle, there have been times when I haven't found Mr. Maleska to be completely fair in his spelling of certain words but have enjoyed them nonetheless. However, I take offense at the answer to 101 Down (Jan. 14)—What a Scot wears under his kilt. If you ask this question of a Scot, he will tell you, "Sir, nothing is worn, it's all in perfect working condition." The answer TREWS is the abbreviation for trousers—which is the British word for pants—which is the British word for underwear—which no true Scot would be seen dead in.

The above blizzard of letters leads me to choose Organizations as the next category simply because another tempest brewed in 1988 when solvers thought I had placed the wrong Nazi in charge of the Gestapo.

My general reply to the would-be Gotchas read as follows:

So many solvers have questioned my "Goering's gang" clue that I am forced to resort to a Xeroxed letter.

The *Columbia Encyclopedia* states: "The Gestapo originated in 1933 under Hermann Goering."

Yes, it's true that the leadership of the secret police was turned over to Himmler in 1936, but Goering was the father of that infamous group.

Monsignor A.V.M. is the president of my Gotcha Club because he has surpassed all other solvers in discovering mistakes in the puzzles. But sometimes even Homer nods. In a 1984 crossword the clue for a six-letter word was "Leatherneck." My error-catcher put in MARINE.

```
            P
    M A R I N E
            R
            E
```

But the correct answer was GYRENE, a slangy word for *marine* (see *Random House, Second* or *New World, Third*). This caused the monsignor to trip up on the four-letter crossing word, for which the definition was "This stack'll crackle." The answer, of course, WAS PYRE.

This next communication might well have been entitled "Hooey!" It comes from G.Q.K. of Middletown, Rhode Island.

> "Chinese Secret Society"—HUI?—the word is *Hawaiian* and is used there today to refer to any group of people knit together for a common purpose, most usually financial, e.g., "The condo is owned by a hui comprised of local businessmen." I tried real hard to fit *tong* into these three spaces!

My sources for *hui* include *Webster's Second* and *Webster's Third*. What confused G.Q.K. is that there really is a Hawaiian hui which has a benevolent purpose and is not a secret; a hui in the Fiftieth State is a firm or partnership.

And now we come to my Nautical critics. Some found their way into the chapter that follows this one, but a few were all at sea. Take P.B. of Wilmington, Delaware, for instance. In 1987 he objected to a statement I had written in a piece about crosswords.

> Gotcha! In reference to your article in the 26 April *Magazine*—a sheet is *not* a rope—it is a line. Any cordage, while ashore, may be properly called a rope, but once aboard a boat or ship (and there's a nice distinction there), it becomes a line. For example, the main sheet is the *line* which is used to adjust the position of the mainsail.
> Sorry about that.

In my reply I told P.B. that he should present his dissent to the editors of the *New World* dictionaries. Under *sheet*, their definition reads: "A rope or chain attached to a lower corner of a sail: it is shortened or slackened to control the set of the sail." Sorry about that!

In 1985 Dr. M.H.M. of Englewood, New Jersey, took issue with all my sources concerning the shape of a *burgee*.

Thank you for your response to my "halyard" letter and the kind comments you made about sailors. I agree that they tend to be very pleasant people.

I hate to be a nit picker, but a burgee is *not* a two-tailed flag (October 17, 1985). In fact a classic book on sailing technique by H. A. Calahan states "the burgee is always triangular in shape" and serves to identify the owner's yacht club. The two-tailed flag of your puzzle is in fact the owner's private signal and is called a fish-tail or swallow-tail.

Does this make the "Gotcha Club"?

Those readers who have a copy of *Webster's Second* are fortunate. That dictionary displays illustrations of two types of burgees: one is triangular, the other is swallow-tailed.

Some fans are regular correspondents. Among them is N.L.D. of East Falmouth, Massachusetts. He chided me on a nautical matter.

I gotcha again. I thought I had straightened you out on using oarlock (thole) as the oar fulcrum. For this use of word, oar would have to be a first-class lever and the water the workload, which is ridiculous. This use of word was started by some ignoramus (at least so when dealing with the simplest of mechanics). *Question:* Who did in fact start this?

The correct answer of oar's fulcrum, as I stated before, is the water. The oar is a 2nd class lever with the water as the fulcrum and oarlock is the workload and hands the power (source).

Here's how *New World, Third* defines *thole:* "a pin or either of a pair of pins made of metal or wood and set vertically in the gunwale of a boat to serve as a fulcrum for an oar."

A.S. of Roslyn, New York, was impelled to write when a puzzle referred to *dead reckoning*.

The puzzle requires a 4-space answer to "___ reckoning" and is solved by DEAD but this is not historically correct if the reference is to a type of marine navigation. The Chapman's source book, used extensively in boating, refers to *DED. reckoning,* as an abbreviation for *deductive reckoning*.

The source book to which Mr. S. refers has an interesting theory, but it is dead in the water as far as the lexicographers are concerned. As an example, the following is from *Random House, Second:*

> *Dead reckoning.* Navig. calculation of one's position on the basis of distance run or various headings since the last precisely observed position, with as accurate allowance as possible being made for wind currents, compass errors, etc.

Webster's Third gives an equally elaborate definition and adds: "broadly, guesswork."

On the subject of navigation, N.B. of Naples, New York, was understandably confused in December 1987 when DORAN was the answer to the clue "Navigational device." She wrote: "On our sailboat our navigational device is *loran*."

As happens many times, the fan is correct but so am I. Again, I quote *Random House, Second:* "*Doran.* . . . an electronic device for determining range and assisting navigation, employing the principle of the Doppler effect. *Do*(ppler) *ran*(ge)."

Loran, by the way, stands for *L*ong *r*ange *n*avigation and involves radio signals from two or more fixed transmitters.

Since sailing is a sporty activity, let's turn to Sports in general and start with baseball.

R.J.S. of Staten Island sent me the following letter in 1989.

> I enjoy dearly trying to solve your daily crossword puzzles, and your edition of today was no exception. As a matter of fact, I was able to complete today's heady puzzle.
>
> I do, however, take exception to the answer for 7 Down, "Catcher's equipment." Your answer, PADS, does not fit the requirements of the clue, inasmuch as pads are never referred to as part of, or in total, the equipment worn by catchers. A more appropo clue might have been "Goalie's equipment," referring to the pads worn by ice hockey goalies.

In baseball, catchers wear chest protectors and shin guards. *Random House, Second* is one of several dictionaries that define those articles as *pads*.

• • •

Perhaps B.K. thought that he had caught me in a trap when he communicated as follows:

> In the puzzle of the Tuesday, October 4 edition, the clue "trapshooting" is given for 49 Across. The correct answer appears to be SKEET.
>
> Skeet is a form of target shooting in which two targets are launched simultaneously from separate locations. In trap, only one target is launched. Those familiar with both sports will tell you that the difference is considerable. Both, of course, involve the use of weapons, but then, so does public education.

Mr. K.'s last sentence is a puzzle in itself. Did he know that I once supervised thirty-seven schools in the "Fort Apache" area of the Bronx?

At any rate, he was shootin' from the hip. *New World, Third*; *Random House, Second;* etc. declare that skeet is a form of trapshooting.

This next one relates to football. It comes from J.S.H. of Scranton, Pennsylvania.

> Ha! Ha! I finally caught you in an error. In the puzzle which appeared in Saturday's *New York Times* (6/29/85)—Cappelletti of Penn State fame is *John,* not GINO, the latter being Marchetti of the Baltimore Colts and Fast Foods Restaurant fame.

Well, J.S.H., the laugh's on you. There are two Cappellettis of football fame. Your Nittany Lion, John C., won the Heisman trophy in 1973. Gino C. was one of the New England Patriots in the sixties. He happened to have the same given name as the illustrious Mr. Marchetti.

Amy Alcott is a professional golfer who has won many Ladies Professional Golf Association tournaments. But her name was not familiar to dozens of puzzle solvers in 1988 when my clue for AMY was "Lowell or Alcott."

Perhaps the reference to poet Amy Lowell triggered off an

association with author Louisa May in the minds of many fans. I have chosen two typical letters on the subject. The first comes from S.J.

> AMY seems to be the answer (as in *Amy* Lowell). *May Alcott* was Louisa's sister and Bronson's daughter; *Amy March* is her fictional prototype.
>
> As a fact-checker it is my job to find mistakes; every once in a while it's fun. . . .

M.J. of Houston, Texas, teed off as follows.

> This is the third time in recent months that a crossword puzzle edited by you has used a clue of "Alcott" to refer to Amy.
>
> Twice this occurred in puzzles appearing in the Sunday *Houston Post Magazine.* I did not write immediately, sure that other Alcott enthusiasts by the legion would already have done so.
>
> Now in today's *New York Times* it has happened again.
>
> Louisa May Alcott never had a sister named Amy. The only Amy in her life was the character in *Little Women* whose name was Amy March.
>
> Could your puzzlers stick to Lowell and Carter as clues instead?
>
> It would dismay me to have my trust in you shaken.

The game that Mark Twain called "a good walk spoiled" generated another leaping letter in 1988. E.M.A. of New Haven, Connecticut, wrote:

> Referring to your puzzle January 26, 24 Down—Golfer's number 4 wood, which you said was CLEEK.
>
> According to my *Webster's New Collegiate Dictionary* they define *cleek* as an "iron club with a straight narrow face and a long shaft."
>
> The above for your information.

Unfortunately, my correspondent had used an abridged dictionary. *If* she had consulted *Webster's Third*, she would have found these two definitions:

a. A narrow-banded driving iron formerly in use for short drives
b. A number four wood

• • •

Lately, the salaries and awards given to professional athletes have stirred up discussions on Money, so I now segue into that area.

In a 1989 puzzle, RIN was defined as "Part of a yen." Both are Japanese coins.

For some strange reason, D.M. of New York City thought that a rin belonged in Chinese wallets. He wrote:

> The crossword puzzle of 10-20-89 has an error: 7 Down the clue should be "Yuan" not "Yen." The yuan is Chinese currency and its components are rin; yen is Japanese and its long-ago components were sen.

Also in 1989, when MINT appeared in a puzzle, I hit upon a humorous clue: "The buck starts here." Silver dollars and the Susan B. Anthony were on my mind, but L.G. (address unknown) took a leap.

> "Bucks" are not minted. They're produced at the Bureau of Engraving in Washington, D.C. Coins are minted. Tsk! Tsk!

Shifting from mercenary matters to aesthetic ones, I begin with my Leapers in the field of Music.

Someone once described the oboe as "an ill wind that nobody blows good." The instrument is also hard to pin down. Every time I find a new clue for it, somebody bats it down. For example, a fan whose salutation to me is "Hi buddy" and whose sign-off is Rex declares that an oboe "ain't no contrabassoon." His assertion is contradicted by *Webster's Third*, which calls the instrument "the largest member of the oboe family."

D.H.W. of Troy, New York, is so upset about two of my definitions for *oboe* that I wonder if my source (*Webster's Third* again) is correct.

> A *musette* is not an *oboe*. It is a bagpipe, sometimes called the "French" bagpipe and was most common in the 17th and 18th centuries. (See puzzle for 4/11/88.)
>
> And while I am on the subject, a *contrafagotto* also is not an *oboe*. It is a large, or double, bassoon. It is to the usual bassoon as the contrabass is to the cello.
>
> These instruments are never interchangeable in a musical

context. Though the world does not shake from their confusion in a crossword puzzle, the frequent recurrence of this solecism is an irritant to one trying to solve your puzzles.

It should be noted that *Webster's Third*'s first definition for *musette* is "a small bellows-filled bagpipe . . ." and the next definition states that the "small simple oboe" is also called a musette pipe.

When NATURAL popped up in a 1991 puzzle, I found an interesting definition in *Random House, Second:* "a white key on a piano, organ, or the like." When I used that clue, R.E.H. of Glen Cove, New York, objected.

> As a purist, I must fault your clue for NATURAL as a "white key on a piano." I taught piano and E was often called "D double sharp," and even more common C was B# and F was E#. I felt obliged to tell you this!
> But keep up the good work. Do not let this inhibit you.

J.B. has a problem with the instrument known as the human voice. In 1989 he asked:

> Are you perhaps confusing *trill* with *tremolo* (April 25)? A trill is not a vibrato, but a tremolo might be described as an exaggerated vibrato.

In a polite letter to J.B., I explained that *New World, Third* and *Webster's Third* were among my sources.

Dr. S. from a town in Connecticut maintained that I was wrong when a puzzle gave Verdi as the composer of *Don Carlos*. When I sent him proof, his penitent response read as follows:

> I dispatched my note in haste and I apologize for having wasted your time with my erroneous triviality.
> I feel embarrassed and duly chastised.
> Since I am known locally as something of an "opera mavin"— could we perhaps just drop the matter?

I promise that I will be much more circumspect in the future in scrutinizing your editorial acumen.

Mrs. J.H. of New Rochelle, New York, was equally as rash as Dr. S. In 1985, she had orthographic problems.

> The puzzle (Sept. 12) referred to the opera *Otello* (sic). I believe the usual spelling has only *one L* (Otelo). Thanks for all you do for puzzles.

Note: If Verdi had been a Spaniard, Mrs. H.'s spelling would have been correct.

Spelling also undid K.V.K. of Westport, Connecticut. He wrote:

> In the answers for the puzzle of January 5, 1988, I wish to point out an error. The answer for 63 Down should be DOS, not DAS, as in John Dos Passos.

The answer was DAS *Rheingold,* not DOS *Rheingold.*

A plural form confused F.H., and who could blame her? The clue for ETUDES was "Chopin opera." (plural of *opus*). She fell for the fooler as follows:

> In the Thursday, Nov. 17, you had a question of Chopin opera, and the answer was ETUDES. Chopin never wrote an opera and Etudes are compositions.

M.M. of New York City leaped because he failed to realize that two different composers often use the same title.

> As an inveterate addict of the daily and Sunday puzzles, I am occasionally disturbed to discover entries which, in my view, are inaccurate (or at least misleading). But I have refrained from writing because reasonable men can often differ on such arcane matters.

I am writing this time because a gross error in Saturday's (November 4th) puzzle leaves no room for any reasonable difference of opinion. While Tosti composed countless Neopolitan songs, he most assuredly did not write "Mattinata," which was composed by Leoncavallo. Those of us who look forward each day to your puzzles rely on their (and your) scrupulous accuracy. That makes this disappointment even more disturbing.

My sources for the Tosti title were *The Cyclopedia of Names* and *Webster's Biographical Dictionary*.

The double trouble of Mr. M. above was also experienced in 1991 by C.B. of South Orange, New Jersey.

After so many years of enjoying the wit and ingenuity you incorporate into the puzzle definitions, I can't resist the temptation to tweak you about one of your very rare trip-ups. In the puzzle of June 15, 1991, you had "Wabash Moon" as Morton Downey's theme. Although none of my many reference books give me any help in documenting it, I am sure, to the point of John McLaughlin's metaphysical certitude, that Downey's theme was "Carolina Moon."
This small fall from grace diminishes my ongoing admiration for your work much less than a whit. Happy ongoing wordsmithing!

My admiring fan felt abashed when he was told that Mr. Downey had two theme songs—"Wabash Moon" and "Carolina Moon," as explained by David Ewen in *All the Years of Popular Music*.

Similarly, in 1988, L.C. of Katonah, New York, was fooled by likenesses. The clue in a Sunday puzzle asked for the name of the songwriter who wrote the music for "Let's Fall in Love." Here's part of Mrs. C.'s letter.

I tried to stretch *Cole* and shorten *Porter* to no avail. Neither would fit into five boxes. Considering "Let's Fall in Love" is one of Porter's most famous songs, you're bound to get many of these letters. Oh well . . .

Mistaken clue notwithstanding, my husband and I enjoyed solving the puzzle.

P.S. To be precise, Porter's song was titled "Let's Do It." The *sub*title was "Let's Fall in Love."

I'm not sure about Mrs. C.'s claim concerning the subtitle but I do recall that the lyric ended with "Let's fall in love."

The five-letter answer to the clue was ARLEN. Ted Koehler wrote the lyric for Harold Arlen's music, and the song was introduced in a 1933 motion-picture musical by the same name. Since Cole Porter's "Let's Do It" came out in 1928, perhaps the final phrase of that song still rang in Mr. Koehler's head when he sat down to write the words for Arlen's score.

I have an interesting anecdote concerning Harold Arlen. When he and Johnny Mercer created "Come Rain or Come Shine," I was the first person to hear that classic from the 1946 musical entitled *St. Louis Woman!*

How did that happen? Well, the book for the musical was the product of my colleague and friend, poet Countee Cullen, when we taught at Frederick Douglass Junior High School in Harlem. After school, Countee would read to me the part of the script that he had just written and he would ask for my suggestions and criticisms.

Then a tragedy occurred. Mr. Cullen died suddenly of uremia during the Christmas holidays. On his deathbed he asked that I finish the last scene of the last act. Subsequently, I took a leave of absence from the school system and showed up at the Martin Beck Theater, where I met such stars as Pearl Bailey, the Nicholas Brothers, and Rex Ingram. Best of all, I became acquainted with Messrs. Mercer (extrovert) and Arlen (introvert).

Late one afternoon I was sitting in the back of the theater and watching Ms. Bailey rehearse when my two musical friends sat down next to me. They were all smiles. "Gene," the extrovert said, "We've just written a new song, and we think it should be the finale. In fact, it might be sung earlier and then reprised. You wanna hear it?"

Did I? Of course! They took me around the corner to a tiny office that they had rented and turned on a recording that they had just made. Arlen's piano-playing and Mercer's singing voice combined on "Come Rain or Come Shine." I can still see the two of them watching my countenance intently as I listened, and I'll never forget the smiles that wreathed their faces when I shouted: "Wow! You've got a hit!"

The late Sammy Cahn was one of my pen pals. He once told me that many people incorrectly call him a songwriter—a designation that he felt should be reserved for composers like Arlen or Jimmy Van Heusen. Sammy preferred to be called a lyrist. In that connection, here's a letter from A.F. of Poughkeepsie, New York.

Is there a misuse of the word *lyrist* in the June 17 crossword? 13 Across and 16 Across use the word *lyrist* to mean one who writes lyrics. But a lyrist is one who plays the lyre. I believe that *lyricist* is what is meant.

A.F.'s definition for *lyrist* is given as the first one in most dictionaries, but mine and Mr. Cahn's are also acceptable. Incidentally, *Random House, Second* defines *songwriter* as follows: "a person who writes the words or music, or both, for popular songs." Once again, sloppy folk usage has blurred old distinctions.

While we're on the subject of popular songs, I have a book called *The Beatles A to Z*. Therein "Maggie Mae" is called "a traditional Liverpool sing-along song which The Beatles performed as early as their Quarrymen years." The book also states that The Beatles recorded the song in 1970 as part of the "Let It Be" album.

M.L. of Brooklyn took a leap on the above subject.

I am writing about a glaring error which occurred in the crossword puzzle of October 18, 1983. The error was in clue 61 Down " 'Maggie ____,' Beatles Recording." The answer was MAE, however, "Maggie Mae" is not a Beatles recording, but was recorded by Rod Stewart in the early 70's after the Beatles had disbanded.

But A.J.C. of Huntington, New York, threw some light on the situation.

Yesterday's puzzle contained a clue which I felt could have been somewhat clearer. As a matter of fact, for all I know, you could have been entirely correct in calling "Maggie *Mae*" a Beatles tune. Perhaps the boys from Liverpool (or one of them) did write the song and it was probably recorded on the flip side of one of their bigger hits.

However, I thought it would have been much clearer for the puzzle solver (at least this puzzle solver) if the clue had been " 'Maggie ____,' a Rod Stewart hit." I do believe the song is more closely associated with the artist who made it into a hit than with the person who wrote it.

"Volare" is another popular song that evoked corrections from would-be Gotchas when I described it as "Dean Martin hit." Typical of all the letters was this one from F.R. of Spring Valley, New York.

Gotcha?
"Volare" was introduced by Domenico Modugno in 1958. This record became a huge hit and was responsible for the popularity of the song. Today, the song is generally associated with Mr. Modugno, and not Dean Martin.

Perhaps you mean "That's Amore," which is associated with Mr. Martin.

According to David Ewen, noted historian in the field of popular music, Mr. Martin and Mr. Modugno made separate recordings of the song in the late fifties. Mr. Modugno had joined with Mitchell Parish in the creation of the song. It was also called "Nel Blu, Dipinto di Blu."

ALAN is a name that constantly appears in puzzles. As a result, we constantly give publicity to actors Alda, Arkin, Autry, Bates, Mowbray, Rachins, and Thicke.

Authors Paton and Villiers also get mentioned as well as comedian King and astronauts Bean and Shepard. Also there are lyrist Lerner and poets Seeger and Dugan—not to forget senators Cranston and Simpson.

Still eager to introduce a different *Alan,* I discovered pianist

Feinberg in 1990. That citation brought forth two letters. The first came from E.K. of Houston.

> I think I have caught you, for once, in a mistake. 48 Across—pianist Alan *Feinberg*. (sic)
> Having enjoyed the wonderful piano of a Mr. Alan *Feinstein* in Houston, I am sure that was the artist you had in mind.

The second letter was written by pianist Feinberg himself.

> I cannot tell you what a thrill it was to discover my name in the Monday, March 12 puzzle. I'm a great puzzle fan, and discovered that many, many of my friends are also—judging by the number of calls I received. It made my week! Thanks.

Several years ago I looked into *Webster's Biographical Dictionary* for a less familiar definition for RAVEL and found that he had written a set of songs called "Sheherazade" (1903). When I referred to that work, a half-dozen Leapers popped up. All of them were devotees of Rimski-Korsakov. Here's a sample:

> Sir: Referring to today's puzzle, the answer to 21 Across works out as RAVEL—which I am sure will be in accordance with the author's and your intentions. Well, that's wrong! The *composer of* (Sheherazade) was *Nikola Rimski-Korsakov*—not *Ravel*. It's fine to make the puzzles difficult but get your facts straight.

It should be indicated that Rimski-Korsakov composed a symphonic poem entitled "Scheherazade"—a spelling slightly different from Ravel's.

Sometime in the eighties, constructor Maura Jacobson's puzzle featured puns on celebrated people's names. One clue read: "Composition by John Fillup Sousa." The answer was PUMP AND CIRCUMSTANCE. She and I both felt that the puns on *Philip* and *Pomp* were a great match. We also assumed that all solvers would give us credit for having once marched in a high school graduation line while the orchestra played Elgar's work.

We were wrong in thirty-six instances! Three dozen solvers

gleefully demanded Gotcha certificates. Instead they received a photocopied letter saying in effect, "We know, we know."

Literature has attracted a goodly number of Leapers. The first to jump was a man from Braintree, Massachusetts; unfortunately, I have lost his letter, but here's the story.

The word WASP appeared in a daily puzzle. Tired of definitions like "Hornet" or "Stinger" or "Yellow jacket," I dredged my mind and remembered that Alexander Pope had been called "The Wicked Wasp of Twickenham." And so, my clue was "Epithet for Pope."

My Braintree critic smugly reminded me that Alexander Pope was not a Protestant but a Roman Catholic!

In my reply, I quoted a Pope couplet:

> A little learning is a dang'rous thing;
> Drink deep, or taste not the Pierian spring.

That Leaper was probably without professional credentials. But in 1979 the entire English Department of a highly regarded Massachusetts college signed their names to a letter that erroneously accused me of a gaffe. The definition in question had been "Poem by Spenser," requiring ASTROPHEL as an answer. The professors stated that the poem had been written by Sir Philip Sidney. Not so! His work was *Astrophel and Stella*.

HORSE was the entry in a 1989 puzzle. The clue read: "Richard III's need: Act V, IV, 7." Whereupon S.A.R. of Newburyport, Massachusetts, wrote:

> Re: Clue 14 D in Sunday's puzzle (3/19). Richard III wasn't H-O-R-S-E-L-E-S-S at the end of Act V, he was dead. He was horseless at the end of Act IV.

That letter gave me a scare. I turned to my book of Shakespeare's plays and found Act V of the drama about the deformed monarch. Sure enough, Richard's steed is slain and he is forced to fight on foot. Twice he cries out: "A horse! A horse! My kingdom for a horse!"

Then in Scene V, the king is killed by Richmond and the play ends. Whew! Apparently S.A.R. mixed up Scene V with Act V.

In 1985 A.M.B. of Tucson, Arizona, became confused, too. This time a title caused a leap.

> Twice in the past few months the *New York Times* crossword puzzle has mentioned *The Boys of Summer* as having been written by Roger or E. J. Kahn; the author of this book is Roger Angell.

Roger Angell wrote *The Summer Game*. My clues had correctly stated that Roger (not E. J.) Kahn was the author of *The Boys of Summer*.

Memory lapses occur to all of us. We are certain that we still hold in mind a certain passage from literature, for example, and then we look it up and discover that we had mangled the original text. This happens to many of my Leapers. For instance, J.B.S. of Newark was sure that Alexander Pope had written: "A little *knowledge* is a dangerous thing"—not "a little *learning*."

Most people misquote Gertrude Stein's "Rose is a rose is a rose." They think that the line begins with the article *A*. But J.R. of Buffalo knew better; however he forgot the end of the line.

> The crossword puzzle for 24 April, contains an error *viz*: No. 46 Down "pair in a Stein line," is *not* A ROSE. The line, according to Stein reads: "Rose is a rose." (no *a*)

"A little learning" has the danger of causing a tiny leap on occasions. R.J.P. of Key Biscayne, Florida, had that problem. Although he remembered T. S. Eliot's comparison of fog to a cat in "The Love Song of J. Alfred Prufrock," he apparently had no knowledge of Sandburg's "Fog." In that gem, the poet had written:

> The fog comes
> on little cat feet

Here is part of R.J.P.'s letter.

> 61 *Across:* Means of locomotion in Sandburg's "Fog" (CAT FEET). Shouldn't it be T. S. Eliot ("Let us go then you and I . . ." etc.)?

Incidentally, T. S. Eliot's lines are:

> Let us go then, you and I,
> When the evening is spread out against the sky
> Like a patient etherized upon a table;

About a dozen lines later, the poet goes on to say:

> The yellow fog that rubs its back upon the window-panes,
> The yellow smoke that rubs its muzzle on the window-panes,
> Licked its tongue into the corners of the evening, . . .

R.J.P. is excused for making "a sudden leap" (phrase used by Eliot later in the passage on the catty fog and smoke). At least, Mr. P. gave me good reason to quote some great lines of poetry.

Confusing one poet's lines with those of another also caused Lesley M.H. of Mercer Island, Washington, to join a crowd of Leapers.

It's a long time since I wrote you to correct something in a crossword puzzle, and although at times I've thought you sailed a bit close to the wind, there was enough uncertainty that I thought it not worthwhile to cavil.

But this time it is difficult. All my Scottish ancestors, the Munroes and the Reids, have risen in me and said, "Nae, nae, it canna be. Lassie, ye must write him and mak it richt." I refer to the *New York Times* Crossword puzzle in the *Seattle* [*Post-Intelligencer*] for March 10, in which 28 Across says "____ a body meet a body" and I naturally put in the correct three letters, i.e., *gin*. To my horror I found that it required IF A, which I can only think is a horrible Americanization.

> Gin a body meet a body
> Comin' thro the Rye.
> Gin a body greet a body
> Need a body cry?
> Ilka lassie has her laddie
> Nane they say hae I
> But a' the lads they smile at me
> When comin' thro' the Rye.

> Amang the train there is a swain
> I dearly lo'e mysel'
> But what's his name and whaur his hame
> I dinna care to tell.
> Ilka etc.

I grew up in a Canadian city with a large Scottish population and I had two Scottish brothers-in-law, one of whom had such a broad brogue that he was sometimes incomprehensible. It was a musical city and my family was musical and folk songs, English, Scottish and Irish were second nature to us. "Comin' Thro' the Rye" is a Scottish dialect of English and it ought not to be interfered with.

All good wishes.

P.S. Robert Burns wrote a poem about me—at least, that's where the family got my first name!

Lesley M.H. and many others couldn't be blamed for not knowing that in 1796 James C. Cross wrote "The Harlequin Mariner." His song begins:

> If a body meet a body going to the Fair,
> If a body kiss a body need a body care?

My sources say that both Burns and Cross built their "body" songs on the refrain of an old ditty of unknown authorship. It was called "The Bobtailed Lass."

Names of characters in books, poems, etc. cause lots of literary leaping. For example, J.S. of Oceanside, New York, wouldn't change her mind when a puzzle stated that Amy was the youngest of Alcott's March girls.

> Although it's been a long time since I first read *Little Women*, I don't think the story has changed. At that time, Beth, not Amy, was Mrs. March's youngest (Sunday, May 3–8 Down) and I think she still is.

Sometimes I lay a little trap to find out who's paying attention. *Esther Waters* is probably George Moore's greatest novel. And so, when ESTHER appeared in a puzzle, I discombobulated a number of solvers, including E.H. of Providence, Rhode Island.

In reference to crossword puzzle dated 2/7/84; who is ESTHER WATERS? (42 Across—"Waters and Williams")? Did you mistake *Esther* for *Ethel* Waters?

Occasionally, literary characters' names undergo changes in spelling because of their appearances in English and in foreign languages. *Tristram* is a perfect example. W.M.B. of Brooklyn objected to that spelling in 1984. Apparently, he was more familiar with Wagner's *Tristan and Isolde* than with E. A. Robinson's "Tristram." My *Cyclopedia of Names* lists sixteen spellings for the hero of medieval legend and romance. That reference book also notes that the hero's girlfriend is *Isolt, Iseult,* or *Isolde.* It's no wonder that confusion reigns!

The same Lesley M.H. who was double-crossed by James C. Cross a while back sent me another complaint in 1989. She objected to my statement that *Oriana* was one of the epithets for Elizabeth I. She maintained that *Gloriana* was Spenser's name for the queen—and she was right. But *Oriana* was also correct according to various sources, including *Webster's Second.*

Oleg Cassini is a famous designer, but few people know that Igor Cassini is a reputable columnist. In a 1988 puzzle, I defined IGOR as "Cassini or Stravinsky." B.P. of New York City cut out the puzzle, circled the clue and wrote: "How could you? Were you on vacation when this was okayed?"

Five other solvers took the leap with B.P.

This letter from T.K. of Glen Head, New York, reveals how even the best of us can jump to conclusions if we assume too much.

Number 46 Down asks for the queen of whodunits and the answer appears to be ELLERY. If that answer is correct and it refers to Ellery Queen, it should ask for the king of whodunits. Ellery Queen is a male detective and the authors were two brothers named Lee (I believe). I was misled in the beginning and put down Agatha (as in Agatha Christie), but it became apparent that was not correct. Ellery seems to fit in.

It should be emphasized that the clue was "*Queen* of Who-dunits"—not the *q*ueen of whodunits.

Probably the greatest and funniest example of the danger of making assumptions is a letter written by J.M. of New York City. Whenever I give a talk on crosswords, I always save J.M.'s letter to the end and invariably it causes the room to rock with laughter.

The problem started when the word *poesy* appeared in a Sunday puzzle by John Samson. One of the chief definitions for that word is "precious or sentimental poetic writing." Personally, I always associate *poesy* with such writers as Thomas Carew, John Suckling, and Richard Lovelace—a group called the Cavalier Poets. Lovelace is the one who wrote:

> Stone walls do not a prison make,
> Nor iron bars a cage

He also penned:

> I could not love thee, dear, so much
> Lov'd I not honor more.

At any rate, I decided to define *poesy* as "Lovelace's forte." So far, so good, but when J.M. curled up with the Sunday puzzle in her apartment, the crossing word for POESY immediately gave her the PO starters for a five-letter word. Apparently, she had no knowledge of Richard or had forgotten about him; but she did know about Linda Lovelace. Immediately, she wrote *porno*. Seething with anger, J.M. rushed to her typewriter and sent me an immortal reprimand.

In over fifteen years I cannot recall being offended by a crossword puzzle until today's. If I read it correctly, the clue for 20 Down is Lovelace's forte, and the five-letter answer is *porno*. I find this appalling. Ms. Lovelace has stated that she was abducted, drugged, beaten and otherwise physically abused during the period of time certain films were made. This is a forte? Even if one does not believe her story, I think Ms. Lovelace has been humiliated enough without her unfortunate life being reduced to a degradingly flippant clue in the *Times* crossword puzzle. Mr. Samson's forte is bad taste.

>t>120

t>120

>t>120

t>120

t>120

t>120

P.S. Sometime later, perhaps after discussing her indignation with friends, J.M. was overcome with embarrassment. She sent a telegram asking me to disregard the irate letter.

Not to worry, J.M. I don't know who you are, nor do I wish to investigate. We all fly off the handle occasionally so there's no need to be ashamed. My listeners and readers join me in thanking you for having inadvertently provided us with a cue for laughter.

The Holy Bible is the all-time best-seller, even outdoing *Gone With the Wind*. Therefore, at this point it seems appropriate to follow up Leapers' letters about literature with their messages on scriptural subjects.

In the beginning is Genesis, so let's start there. E.L. of Philadelphia disagreed with me concerning the time when the stars were born.

In the puzzle for March 31, 1985, the clue for 70D was "Fourth day creations." The solution was STARS. I consider this to be in error, because according to Genesis 1:20 and 21, on the *fourth* day, He created the waters, the great whales, and every living creature that moveth. It was on the *third* day, also, according to Genesis 1:16 "He made the stars also." Please advise.

Admittedly, the start of the Old Testament is confusing, but since not one of the thousands of members of the clergy objected to my clue, I'll assume that I was correct.

In a 1989 puzzle, SETH was defined as "Adam's third son." E.L. of Aventura, Florida, wrote:

[The clue for] 36 Across should read "Noah" and not "Adam." According to the Bible the sons of *Adam* were *Cain* and *Abel*.

My husband and I enjoy working on the puzzles.

In my reply, I referred Mrs. L. to Genesis 4:25.

• • •

R.J.M. of Madison, New Jersey, had also forgotten about Seth back in 1987. When the November 24 puzzle described "Cain" as "Adam's eldest," Mr. M. wrote:

> In the crossword puzzle for this date, the response for 48 Down works out to be ELDEST. However, since the reference is to 1 Across, "Cain" and, by inference, 26 Across, "Abel," *elder* would be the better answer. However, since *elder* would not fit in the solution diagram, a different definition altogether is called for.

Several other Biblical Leapers had arisen in 1987 when "A time to ____" appeared in a puzzle and the three-letter answer was SEW. R.F.D. of Scotch Plains, New Jersey, was among the solvers who apparently got mixed up by Matthew's "They sow not, neither do they reap."

> In Today's *New York Times* puzzle (8/13) number 29 Down— you had better read your Bible better. It reads, "a time to s*o*w" as in seeds being planted.
> I enjoy your challenging puzzles and find that they keep my mind alert during the lulls at work.

The quotation from Ecclesiastes 3:7 is "A time to rend and a time to sew."

All my reference books list the seven deadly sins (or capital sins) as pride, covetousness, lust, anger, gluttony, envy, and sloth. Perhaps C.L. of Whitestone, New York, was really quarreling with the theologians when she objected to one of my clues.

> In reference to the crossword puzzle in the *New York Times*, Oct. 10, 1988. 58 Across—a deadly sin; solution—ANGER. Anger is no sin at all; it is a feeling. You might like to "look it up."

How did the "deadly" list come into existence? Perhaps some erudite reader will inform me. In any case, I suppose it's inaccurate to classify C.L. as a Leaper.

• • •

Another non-Leaper, I must admit, is R.R. of New York City. In 1990 he sent me an interesting letter.

> A clue and its answer in the puzzle of the 5th April perpetuates the common misconception that "Pride goeth before a fall." It doth not.
> (5 April 1990) 56A—Fall cometh after this: PRIDE
> Actually, upon the authority of The Holy Scriptures, that which "a fall" cometh after is "a haughty spirit."
> Proverbs (of Solomon), 16:18—
> "Pride goeth before destruction,
> And a haughty spirit before a fall."

Actually, I was quoting some old English proverbs, one of which is "Pride goeth before a fall."

NER creeps into puzzles from time to time. Sometimes the clue is "Grandfather of Saul" (1 Chronicles 8:33 or 9:39). At other times, the clue is "Uncle of Saul" (1 Chronicles 9:36) or (1 Samuel 50). Whenever I refer to NER as an uncle, a host of solvers yells "Grandfather," and whenever I yield to that crowd, the other side says "Uncle." Sometimes I wish both factions would give up and reread their Bible.

Another generator of dozens of letters is the abbreviation APOC. The problem is that the shortened form stands for either *Apochrypha* or *Apocalypse*. The latter is another title for the Revelation of St. John the Divine, which is listed as the last book of the New Testament.

When I was a freshman at Montclair State College in New Jersey, one of my professors said that the story of Adam and Eve was a myth. After class, I objected strongly and he calmed me down by stating that I was entitled to my opinion.

I mention the incident because I don't want any letters criticizing me for adjoining the previous section on the Bible with the present one on Mythology.

Also, it should be stressed that ancient myths and legends are nebulous fields and sources often differ. My chief reference books in this section are the *Columbia Encyclopedia, Brewer's Dictionary of Phrase and Fable,* and Kravitz's *Dictionary of Greek and Roman Mythology.* Also, I consult such dictionaries as *Random House, Second; New World, Third;* and *Webster's Second.*

Let's start with some correspondence between me and I.J. of Chevy Chase, Maryland. In 1991 a *Times* puzzle stated that Echo was a nymph pursued by Pan. Mr. J. then maintained that Narcissus was Echo's chaser—not Pan. The latter, he declared, pursued Syrinx.

My reply read as follows.

Pan pursued lots of nymphs, according to my reference books.

'Tis said that Pan was an awful lecher;
He ran after Echo but failed to kecher.
'Twas Echo who pursued Narcissus;
Alas, she failed to be his missus.

Mr. J. remained unconvinced. He wrote:

I regret to say that neither your "referral books" nor your delightful quatrain legitimately support the "Pan-Echo" connection.

Had he not pursued Syrinx into the reeds, we should never have had Pandean pipes.

Let us, therefore, leave Echo to "pan-ic" after Narcissus!

Here's how Kravitz describes Pan: "a lecher, with goat's legs and horns, he pursued many nymphs, including Echo, Pithys and Syrinx—though not always successfully."

Mr. Kravitz's comments on Echo are also interesting: "Hera suspected her of conspiring to conceal one of Zeus's dalliances, and took from her the power of normal speech, leaving her able only to reply to others, and unable to remain silent after others spoke. When Narcissus spurned her love, she wasted away."

I advise Mr. J. to reread that last sentence.

A.F. of Poughkeepsie, New York, took another leap in 1988.

Have I got it wrong? Iphigenia wasn't *saved* by Aulis (50 Across in today's puzzle). She was *sacrificed* by her father, Agamemnon, so there would be winds to take the Greek fleet to Troy. If that's salvation I want none of it.

Again I quote Kravitz re Iphigenia: "Her father tried to sacrifice her to Artemis but she was saved at the last minute when the goddess substituted a deer."

Sometimes it's hard to remember the Greek names of the gods and goddesses and their Roman equivalents. In 1986 S.W. of Davis, California, was sure that I converted Greeks into Romans and vice versa, but in actuality she was the one who had things backwards.

May I draw your attention to Crossword 26 Down of Friday, June 20: Persephone's mother is actually Ceres, whereas Demeter is the mother of Proserpina. Trifling matter of the differences between Greek names and Roman names of corresponding cult figs.

Now let's get it straight. Demeter was the mother of Persephone. Both were Greek deities. Demeter's Roman name was Ceres, and Persephone became Proserpina in Caesar's land.

In the following instance, the fault for the confusion is mine. My clue in a 1986 puzzle was "Father of Diomedes" and the answer was ARES. From Mount Vernon, New York, came a postcard signed by W.E. and claiming that the proper answer was Tydeus.

The problem is that there was more than one Diomedes. Mine was a Thracian king who owned horses that fed on human flesh. The eighth labor of Hercules (or Heracles) was to kill those beasts. The Diomedes to whom W.E. refers was a king of Argos who played a leading role in the siege of Troy.

Among the nine Muses, the one who receives the most publicity from crossworders is Erato—mainly because her name begins with a vowel, contains two oft-used consonants, and alternates vowels and consonants.

Recently, I discovered that the Muse of lyric poetry was not the only Erato. One of the Dryads bore the same name, and there was even a Naiad named Erato.

Armed with the above knowledge, in 1986 my clue for ERATO was "One of the Dryads." Scores of Gotcha letters poured in. Most fans were absolutely sure that I had goofed, but Monsignor A.V. M. (President of my Gotcha Club) had learned from experience that I sometimes had hidden aces up my sleeve. Note the last stanza of his poem.

YOU DID IT TO A MUSE?

The NAIADES were nymphs of springs and fountains;
OREADES preferred the hills and mountains;
The DRYADS, whom the Greeks called DRYADES
Were happiest around the Grecian trees.

ERATO, who was MUSE of poetry,
Was higher as regards divinity;
With her eight sisters, MUSES of some fame,
She shouldn't have to bear that DRYAD name.

The Greek God mess makes very little sense,
And that is why, while meaning no offense,
I'm certain you must own another book
Which proves that you are safely off the hook!

Mrs. J.M.C. of Dime Box, Texas, was less circumspect than the monsignor.

The Austin *American Statesman* publishes a *New York Times* crossword puzzle each week in a section of their newspaper called, "Onward." This is done each Tuesday. Lately, I have been running across errors in definition that are very irritating, but I have let it ride. Yesterday, July 29, there were two blatant errors. The puzzle was called "Fair Game," and was created by Jeanne Wilson. Both errors were of Greek mythology. One was 119 Across. The clue was "a name for Aphrodite." Since Aphrodite was the Greek goddess of love, I immediately thought of Venus, the Roman goddess for love. I checked both the latest collegiate dictionary and *Bulfinch's Mythology*, and that was correct. The word worked out URANIA. *She* was the Greek *muse* for astronomy. The second error was 29 Down, and the clue was one of the Dryads. I checked out Bulfinch again and

the Dryads had no names. They were wood nymphs that died
when the trees they inhabited died or were cut down. The
dictionary confirmed that they were wood nymphs. The word
worked out ERATO who was the *muse* of lyric and love poetry. I
cannot figure out why you let this slip by you unless you have
assistants who do not know their mythology and neglected to
check it out.

With regard to *Urania, Webster's Second* is one of the reference
books that give the name as an epithet of Aphrodite. Of course,
all my sources also state that another Urania is the Muse of
astronomy.

It follows naturally that a section on fans' mythological misap-
prehensions should lead into a review of Leapers' letters in the
area of Latin.

In 1985, F.T.T. of Haddon Heights, New Jersey, mixed up
Latin and English.

A recent Sunday puzzle of your composition contained the
following:
Clue: "like Ben Jonson"
Answer: RARE
No doubt you refer to the inscription on Mr. Jonson's tombstone, "Orare Ben Jonson." Surely you are aware that the word
orare is a Latin exhortation to "pray for Ben Jonson." It has
little to do with a scarcity of the old boy.

All reference books carry "O rare Ben Jonson!" When Francis
Bacon wrote that tribute, he was stating that the dramatist-poet
had been an unusual or extraordinary man. If Bacon had been
asking us to pray for Jonson, he probably would have inscribed,
"Ora pro Ben Jonson."
Orare as a Latin infinitive does appear in old proverbs like
"Laborare est orare" or vice versa.

In 1990 a clue for ALIA caused J.D. of Providence, Rhode
Island, to leap to his stationery.

There is an error in the diagramless of May 20 by Arthur
W. Palmer. The clue for 58 Down is "Part of et al."
I've published enough technical articles to know that the ab-

breviation *et al.* is meant to refer to other *people* (plural) and not to other things. As such the plural becomes *alii.* So the abbreviation *et al.* stands for *et alii.*

I'm sure that somewhere, sometime I read a long article on the plural of *alios.* It was all rather complicated, but a quick check in a dictionary will tell you that it is *alii.*

All my up-to-date reference books state that *al.* is an abbreviation for *alii* (other people) or *alia* (other things).

Along the same lines, another letter came from an anonymous solver in 1986.

> In today's puzzle the answer to the clue—"and others, abbr."—was ETC. Isn't the proper abbreviation for "and others" *et al*(?) while *etc.* means "and so forth"?
> Don't mean to be picky but I do the puzzle every day and love the exactness of it.

If my correspondent had consulted any good dictionary, he or she would have discovered that *et cetera* literally means "and others." Freely translated, the phrase becomes "and so forth."

The motto of Massachusetts is "Ense petit placidam sub libertate quietem." The translation is "By the sword she seeks quiet peace under liberty." In 1985, H.E.G. of East Greenbush, New York, informed me gleefully:

> I found an error in the puzzle in the daily *New York Times;* almost immediately I might add.
> No. 13 Down: "———petit placidam"—I believe this should be *esse* and not ENSE.

H.E.G.'s mistake makes some sense of a sort. According to him, the Bay State's motto should be: "To exist, she seeks quiet peace under liberty." Not bad!

In connection with the preceding letter, part of a 1989 message from R.M.R. of Albuquerque, New Mexico, reads: "*Esse* means 'to be,' an infinitive—it does not mean 'being.' The word in Latin for 'being' is *ens*."

R.M.R.'s letter is a typical example of the exclusionary reasoning of many Leapers. They believe that if *A* is equal to *X*, then *B* cannot also equal *X*.

It is true that *ens*, the present participle of *esse*, means "being," but it is also a fact that the infinitive *esse* has been transformed into a gerund meaning "being, existence, essence." Early philosophers, skilled in Latin, played a large part in the change. Incidentally, altering the part of speech of a certain word has often occurred in English, too. As one quick example, I cite "make a *go* of it."

A while back, Julius Caesar was mentioned. His name comes up again in a letter from W.J.H. of Great Neck, New York.

> There was an error in your quotation of J. Caesar's famous commentaries. See puzzle of 8/23/91, 66 Across. The quote *should* read "Omnis Gallia . . . divisa (*in tres partes*)."

My source for the opening sentence of Caesar's *Commentaries* is Bartlett's *Familiar Quotations*. The text reads: "Gallia est omnis divisa in partes tres."

One of my colleagues has said that editing crossword puzzles sometimes resembles fishing: you drop your line and see what happens. Earlier I noted that I catch a legion of Leapers when I define *Erato* as "A dryad or naiad." The same thing happens when the clue for AVE is "Cato's goodbye" or "Fabius's farewell." Here's a typical letter. It came from G.L. of Princeton, New Jersey.

> This is the letter I always say I'll write and never have done, before today, that is.
> When I learned Latin over thirty years ago, I was informed *ave* meant "hail" as in hello and *vale* meant "farewell." "Ave atque vale" makes clear that the *vale* is the farewell part. *Ave Maria* doesn't mean "good-bye Mary" and valedictory speeches are the graduation farewells.
> Because of my faith in the *New York Times*, when I saw the

clue for 24 Across in yesterday's puzzle, I thought, "He can't want *ave*. That's wrong."

Please justify your usage to me so I can lessen my skepticism.

Here's a copy of an answer I wrote in 1989 to an *ave* Leaper who gloated that after ten years he had finally earned a Gotcha certificate.

Thanks for your interest in the puzzles, but you still haven't found a mistake. I studied Latin for eight years and taught the subject. During that time, I learned that the Romans used *ave* in two ways. It meant "hello" and "goodbye."

The more formal *vale* was also used for farewells especially when addressing the dead at funerals. For some reason, Romans preferred *ave* for "farewell" when leaving a friend in the *morning*.

By the way, it's fascinating that Italians now use *ciao* to mean "hello" or "goodbye."

In 1985, G.B. could not believe my clue for SEMPER PARATUS.

Please excuse me for pointing but the crossword puzzle published in the *New York Times* on my birthday, March 13, puzzled me more after I solved it than before.

45 Down "——paratus (plea at law)" worked out to be SEMPER PARATUS. Did I miss something? What will the Coast Guard think?

Thank you for answering my last letter concerning nautical "sheets" vs. "sails." Being your pen pal is a mixed blessing. I enjoy broadening my mind but it cost me since I bought four copies of *A Pleasure in Words* as excellent Christmas gifts.

Keep those words a'crossing!

G.B. was half right. The Coast Guard does boast that it is "always ready," but *semper paratus* is also a legal plea in which the defendant alleges that he or she has always been prepared to meet the court's demand. My source is *Webster's Third*.

Now let us move on to living Foreign Languages starting with a few of Latin's direct descendants.

Whenever I want to find out how many solvers need to brush up on their French, I publish "raison d'————" as the clue for ETAT. J.K., of Woodridge, New York, became one of the Leapers who fell for the trick in 1983.

> Incredible error in today's puzzle! 52 Down calls for "raison d'*etre*," but it really should call for "coup d'*etat*," if you want it to agree with 57 Across (ARNE) and 60 Across (SAR). Gotcha!
> Thanks for all the challenging puzzles!

A.B. of Stamford, Connecticut, sent a terse reaction to the same fooler.

> By now I am sure that half of your fans have written to tell you that this kind of thing can spoil a guy's whole weekend.

For those readers who are not familiar with Gallic phrases, let me add that *raison d'etre* means "reason for being" and *raison d'etat* means "reason of state." The former is in general use, but the latter is a diplomat's justification for an action taken.

The chairman of Foreign Languages in a New Jersey high school wrote a rather patronizing letter when he thought that my clue was Latin instead of Italian. The definition read "March 15 in Roma" and the answer was IDI.

> Beware the *Idi* of March, sir, for they do not exist! I was indeed distressed to find this form as part of the solution to yesterday's crossword puzzle. For future reference, please note that the word *Idus* is already plural in form as it is a fourth, not second, declension noun in Latin. Its forms therefore are *Idus, Iduum, Idibus, Idus, Idibus.*
> If I can be of any further help, please do not hesitate to call or write.
> P.S. Perhaps "Amin" would have been a better clue here.

Actually, this Leaper was somewhat justified because the Latin word for *Rome* is the same as the Italian word. But it's reasonable to expect that a foreign-language chairman would keep the duplication in mind.

By the way, since Idi Amin is such a villainous person, I always try not to give him publicity when his given name or surname appears in a puzzle. Some other clues for IDI are "*Marzo quindicesimo*" or "*Gennaio* 15, in Genova."

As for AMIN, I was delighted when *Amin Gemayel* became president of Lebanon.

Folk usage caused R.G.C. of Philadelphia to become a Leaper a few years ago.

> May I point out an error in today's puzzle? The clue for 79 Across "Comedia Dell' " works out to ARTES. Even if a plural were wanted—although a plural for this word does not exist— the Italian plural of *arte* is *arti,* not *artes.* The word then is "Commedia Dell'arte."

Strictly speaking, Mr. C. is correct, but so many educated Americans have used *commedia dell'artes* that modern lexicographers have given in.

Turning to German, two Leapers are worth mentioning. In 1988, a clue for STAAT read: "Hamburg is one." A.L. of Charles City, Iowa, objected: "Hamburg should be *stadt* not STAAT. *Stadt* is German for city."

A.L. forgot that Hamburg is not only a city; it's a *staat* (state).

In the same vein, M.Y. of Dayton, Ohio, was unaware that *nein* and *kein* are both German words for "No."

About three-fourths of our words have come down to us, either directly or indirectly, from the Romans. Therefore, it seems logical to follow sections on Latin (and other languages) with one on Vocabulary.

Let's start with *eat,* a simple word with many meanings. Here's a nasty letter from R.W.N. of St. John, Missouri.

> I've considered writing to you in the past; now, I have absolutely no choice.
> Do you *really* edit these puzzles? Do you merely glance at them and hope they're all right? Do you farm out the job to someone that you hope is doing it right? Are you taking money under false pretenses?

The cause of my umbrage is the April 6 crossword, in which the clue for 12 Down is "eat" and the answer is (supposedly) HAVE. Come on, now!

If those words are even vaguely synonymous, then why does our language have this expression: "You can't *have* your cake and *eat* it, too."?

Such slovenly material is unfit for publication under the aegis of the *Times*.

I suggest you pay more attention to your job—that way, you may get to keep it.

My reply reveals that R.W.N. had struck a sensitive nerve. Since I take pride in my careful attention to the details in each puzzle, I resent being labeled as a negligent, lazy editor.

You *have* the dubious "honor" of *having* written to me the most vitriolic, insulting letter that I *have* ever received in my eleven-year tenure as Puzzles Editor.

As any philologist or lexicographer knows, individual words sometimes take on scores of meanings—often contradictory as in the case of *cleave* or *ravel* or *scan*.

Among my many sources for *eat* as a synonym for *have,* I cite the new Second Edition of the *Random House Dictionary*. There, under *have,* the eleventh definition is "to partake of; *eat* or drink."

I am the opposite of *slovenly*. I am *meticulous*.

In 1989, I.A. of New York City also took objection to a particular use of *eat*.

The clue at 55 Across is "grieve bitterly," and the answer, according to the puzzle, is EAT ONES HEART OUT. I believe that this is incorrect. To "grieve bitterly" would be to "cry ones heart out." The correct clue for the answer given would have to be "show extreme jealousy," as the phrase "eat your heart out" is usually used smugly by a "have" to a "have not."

Webster's Third defines *eat one's heart out* as "to grieve bitterly and without hope." *Random House, Second* says: "to grieve inconsolably." In cases like this, I usually tell the fans that they should inform me if they ever receive retractions from the editors of the dictionaries.

• • •

ANODE is a word that often appears in crossword puzzles and causes Leapers to hit the ceiling. The following letter from M.F. of Mount Vernon, New York, is typical of many I have received.

> You score very high in editing *Times* crossword puzzles. Unfortunately, those who do so well so consistently are doomed to expectations of perfection. Even small errors become unforgivable. But what about large errors? What are we to think of them?
> Take today's *Times* crossword: The clue for 29 Across is "Battery's negative terminal." That is, of course, the cathode. But the puzzle solution tells us it is the ANODE.
> Tsk, tsk, tsk.

The problem is that there are two kinds of *anodes,* as indicated by the following definitions in *Webster's Third:*

a) the positive terminal of an electrolytic cell
b) the negative terminal of a primary cell or of a storage battery that is delivering current.

Sometimes the use of an unusual word in a puzzle will bring forth a letter from a fan who is probably using an old or inferior dictionary. Perhaps that was the case in 1985 when an objection to VANDALIC came to me from T.C., a magazine editor.

> Come, come; it isn't fair to rope in a made-up word, as *vandalic,* in the September 29 issue of the *Magazine.* My unabridged Webster's does not list such a word. The proper word is *vandalish* or *vandalism.*

Amazingly, *vandalic* appears in all my dictionaries. *New World, Third* defines it as "ruthlessly destructive."

Similarly, an uncommon clue for BLENCH generated a letter from D.S. of Boston, Massachusetts.

> The clue for 8 Down of the 11/26/87 puzzle was "whiten"—your answer, BLENCH. According to *Webster's Ninth New Collegiate*

Dictionary (1986), *blench* means to "draw back or turn aside from lack of courage: Flinch, "—not an appropriate clue from "whiten." If one wanted to whiten something, for instance almonds, one would blanch them. (*Blanch:* "to take the color out of . . . to make ashen or pale . . . to become white or pale.")

Again, all my dictionaries carry both D.S.'s *blench* and the one that means the same as *blanch*.

Another example of either misreading a dictionary or having access to only an inferior one comes from the following 1987 letter by V.L.B.

I wish to call your attention to the fact that WANEY (April 25th puzzle) is not a definition for "decreasing." *Waney* means: "having a wane or natural level, as a plank or board, hence making poor lumber because of irregularities of the surface, as a log." Your people must have had in mind: *waning* as a definition for "decreasing."

My lexicons allow V.L.B.'s "timbery" description as a second definition for *waney*.

Now and then, even the sharpest members of my Gotcha Club take a leap. F.I. of New York City was fooled when the clue read: "Samoan's starchy fare." Naturally, she expected *taro* to be the answer. Here's her clever note: "Here we go again. One man's 'talo' is another man's 'poi-son.' "

My source for *talo* was *Webster's Third*. The word ranks with dryad *erato* and with *ave* defined as "Goodbye, to Galba." All three are sure to draw forth letters from Leapers.

Another of my keen solvers, R.R.R. of New York City, was thrown for a loss when "Partlet or pullet" was the clue for HEN. He wrote:

In today's crossword puzzle, for the life of me, I cannot see any correlation between the definition and the answer to 11 Down: a *partlet* was what we in Italy used to wear in the Middle Ages rarely while tending to our pullets in the henhouse.

Webster's Third lists two words that are spelled *partlet*. They come from entirely different sources. The first is "a covering for the neck and shoulders worn chiefly by women in the 10th century. . . ." It stems from the Medieval French noun *patelette* ("bound of cloth").

The second one is derived from *Pertelote,* the hen that was the favorite wife of the rooster named Chanticleer in Chaucer's "Nun's Priest's Tale."

Speaking of chickens, in 1984 the clue for ROOST was "Place to lay an egg." M.S.B., who described herself as a farm girl, objected courteously:

> Oh dear! So many broken eggs! A *roost* is a "perfect place" to sleep, but a terrible place to lay an egg. A *nest* is a perfect place to lay an egg.

M.S.B.'s statement was accompanied by two sketches: one showed a bird standing on a perch (which she called a roost) and the other showed a bird apparently laying an egg in a nest.

Like many other Leapers, my correspondent was half right. She forgot that a roost is also a large cage, house, or place for fowls or birds.

R.P. of Roslyn Heights, New York, apparently has a hang-up on *apprehend*. Perhaps he thinks that the verb means "arrest" and nothing more. Here's his 1987 missive.

> In your puzzle of 4/29/87 the clue for 12 Down (INTUIT) I believe should have read: "*Comprehend* sans reasoning" as opposed to *apprehend* . . .
> Is this a "Gotcha" or is it me?

Webster's Third defines *intuit* as follows: "to know or apprehend directly . . . ," and all my dictionaries state that the verb is a synonym for *perceive* or *understand*.

In 1988, my clue for WELSH was "Kind of rabbit." S.B. of New York City sent a stern reprimand.

I draw your attention to the crossword puzzle in today's *Times*. The answer to clue 60 Across, seems to be WELSH.

I would like to point out, that the actual name of that dish is *Welsh rarebit*, and has nothing, I repeat, nothing to do with rabbits.

If my critic had looked into any good dictionary, she would have discovered that *Welsh rabbit* was the original humorous designation for the dish of melted cheese often mixed with beer or ale and served with crackers or toast.

New World, Third states that *Welsh rarebit* has evolved through "faulty etymologizing."

By the way, the anonymous jokester who named the cheesy concoction is no friend of the good citizens of Wales.

S.R. of Bristol, Rhode Island, probably has an old dictionary. Here is part of a letter he sent in 1989.

Gotcha—Sept. 17 puzzle, 91 Down. *Paddy* is not a rice field! *Paddy* is the Asian word for rice. One can have a paddy field, but not a rice paddy.

I will grant that the error is very common.

The original meaning of *paddy* was "rice," as S.R. asserts. However, by association or metonymy, folks began applying the name to the field in which the cereal grass grew. As a result, in new dictionaries like *Random House, Second* the first definition for *paddy* is "rice field."

Incidentally, *Webster's Third* lists four other words spelled *paddy*. The first is a bird known as Java sparrow; the second refers to a baby's hand; and the third is an adjective meaning "*like a pad.*" The last means "Irishman" and, by slangy extension, "policeman" or "cop." A further extension is the use of *paddy wagon* for the patrol wagon of yesteryear.

Let me hastily add that the latest lexicons like *New World, Third* are careful to state that *paddy* for "Irishman" (from *Padraig*, the Irish form of *Patrick*) is "a patronizing and formerly derisive term"). Why "formerly"? Probably because it's no longer used.

Coming back to *Webster's Third*, I should also note that a shortened form for *paddywhack* is *paddy*. It can mean "fury or temper." As a verb it becomes "*thrash, spank, paddle.*"

• • •

At the end of 1988, P.H.B. of Port Washington, New York, demurred justifiably but was still a Leaper.

> First of all: Merry Christmas! As one of the millions who daily solve your puzzle (with or w/o dictionary) I am again questioning a clue. 38 Down on yesterday's reads: "fissure" which could be *rift* or *rent* whereas the proper answer REFT should be past tense or participle of *reave* or perhaps *robbed of something*. I wonder how many others wrote too?!

P.H.B.'s problem is that he apparently does not have access to *Webster's Third*. That dictionary declares that *reft* means "Cleft, fissure" and adds that the use of the word is "probably influenced by *cleft* or *rift*." I should add that *Webster's Third* states that another *reft* is the past tense of *reave*.

M.M. of Staten Island is one of many solvers who sometimes forget that a word often has many meanings. In 1987 he wrote:

> I believe the definition should have been "conce*p*t" instead of "conce*it*" as my solution of the puzzle yields the answer IDEA.

My guess is that M.M. equates *conceit* with vanity and has forgotten or has never learned that a conceit is an idea—usually a fanciful one.

Somewhere along the line, many young people are criticized by oldsters when they use *intermural* for *intramural*. The corrections are so ingrained that they grow up thinking that *intermural* is a nonexistent adjective. In fact, *New World, Third* fails to list the word!

In 1984, I used INTERMURAL in a puzzle and defined it as "Describing some sports." To my amazement, about a dozen solvers leaped. One of them was Mrs. D.W.B. of Cleveland Heights, Ohio.

> I do believe you've let them get something past you again, and I wish you wouldn't: you see, after spending the summer

out of reach of *The New York Times,* the 9/30/84 puzzle was my
first in three months and I've got so much to catch up on that
even looking at the puzzle was a luxury, and where am I supposed to find the time to be picky?

   . . . but I can't help it. You mustn't let them substitute *"intermural"* (114 Across) for *"intramural";* it won't do.

Webster's Third defines *intermural* as "between the walls" and
notes that *intramural* can mean "within the walls." Thus, if some
freshmen at a high school play other freshmen or even upper-
classmen, it's an *intramural* game because it is literally "within
the walls" of a single school.

Random House, Second says the following about *intermural*: "of,
pertains to, or taking place between two or more institution cities,
etc.: *an intermural track meet."*

Several letters also came to my desk when I defined SCANS as
"reads cursorily." G.G., a loyal solver from the Bay State, was
among the Leapers.

   No, no! *Skims,* maybe but it doesn't fit the crosswords. Scan-
ning is a very detailed, cautious reading.

   I suppose everybody is at you about it. Sorry to add to the
din, but I do feel it's the duty of all of us to keep you on your
toes!

The problem is that *scan* has two diametrically opposite meanings. Typical words of that sort are *ravel* ("tangle" or *"un*tangle")
and *cleave* ("split" or "stick to").

   J.T. of New York City calls such words "antilogies" (contra-
dictions in terms or ideas) and includes the following in his rather
extensive list:

Buckle	Fasten together; fall apart
Downhill	Getting easier; getting worse
Enjoin	Command to do; forbid to do
Handicap	Disadvantage; advantage (as in golf)
Overlook	Watch over; ignore
Trim	Cut down; embellish, as a tree

• • •

In 1990 the clue was "Eject violently" and the answer was ERUCT. The *C* was crossed by the same letter in FINCA, defined as "Mexican estate." Even though P.G. of New Canaan, Connecticut, knew the Spanish word he couldn't believe *eruct*.

> The Sunday Puzzle; clue/clew Number thirty-nine, Mexican estate is "fin*c*a" not "fin*p*a"!
> You are not double checking. I'm going to watch you like a hawk.

I.S.G., a professional engineer of Cranbury, New Jersey, took me to task on a matter involving his line of work.

> 1 Across in one of last week's puzzles had as an answer BRAZE.
> The definition was "solder . . ."
> Please be advised that soldering and brazing are two distinctly different processes separated at 450° C.
> It is a technological faux pas to use *solder* and *braze* interchangeably in a definition.

Once again, I believe it's a case of generalization coming about because of folk usage. *Webster's Third* defines *braze* as follows: "to solder with an alloy (as hard solder or brass) that is relatively infusible as compared with common solder."
I also learned from *New World, Third* that *braze* has a second meaning: "to make hard like brass."

Again, folk usage may be a factor that has caused D.R. of Spring Valley, New York, to become a Leaper. His clever letter reads:

> "tire part" = lug?
> Saturday, Feb. 10, 1990
> As a lug who's lugged many a tire, I can assure you there are no lugs on same. There aren't any on the tire rims, either.

The threaded lugs are on the wheel base, which stays on the car when changing the tire. The lug nuts go onto them, against the tire rims.

Tiresome, but true.

But here's what *Webster's Third* says about *lug:* "A projection or ridge on the rim of a wheel (as of a tractor) or on a rubber tire to increase traction."

Now here are three examples of fans who leaped before waiting to see the answer. First, let's consider one from R.A.Z. of New York City.

I am writing to point out an error in the puzzle published on today's date. The clue for 71 Across is "High nest." The obvious answer is *aerie*. However, I believe that the correct answer for 50 Down is ENROBE. This leaves EERIE as the answer for 71 Across.

I always enjoy your puzzles and hope that this time I "gotcha."

Next comes one from F.G.I.-W. of Switzerland.

Okay, I didn't merit a "Gotcha" last time (bandito/bandido). But 31 Down in the *International Herald Tribune* you clue as "friends in Firenze," whereas you should have indicated "friend," in the singular, since 47 Across is *dot*. Right? Still your fan in Switzerland.

Thirdly, I present a double-complaint from A.Z.L. of Hartford, Connecticut: "LEHR for comedian? RIMIFY for branch out? Surely you take liberties."

Mr. Z. assumed that *aerie* was the correct answer for "High nest," but this time the right response was EYRIE.

My Swiss correspondent wrote *dot* as the answer to "Morse code E." This caused the vertical crossing word to become *amico*. But the correct word was DIT. Thus AMICI emerges as the response for "Friends in Firenze."

Ms. L. is probably a young person who has never heard of Lew *Lehr,* the comedian who died in 1950. She probably thought that I'd misspelled Bert Lahr's surname.

As for *rimify*, the answer was really RAMIFY. The crossing looked like this:

```
          I
          R
R   A   M   I   F   Y
          S
```

The crossing word, IRAS, was defined as "One of Cleo's attendants." Ms. L. entered *Iris* instead of *Iras*.

The preceding error reminds me of another by Mrs. W.T.S. of Erir, Pennsylvania. Here's her letter.

I call your attention to the enclosed puzzle. Number 78 horizontal—MULE should really be *mewl*. Nowhere in any dictionary is the meaning of the word *whine* spelled *mule*.

Mrs. S.'s confusion arose from the fact that she did not know that a century plant is a PITA—not a *mita*—and she was unaware that to whine is to PULE.

```
P   U   L   E
I
T
A
```

Similarly, an anonymous fan from Westchester, New York, did not know that a "Whipstitch" is a SEC (short for *second*) as well as a seamstress's overcast. Hence, she criticized me for not knowing Lil Abner's creator. Her answer read:

```
        S
        E
A   L   W   A   P   P
```

• • •

Have you ever felt so sure about the meaning of a word that you don't bother to look it up and then discover that you're dead wrong? W.W. of Jamaica, New York, had such an experience in 1982 when he wrote:

> I enclose crossword puzzle for Thursday, August 6, in the *New York Times*. The clue for 27 Across is "coming twice a year." The answer, the wrong answer, is BIANNUAL.
> *Biannual* means every two years. *Semi-annual* means every half year. Therefore the clue should have been "coming every two years."

Let me set the record straight:

> Biannual   Occurring twice a year
> Biennial   Happening every two years

Solstices are *biannual* events. One comes in the winter; another comes in summer.

Some flowers that skip a year when blooming are *biennials*.

In 1989 M.K. of Amherst, Massachusetts, informed me that SWEETS as a synonym for "darling" was not listed in *Random House, Second* or *Webster's Third*. He was mistaken, but it is easy to understand the reason. Both dictionaries carry *sweets* as a sub-entry under the noun *sweet*.

The *sweet-sweets* matter reminds me of the *smith-smithy* debate with Professor A.R.B. in 1985. She wrote:

> In the Dec. 8 puzzle, p. 156, down, #11, no doubt you mean *smith,* not SMITHY.
> Consult William Safire!

I kept a copy of my reply. Here it is.

> Thanks for your interest in the puzzles and for taking the time to write. As for SMITHY, I have several dictionaries that support my clue. For example, *Webster's Third New International*

and *Webster's New World* state that *smithy* is not only the workshop
but the *smith* himself. If Mr. Safire disagrees, I challenge him
to a logomachy at thirty paces.

Once in a while an Englishman gets into the Leaper act because
of differences in British and American colloquial language or
outright slang. The following example comes from M.F., who
has settled in St. Simons Island, Georgia.

> I've written in the past about this to Will Weng and Margaret
> Farrar and now, alas, I have to write to you:
> As an Englishman, I must tell you that 7 Down in the attached
> puzzle is incorrect in its spelling. If you are "bananas" in the
> U.K., you're "Ba*r*my"—if the weather is warm and a bit tropical,
> it is "Ba*l*my."
> If you would use the correct word in the future it would be
> balm (not barm) to my soul.

My clue for BALMY was "Bananas." In my reply to M.F. I
stressed that the clue did *not* say "Bananas in the U.K." I think
I also told him I liked his *barm-balm* pun.

M.B. of Port Washington, New York, is one of my faithful solvers. Since he once received a Gotcha certificate, he has often
tried in vain to catch me again. Here's an example. He objected
to using "O.K.!" as a clue for ROGER.

> Ha! Gotcha!
> 50 Down in 10/21/86 *Times*. *Roger* means only that "I have
> *received* and *understood* your message."
> It does not connote approval or agreement.
> When do I get my oak leaf cluster?

Mr. B. may need an updated dictionary like *Random House,
Second* or *New World, Third*. Even *Webster's Third* (copyright 1961)
allows "O.K."

• • •

The *Times* syndicates my puzzles to several hundred other newspapers, including at least one in Los Angeles. A.D. of that city
wrote to me as follows:

To the best of my knowledge, there's an error in the puzzle which ran in the *Los Angeles Herald Examiner,* dated April 10, 1985.

The clue is: "Additions to ltrs." And the answer turns out to be PSS.

A *PS* is short for *Postscript.*

Sometimes one adds an additional postscript, in which case it becomes a *Post postscript,* or a *PPS.*

I realize you can't answer individual letters, but I'm truly puzzled as to what *PSS* could stand for.

Help!

I referred A.D. to *Webster's Third* and other recent lexicons that carry *P.SS.* as abbreviations for *postscripts.*

I'm reminded that I recently received a letter from one of my regular puzzle constructors. She appended three different postscripts and then added still another. It read: "I apologize for using so many P.SS."

Still on the subject of the English language, we proceed to Diction and Grammar. In this area, most of the Leapers are old-fashioned people who insist on the strictures they were taught to observe many years ago and refuse to go with the flow. I must admit that I was one of that self-righteous crowd myself until I wrote *A Pleasure in Words.* Research involved in the writing of that book impressed upon me the fluidity of our language and the fragility of rules prescribed by protectors of an artificial *status quo.*

Here's an excellent example of what I mean. As a Latin major in college, I knew that an *agendum* was a list of things to be done. Therefore, any committee that I headed had an *agendum*—not an *agenda.* And my dictionaries in those days supported my argument that *agendas* was a monstrosity created by ignorant people.

R.J.H. of California wrote the following letter in 1989—not 1929.

I charge you with slaughtering the "King's" English, more aptly put, Webster's rendering of it. There are two words in question. They are your renderings of:

44 Across: W. German state. Translation works out to
              HESSE. The official name is *Hessen*.

45 Across: Programs for committees. Translation works out
              to AGENDAS. There is no such word. *Agenda* is
              the plural for *agendum*. If one were to use your
              translation, *agendas,* it would be quite alright to
              say "datas" . . . and we know that would be bad
              English. Yes?

Have I gotcha? In addition to being a purist, I'm also an
arrogant . . . else why would I "work" my puzzles in ink?

Mr. H's criticism of *Hesse* is hardly worth discussing. Suffice
it to say that my solvers are Americans. Even those of Teutonic
background know that *Hesse* is English and *Hessen* is German.
As for *agendas,* see any modern lexicon.

Mrs. J.H.H. of New Rochelle, New York, was certain that *emanate*
and *erupt* were intransitive verbs. Her postcard read:

Another protest against defining a transitive verb by an intransitive and vice versa. Nov. 1 puzzle, Down (1) threw forth;
Down (40) give off.

Webster's Third gives the following examples of how the verbs
in question can take an object: "The serenity he emanated
touched her so warmly" and "The volcano erupted lava bombs."

M.B. of Englewood, New Jersey, thought he had run into a typo
in 1989. The clue for LSTS read: "W.W. II craft." Mr. Beck
consoled me briefly: "Not to worry—proves you to [be] human
like the rest of us!"

Possibly because of expressions like "arts and crafts" sailors prefer such sentences as this one that I have found in *Random House,
Second*: "The craft were warned of possible heavy squalls."

In connection with the above, here's a letter from G.P.P. of
Concord, Massachusetts. Please note the year that Mr. P.'s lexicon was published!

According to Mr. W.'s New International 1926, the plural of *arapahoe* is *Arapahoes*—how come you let the constructor get away with *Arapahoe?*

Modern dictionaries, such as *Webster's Third* and *Random House, Second* give either *Arapahoe* or *Arapahoes* as the correct plural for the Algonquian group. When considered collectively, *Arapahoe* is preferred. An example is: "Oklahoma and Wyoming are states in which the *Arapahoe* live."

M.A.S. of Stony Brook, New York, registered a linguistic complaint as well.

Today's crossword (8/29/87) has, I think, a mistake: 19 Across "Ain't, properly" should not have the answer ARENT! "Ain't" properly should be "am not" or maybe "is not," but it certainly isn't "aren't"!

In its discussion of the versatile solecism, *Webster's Third* gives first billing to *aren't* as one of the many acceptable contractions that *ain't* replaces. An example is: "Things *ain't* what they used to be." Here are some other ways in which *ain't* has been employed:

Ain't it the truth? (Isn't)
That batter *ain't* got a chance. (hasn't)
Don't tell me we *ain't* reached New York yet. (haven't)
I *ain't* talkin'. (am not)

Spelling is the field in which puzzle constructors and editors must be as close to perfection as humans can be. It is also the easiest area for a solver to check in a dictionary. Nevertheless, it has its share of Leapers. Let's start with one from Harwich, Massachusetts. Part of the letter reads:

It grieves me to see a simple spelling mistake under your illustrious name! The spelling habits of too many in the print medium and elsewhere are unnecessarily weird—let's hope the mistake enclosed here was due to a typesetter's slip!

Our Harwich fan is referring to an unusual clue for MALE. The definition was "Maldives capital," but the leaper maintained that the spelling should be *capitol.* This is a common error. People who fall into the "o" trap should keep in mind that *capitols* are buildings whereas *capitals* are cities or towns. Our *capitol* is in a domed structure atop a hill in our *capital.*

In 1990, Dr. S.B. misspelled *sheik* and thought he had discovered an orthographic mistake in a crossing word.

> Just a brief note of mild outrage (how's that for an oxymoron!) about your misspelling error (how's that for a pleonastic redundancy!) in last Sunday's crossword puzzle: 33 Down should have been "misch*ie*vous" (not "misch*ei*vous"). What happened?

Here is my answer to the good doctor:

> Thanks for your interest in the puzzles, but hereafter to avoid embarrassment (and also to save me the time it takes to reply) please wait until the answer is published a week later.
> In the case of MISCHIEVOUS, you misspelled the crossing word (SHEIK). Thus, *mischievous* came out as *mischeivous.*"

Another physician, H.S. of Syosset, New York, jumped the gun, too.

> "Gotcha" again! In today's puzzle you used OPUSES as a solution to "musical works." The plural of *opus* is *opera.*

If Dr. S. had consulted a good dictionary, he would have discovered that both *opera* and *opuses* are acceptable plurals for *opus.*

Similarly, in 1984 D.F. was too enamored of Latin. Here's his letter.

"O Tempora, O mores, O dei immortales."

The plural of *onus* is *onera*. Any Latin scholar knows that. And there's no two ways about it.

In this case, all modern dictionaries give only *onuses* as the plural of *onus*. The word has been completely Anglicized.

I am reminded of *iter*, the Latin word for a passage or road. Its plural, *itinera*, is the source of *itinerant* and *itinerary*.

But *iter* has been taken over by the medical people. To them, it's a brain passage. In that sense it has followed the lead of *onus*. Its plural is *iters*.

Probably the fan's small dictionary was the cause of the following 1988 letter from J.A.T. of Mesa, Arizona.

This is the third time I'm writing to you thinking I've caught you in a mistake. The first two times you pointed out the error of my ways. But this time I'm almost sure I'm correct. If not, I'll consider that a third strike and I won't pester you anymore. I'll still tackle the puzzles, but won't contest any answers.

The puzzle I question this time is the one slugged "Academe." For 96 Down ("clumsy"), I've got *inept*. For 107 Across ("Broadway's Juliet: 1934"), I put *Katharine Cornell*.

If I'm correct the *E* in *inept* clashes with the *A* in *Katharine*. Right or wrong, I very much enjoy your puzzles.

All unabridged dictionaries give both *inept* and *inapt*, but I must admit that I had never heard of *inapt* until a day when I was constructing a puzzle and needed an *a* as the third letter of the word. Although it was a good feeling to find *inapt* in my unabridged dictionary, I have yet to meet the adjective in some writer's work or to hear it in conversations.

As noted before, when thousands of educated people spell a word differently from what is considered to be the norm, then the second spelling becomes acceptable. Here are a few examples based on Leapers' letters.

zero	*aught* or *ought*
Cuban dance	*rumba* or *rhumba*

| prance | *tittup* or *titup* |
| abstain from | *forgo* or *forego* |

That last deviation is especially irritating to purists who delight in noting that *forego* has only one meaning: to precede.

Moving on to other categories, I find Royalty next on my Leaper list. In this area, let me first clear up what I call the "Crazy Otto-Otho Problem." Using *Webster's Biographical Dictionary* as my main source, I note that Otho was a Roman emperor who succeeded Galba (A.D. 69). Also there were four Holy Roman emperors of Teutonic origin starting with "Otto the Great."

So far, so good but in Old High German the foursome were Otho I, Otho II, etc. This change of spelling has caused many solvers to pounce. Typical of their "Crazy Otto-Otho" letters is a 1989 one from J. and J.B. of Ferguson, Missouri.

> The definition for thirty-nine down, is "Holy Roman emperor: 962–73," which, as any ink-pen-using *New York Times* puzzle addict knows, is OTTO. However, Otto didn't comport well with the Siberian Huskies, the Big Men in the U.S.S.R., when he crossed down through their territory.
>
> Eventually, in desperation, we turned to his 900-year predecessor-of-sorts, *Otho*, 69–69, who got along famously with the Big Men. Otho deserved better treatment.

The following letter from J.S. of Atlanta was caused by her perhaps having read only part of the clue.

> Please clarify for me. In the puzzle on Tuesday, the 10th, 3 Down, the question was: "Henry the VIII's third." To my best knowledge it was Jane Seymour. The word worked out to be PARR, who was his 6th. Am I wrong?

The clue actually read "Henry VIII's third Catherine." Prior to Catherine Parr, he married Catherine of Aragon and Catherine Howard.

* * *

On the subject of British royalty, here's a letter from a worker at a Pennsylvania paper, one of the many newspapers that belong to the *Times* syndicate.

> We carry your Sunday Crossword Puzzle in our Sunday paper and it is my favorite part of the paper. On Saturday nights, while I check the first papers off the press, all the printers and makeup men hover round my desk because they know that when I reach for the puzzle, the paper's okay and they can go home. I mention that to prove that I'm not looking for errors—but I found one.
>
> In the puzzle for Sunday, 11 March, 2 Down asked for the last Stuart ruler. I wrote in "Mary," as in William & because Queen Mary II, co-sovereign with her husband William of Orange, was the last Stuart monarch in England. I then sat and stared at that corner of the puzzle for 20 minutes because nothing would fit with it. I finally broke down and entered ANNE and could finish the puzzle—even though, Queen Anne, Mary's sister, was her predecessor. I mention this not in a griping spirit, but in the interest of the accuracy you seem to try so hard to maintain. We like to be accurate here, too, even though mistakes sometimes get past the best of us, and my editors agreed—since we do use your puzzle—that I could point the mistake out to you.

My correspondent should have looked under *Stuart* or *Anne* before she leaped. The *Columbia Encyclopedia* is one of the many reference books declaring that Anne was the last of the Stuarts.

Whenever I define DAME as "Spouse of a knight," a half dozen letters from Anglophiles are sure to await me a few days later. The following one from D.R.W. of Point Pleasant, New Jersey, is an example.

> The last time I "caught" you, and became a member of the *Gotcha Club* it concerned the title of the Queen of England. I write today concerning another English title:
>
> In the puzzle of 25 March, 70 Across asks for "Spouse of a knight," the answer wanted was DAME. The spouse of a knight is a Lady, as in Lady Churchill, not a Dame.
>
> A Dame is a female title equal to Sir (a Knight) given a female in her own right, as in Dame May Whitty. Or the title of the *widow* of a Knight.

My *New World* gives four definitions for *dame*. The third one reads: "In Great Britain a) the legal title of the wife of a knight or baronet; b) the title of a woman who has received an order of knighthood (used always with the given name)."

The latter part of the *New World* definition was familiar to me. I knew all about Dame Joan (Sutherland), Dame Agatha (Christie), Dame Myra (Hess), et al. However, the abundance of letters refuting the use of *dame* as a knight's wife caused me to write to my friend David Guralnik, the Editor in Chief of the *New World* lexicons.

Here is his reply.

> Our definition for *dame* is correct. It is the "legal" title for the wife of a knight (see citations in the *OED* [Oxford English Dictionary]), but these days those dames are generally addressed with the honorific "Lady." Our entry at *lady* takes note of that usage.

Rev. T.C.D. of New York City wrote a very nice letter. It concerned another type of ruler.

> In the Sunday *Times* puzzle of Sept. 25, the clue for 72 Down was "Pope: 795–816." The Pope during those years was Adrian, as appears in the list in the Official Catholic Directory, p. viii (New York, P.J. Kennedy & Sons, 1987). The puzzle requires the answer LEO III, who was Pope 816–17.
>
> Since coming to New York about 11 years ago, I have derived much enjoyment, and a dash of education, from working the puzzles you edit. As a sometime editor, not of puzzles but of books, I may be partial to the breed, but I think they go unthanked. Somewhat like actors who are overadulated and well remunerated—when they work—they go unthanked. I remember long years ago thanking Alec Guinness for all the joy and laughter he brought into my life. He was taken aback and said no one had ever thanked him before.
>
> So now, I thank you for such beguiling and innocent joys of working crosswords. Although, I must admit frankly that I sometimes ascribed to you a diabolical cleverness which, I'm sure, you do not suffer.

Maybe there's a hidden hitch involved, but all my sources avouch that Adrian died in 795.

Since we've moved into the area of religious hierarchies, consider this unconsciously humorous letter from a woman in Shreveport, Louisiana.

> In your Fireside Book of Crossword Puzzles Series 143, puzzle 3, you have a word (6 Down)—"Old cowhand"; your answer is IMAN. My new *Oxford American Dictionary* gives the definition for *Iman* (n) 1. The leader of prayers in a mosque. 2. Iman, the title of various Muslim spiritual leaders. Nowhere is cowhand mentioned or cowboy or rough rider.
>
> I am from Louisiana, next door to Texas, and I have never heard such a word mentioned.

As gently and as tactfully as possible, I explained to my confused Shreveporter that "I'M AN Old Cowhand" is a song and that the Muslim spiritual leader is an *imam*.

Now let's delve into a few discussions on American History. We start with an interesting letter from W.R. of Englewood, New Jersey.

> I believe a correction is in order in your Sunday *Times* Crossword. 63 Down calls for the name of the victor at Saratoga, 1777. It was not Gates, which fits the puzzle, but Benedict Arnold. Gates, the commanding general, ordered a retreat. Arnold countermanded the order and attacked. He won the day and lost a leg in the process. It is known as one of the seven decisive battles of the world. It turned the tide of the Revolution. For that act of wise generalship and heroism he was reprimanded by General Washington—he had countermanded the order of a superior.
>
> Arnold was a brilliant and brave field commander and possessed a fair share of vanity. Naturally he was sorely hurt at Washington's reprimand. Shortly thereafter he entered into negotiations for the surrender of West Point.
>
> P.S. Arnold's treason was inexcusable—but what about Washington's treatment of him?

Upon investigation, I found that the true hero of the Saratoga victory was indeed Benedict Arnold. Furthermore, Gates never even took the field. Instead he watched from a distance. But since he was the commanding officer, all reference books give him the credit for the triumph. Therefore, I will continue to use "Winner at Saratoga" as a clue for GATES. One of my reasons is that the definition has a touch of humor: it seems to be referring to a racehorse.

When INS crops up in a puzzle, constructors often define it as "Office holders" or "Electees." Seeking a different clue when a 1984 puzzle on American history contained INS, I consulted an almanac and found that Polk and his colleagues had been elected in 1845. Fine! That would be my INS clue! But I inadvertently confused young B.S. of New Rochelle, New York. He wrote as follows:

> I am a junior at New Rochelle High School and am presently studying James Polk's administration in my American History Honors class. I was amused to see Polk's campaign slogan, "54-40 or fight" regarding the northern boundary of the Oregon country in today's crossword puzzle.
> While doing the puzzle a problem arose concerning 38 Across—"Polk's party in 1945."
> You incorrectly state that Polk was a member of the *Independent* Party. He was really a member of the Democratic Party and an ardent supporter of Jacksonian democracy. At the nominating convention of 1844, Martin Van Buren seemed to be the logical choice for the Democratic candidate but he could not obtain the required 2/3 majority. As a compromise, the convention nominated James K. Polk as its Democratic candidate, thus becoming the first "dark horse" in American politics.
> Hoping to hear from you in regard to this matter.

Even though Mr. S. had placed a *D* where an *S* belonged in the crossing word, it was encouraging to learn that at least one teenager was tackling the *Times* crosswords.

GOTCHAS

Among the crossword puzzle fans, the most astute and the least in number are the members of my exclusive Gotcha Club. They are the people who catch me in an error when hardly anyone else has noticed it. For example, in 1987, when I defined *dodecahedron* as a "twelve-sided figure," T.L. was the only solver to take me to task. Here is the main section of his letter.

> 28 Down should have read *dodecagon,* not DODECAHEDRON. A dodecagon has 12 sides, being a flat figure, whereas a dodecahedron has faces, being a solid figure.
>
> A dodecahedron does have sides: 48, if a rhomboidal dodecahedron. Four for each of its twelve faces; it may also have 60 sides, five for each of its twelve faces if it is pentagonal (as in the natural crystal of pyrite or fool's gold).

Another example comes from B.V. of Canton, New York. He gave me a lesson in *ecology* back in 1983.

In the puzzle in the Large Type Edition of 9/26, 59 Down was defined as "Environment Abbr.," and turned out to be ECOL, short for *Ecology* (obviously).

According to the *Random House* unabridged, ecology is a branch of biology (or sociology). It is not synonymous with *environment*. I am sure you know this and therefore I suppose that this error slipped past you.

Many persons confuse *ecology* with *environment*, including many who ought to know better. I find it annoying.

Similarly, Dr. H.B., a professor of Obstetrics and Gynecology at George Washington University, was one of only two correspondents on what he rightfully called "a grievous error" in 1987. Part of his letter reads:

> The definition for number 49 Across is listed as "hordeolum sound." The answer is listed as OINK, which hardly makes sense when the word *hordeolum* applies only to a type of inflammation, or sty, which is confined to one's eye. *Hordeolum* has nothing to do with pigs or a pig's sty.

While editing over forty thousand definitions for *Times* puzzles each year, I make an average of ten mistakes. The number would be far more if I were not blessed with a diligent, intelligent, and alert proofer named Harriett Wilson. After I have corrected the errors made by constructors, Ms. Wilson fine-combs every page and we go over each item together before sending the finished product to the composing room.

Some of the errors are obvious. For instance, let me cite the case of the great football player, Crazy Legs Hirsch. His first name is Elroy, but in 1986 one of my constructors called him Leroy and the mistake zipped by Ms. Wilson and me. Oh, what a flood of letters poured in! Many of them emanated from Wisconsin, where Mr. Hirsch had won new fame as a coach. Here's a copy of my reply to the Gotcha crowd.

Dear Friend or Friends,

First, let me apologize for resorting to a Xeroxed answer rather than a personal reply. At this point, I have received about fifty letters concerning the reversal of the first two letters of

Mr. Hirsch's first name, and more corrections pour in every day.

I have just sent an apology to "Crazy Legs." I hope he will be as forgiving and as nice as most of you. To tell the truth, I am glad that the error from a puzzler in Pennsylvania slipped through me and my two proofers because it taught me how many solvers really appreciate the time and effort I take to make the puzzles accurate, interesting and informative. Only two letters had a nasty "For shame!" message. All the other contained encouraging statements like "Keep up the good work!" or "All your puzzles are great. Please do not retire!"

The ironic part of this fiasco is that I idolized Mr. Hirsch four decades ago when I played football for a small college in New Jersey.

At any rate, I am grateful for your interest in the puzzles and I thank almost all of you for your compassion and kindness.

Happy Holidays!

When a mistake is as egregious as the Elroy-Leroy one, the multitudes of letter writers are not admitted to the Gotcha Club. One reason is to prevent my supply of certificates from running out very fast. But the chief purposes are to prevent the certificate's worth from being debased and to retain the elite quality of the club.

To satisfy those who wonder what the certificate looks like, here's a reproduction of same on the next page.

Another of my rules for certificates is "one to a customer." Incidentally, after being caught about seven times by Monsignor A.V.M. of New York, I appointed him president of the Gotcha Club. I must say that all his letters are gracious, humorous, and almost self-effacing in contrast to missives that feel like missiles delivered by solvers who pridefully pounce on mistakes and never add a kind word about the puzzles in general. Most of them happen to be men, usually professionals, who seem to have a need to show how smart they are or to strike out at someone.

To get back to the Elroy goof, one of the most interesting Gotchas came from B.C. of New York City. Here it is.

The Great Maleska!!

I can't believe it! I was just beginning to think you'd *never* flub one. I spend my mornings—from Jamaica to Penn Station,

The New York Times

G O T C H A

C
L U B

This is to certify that

_____

*is hereby granted
membership in the elite
New York Times
Crossword Puzzle Gotcha Club*

Eugene T. Maleska

EUGENE T. MALESKA   PUZZLE EDITOR

_____

DATE

a ritual—with your puzzles, and although you inevitably try to ruin my week with one of your Greek, unpublished Shakespeare and remote northern Italian lake puzzles, I almost always enjoy my little trip a little more working my way through your daily product.

And like I said, I was starting to believe in your mortal infallibility, but this morning the bubble burst!

The combination of 10, 18, 27, 28 and 29 Across: "Crazy Legs Hirsch." The "answer" as it fit in your puzzle was LEROY, but I'm afraid, Mr. Maleska, that the man's name was Elroy!

You don't know what this does to me! I mean our president is lying to us, our city's falling down around us, the Ice Age is closing in on us. And now, this!

Where can a man put his faith any more?

I'll start in again tomorrow hoping that, as time passes into our uncertain future, maybe my reliance on Eugene T. Maleska as a source of stability, accuracy and honest challenge can be restored.

Names of people seem to be my nemesis. Also, I sometimes fail to check on experienced constructors like Alfio Micci. He was born in Italy; hence I thought he was an expert on the Guccis and Puccis. Wrong! Along came a letter from F.I., the vice-president of the Gotcha Club. In part, it reads:

> I'm afraid, as a certificate-bearing member of your Gotcha Club, that I must call to your attention 17 Down in yesterday's puzzle, "Musical Shorthand." Either Signor Micci doesn't know his Guccis from his Puccis, or 17 Across is "parage"! (Emelio is Pucci; *Gucci*'s first name, I believe, is Aldo.)

Ms. I. caught me again when the clue for PAPA read "Waitt role in *The Waltons*." She reminded me that the actor was Ralph *Waite*.

Gladwyn Hill, a retired member of the *Times* staff, is another officer of the Gotcha Club. In 1987 he chided me for misspelling Carry Nation's first name. But, in this case, I was misled by one of my reference books. And in 1988, *Random House, Second* stated that either *Carry* or *Carrie* was okay.

Another of my trusted sources deceived me on the first name of the most famous of the Boswell sisters. In *Tune in Yesterday* she was listed as *Connie*. Here's part of what D.M. of Kinnelon, New Jersey, wrote.

> It seems that the only times I write to you are when I can gloat a bit over what your *Times* colleague, Bill Safire, calls an "I gotcha."
>
> In the Sunday puzzle, 8 vertical, as you may have heard from others by now, is in error, as Miss Boswell always spelled her name with a double *E*, an affectation, of course.

Oh, those proper names! A constructor misspelled director Sam Peckinpah's surname in the diagram and a score of letters said "Don't gimme paw!" after a substitute proofer and I let it go through.

Harriet S. of Sarasota, Florida, was one of the Gotchas. Afterwards, she sent our correspondence to the *Sarasota Herald Tribune*. Here is what they printed.

Funny exchange between Harriet [S.] and the *New York Times* crossword puzzle editor, Eugene Maleska.

Maleska misspelled Sam Peckinpah's last name in a recent puzzle, changing the *h* to a *w*.

"Do you think he yells 'Raw, Raw' at football games?" Harriet asked the editor via a note. "Or was a friend of the Shaw of Iran?"

"I'm very embarrassed," Maleska said in his personally penned reply. "Baw, humbug!"

Sometimes a misspelling occurs because the name in question is unfamiliar. Such an instance occurred in 1988 with regard to the author of a mystery book. C.W. of Nutley, New Jersey, caught us for a good reason.

When it comes to the diagramless puzzles, I'm always sure it's me. When something won't work out, I'm certain I've put the words in the wrong places. And usually I've been right that I've been wrong.

So, I waited for the solution to the above puzzle to see exactly how I had messed it up this time. But, lo and behold, it wasn't me. I was right and I have *A Taste for Death* at my side to prove it.

You probably already know but, please, allow me to also tell you: It's Adam Dalgl*i*esh, not *ei*.

I feel so good. Thank you.

D.C. of New Canaan, Connecticut, caught another surname boner.

Gotcha! Sonny Bono—okay, but if your Victor Bono is the unctuous, obese villain of many grade-B films, he spells it Buono.

S.C. of New York City was "victor-ious," too.

I believe I've spotted an error in today's puzzle. The clue for 10 Across reads "Sonny and Victor," and the letters that fit in the squares are B.O.N.O. If the Victor you're thinking of is the actor in *Whatever Happened to Baby Jane?* and *Hush, Hush Sweet Charlotte,* he spells his last name *B.U.O.N.O.*

If I show undue glee in bringing this lapse to your attention, it is only because such things happen so rarely.

Sometimes a mistake brings forth some interesting new information. Consider the following letters anent a misspelling of Zasu Pitts's first name. The first came from H.R.C. of Gloucester City, New Jersey, and the second was sent by A.L.H. of Donellen, New Jersey.

I believe you have made a mistake in the puzzle of this date, attached.

Ms. Pitts' first name was Zasu, not Zazu. If I recall correctly, I once read that her parents could not decide on her name—one wanted to name her Eliza and the other parent wanted to name her Susan. The compromise was Zasu.

Zasu Pitts' name has one z, not two. She fashioned the name from a portion of her first two given names, Eliza Susan.

My worst boo-boo concerning the name of a person in the public eye did *not* involve spelling. It was sex that did me in!

It all started with Dr. Zhivago. His lover was a woman named Lara, and since that name often pops up in puzzles, the not-so-good doctor's paramour is given an overabundance of recognition. Naturally, I try to use other definitions for LARA. Here are a few examples:

Byron work
Wife of Hermes
"Granada" songwriter
Composer Isidore de ———

You can imagine my delight at the end of 1985 when I discovered in *TV Guide* that someone named *Lara Teeter* was a member of the cast of a certain musical drama. Immediately, I seized upon the name: "Actress Teeter" subsequently became the clue for LARA in a Sunday puzzle.

Thirty letters, mostly from New Yorkers, poured in. Shame! Shame! The thespian's a man—not a woman! I have saved two examples. The first comes from S.W. of the New York City Opera; the other was sent by S.P. of Long Island City.

Thanks very much for the puzzle of Sunday, January 6. It was wonderful!

However, on behalf of Lara Teeter who has performed with City Opera several times, he is a boy!

Regarding the January 5 puzzle in the Sunday *Times*, 115 Across, "actress Teeter."

If I'm doing it correctly, the answer comes out LARA. Lara Teeter was the *male* lead in the revival of "On Your Toes" a few seasons ago. True, names are often strange—all the more reason for checking.

Yes, on Teeter I tottered! In embarrassment, I wrote an apology to the actor and promised to be on my toes in the future. He sent me a gracious reply and even thanked me for giving him so much publicity.

Mr. Teeter's role in a musical reminds me that I've struck some sour notes in Euterpe's field, too. For instance, in 1983 I declared that "Marie" was Tommy Dorsey's theme song. A correction came from New York City's Guy Lucas, one of the bandleader's associates.

"Marie" was one of Tommy Dorsey's biggest hits in 1937, but a theme song? Never!

P.S. I worked with TD, and I'm getting sentimental just remembering.*

D.R. earned a Gotcha certificate for the following letter.

Your puzzle of October 11 contains a definition conveying a common bit of misinformation:

Composer of "My Way"

Answer: (Paul) ANKA

The composer of a song means the writer of the music, as opposed to the lyricist (more properly called the lyrist).

Though often given credit as the man who "wrote" this song, Anka actually took an existing French popular song and—

---

*This was Mr. Lucas's clever reminder that the Dorsey theme song was "I'm Getting Sentimental Over You."

seeing the possibilities of adapting it for Sinatra—supplied the American version's lyrics.

Even the concept for the song was borrowed from the original.

Some trivial cautions for the future: Barry Manilow didn't write "I Write the Songs," and Duke Ellington did not write "Take the A Train" (which Lawrence Welk is said to have introduced as "Take a Train" one night).

The word *composer* got me into trouble in 1990. John Keats once wrote about the "innumerable compositions and decompositions" that his poems experienced before being printed. Was Keats therefore a composer? Perhaps I'm indulging in sophistry, but I think I wasn't completely off base when I stated that Francis Scott Key was the composer of our National Anthem. At any rate, I admitted R.W.M. of New York City to the Gotcha Club after he submitted a dissent.

I must challenge your definition (February 26, 1990, 63 Down) of KEY as "The Star-Spangled Banner composer." Francis Scott Key was, of course, the poet, or lyricist, for "The Star-Spangled Banner." The music, which he did not compose, came from a popular English drinking song, "To Anacreon in Heaven."

Thanks for the many years of challenge and amusement you have provided in the puzzles.

A musical flub of the past came back to haunt me in 1986. As a young constructor in the forties, I idolized Margaret Farrar, the first editor of Simon & Schuster crossword puzzle books and the first editor of *Times* puzzles. In my opinion, she could do no wrong. I tackled all the crosswords that were printed under her name, and whenever an entry or definition was new to me, I copied it down in one of my many notebooks. One day, the word SIAM appeared and the clue read "Tuptim's land." I had no idea who Tuptim was, but I dutifully placed the definition under *Siam* in my notebook for four-letter words.

Four decades later while searching for a new definition for *Siam,* I spotted Mrs. Farrar's clue in the battered old notebook. What a jolt I received when I read the following Gotcha from Dr. M.C.W. of Fairleigh Dickinson University in Hackensack, New Jersey.

In yesterday's puzzle (5/29/86) the answer to the clue for 50 Down, "Tuptim's land," was SIAM. Tuptim and her lover ("We Kiss in a Shadow") were Burmese.

I write only because Margaret Farrar made the same mistake about 30 years ago. In her reply to my note, she explained that she read a *Playbill* for "The King and I," and assumed that all the characters were Siamese. I wonder if you did the same thing?

For further information on Tuptim, here's another Gotcha. The writer is P.A.C. of Mamaroneck, New York.

In today's puzzle the clue for 50 Down is "Tuptim's land"; the answer, in 4 letters, is SIAM. This is not true. Tuptim, the princess in "The King and I," was from Burma.

If Tuptim were Siamese, there would have been no point to the story. The point being slavery and loss of freedom. The entire thrust of the play was a plea for freedom from the enslaved peoples of the world as personified by this young girl.

Sometimes my musical errors are classical. In a myopic moment I let a constructor use Ludwig VON Beethoven in a definition. The spate of "For Shames!" could have filled a VAN!

And then there was the blunder concerning one of my favorite conductors. A Gotcha certificate went to I.A.P. of the City University of New York for this letter.

Given my admiration for you and my affection for the theme of today's crossword, it truly grieves me to have to send you this *Gotcha!*—But: 18 Across! SOLTI, (Sir) George (*b.* Budapest, 1912) . . . Not Rumanian, of course, Hungarian. There *is* a difference.

Señor C.M. of New York City is one of my many loyal fans who are experts on opera. He caught me on the spelling of an aria from Verdi's *Rigoletto.*

The clue for 49 Down ("Cara Nome," for one) should be "Car*o* Nome," since *nome* is masculine in Italian. Perhaps your proofreader should listen to the aria a few times, which would be a delightful way to learn to remember the proper spelling.

Like most others, I love music. However, I am an ignoramus when it comes to many of the instruments. For example, I'm still fretting about *frets* after receiving approximately thirty letters telling me that such ridges are found on guitars or lutes but never on *violins!*

Science, math, physics, and medicine are also fields that contain land mines for one who stands in awe of the Einsteins, Euclids, Oppenheimers, and Mayos.

Take astronomy, for instance. W.C. of Seal Beach, California, gave me a celestial lesson in 1987. He wrote:

> Today's puzzle defines PERIGEES as "points in planets' rounds." The word actually defines a point in the orbit of an *Earth*-based system, i.e., a point in the orbit of our moon or an artificial satellite. The word to describe a similar point in the orbit of a general system (a planet, for example) is, of course, *periapsis.*

With regard to Mr. C.'s last sentence, I'm not sure if he is correct. In *New World* I find *periapsis* defined as: "The nearest point to the gravitational center in the orbit of any satellite." Since a satellite is not a planet, I'm asking all you Sagans out there to set me straight.

Here's an anatomical anomaly. Early in 1987 I sent a Gotcha certificate to M.L.V. of Sacramento for her linguistic lesson. She had written:

> Someone slipped in yesterday's puzzle, titled "Famous Last Words," in which the clue "Place for a bracelet" resolved eventually into the word ANKLE (29 Across). I was so confident of your integrity in these matters that I tried for many minutes to integrate the vertical words into the word *wrist.*
>
> A bracelet is by definition something worn on the arm. The word has its roots in Latin *bracchium* via French *bras* both meaning "arm." Let me illustrate: an ornamental chain, worn around the neck as a necklace, becomes a bracelet if it is doubled around an arm, an anklet worn on the lower leg. The choice of words is determined by the place where the chain is worn. The term *bracelets* is slang for *handcuffs*—but not for *leg irons.*

However, I recently asked M.L.V. to tear up her certificate because *Random House, Second* (published in 1988) admits that there really are ankle bracelets. Folk usage, which is covered extensively in a later chapter, has prevailed again.

Once in a while, a clue that is meant to be humorous or clever turns into a boomerang. One October day, I tossed a cute definition into a daily puzzle, and it bounced back into my face. Monsignor A.V.M., Gotcha Club president, wrote a gentle objection.

> Greetings, after a long silence! It was my sister Mary, who has always had a great interest in things medical, who pointed out AORTA in today's big puzzle (93 Down), defined as "way to a man's heart"; and since the aorta conveys blood just *from* the heart, she feels that only a salmon, which swims upstream, would be likely to favor that definition! I'm sure you'll provide an appropriate reply, probably medical also, but opportunities for writing you are not too many!

As the Monsignor is often wont to do, he appended a verse.

> Is it fair to call
> A *one-way* hall,
> That leads *away*
> *From* a room, let's say,
> "The way *to* that spot"
> When it's really not?

Mrs. P.S., an elementary school teacher in Tobyhanna, Pennsylvania, put in her two cents.

> It is very rare that an error is found in the *New York Times* Crossword Puzzle. Yet, one did occur in the puzzle of Sunday, October 19, 1986.
> I am referring to the clue for 93 Down—"Way to a man's heart." My sixth grade Science students at Coolbaugh Elementary center in Tobyhanna, Pennsylvania, were quick to point out—
> The aorta is an artery; it carries blood *away* from the heart, never *to* the heart.
> Therefore, the answer for 93 Down, AORTA, is incorrect.

• • •

My father had *apnea*. He would snore loudly and then become
strangely quiet for several seconds. Then suddenly he would
exhale explosively. I mention it because of the following letter
from A.Y. of White Plains Hospital Medical Center in New
York.

> In the puzzle of 7/2/85, the clue for 19 Down, shortness of
> breath, has for an answer (I checked it today) APNEA.
> Apnea is the absence of breath, i.e., it describes a patient who
> is not breathing at all. The word for shortness of breath is
> *dyspnea*.

Mr. Y.'s letter caused me to consult *dyspnea* in *Webster's Third*.
There the word was defined as "Difficult or labored respira-
tion—distinguished from *eupnea*."

Because of my given name, I know that *eu* means "well." So
if you are *eupneic*, not to worry: you're respiring well.

To tell the truth, I had never heard of DYNES or ERGS until I
started solving puzzles. After that, I memorized those units. The
former was "forceful" like *dynamite;* the latter had the same letters
as *energy*.

Therefore, in 1986 I was dismayed to learn that a constructor's
clinker had eluded me and my peerless proofer. Mr. B.E., lec-
turer in Physical Sciences at Kingsborough Community College
in Brooklyn, rang the bell on me.

> As a previously elected member of the Gotcha Club, may I
> take exception to 71 Across in the puzzle of Saturday, 1 March
> 1986? The clue "Energy unit" is satisfied with the response
> DYNE. A dyne however is a unit not of energy, but of force.
> Specifically, the dyne is the force required to give a mass of one
> gram an acceleration of one centimeter per second. The energy
> unit associated with the dyne is the erg. An erg is the work
> done (or the energy needed to do this work) when a force of
> one dyne acts through a distance of one centimeter.
> It takes considerable effort to impress this distinction on be-
> ginning physics students. I hope those of mine who are also

puzzlers do not show up on Monday insisting they were right after all.

In my reply, I wrote:

You have my permission to read this letter to your students.

Dynes are units of force
Of course
Ergs are in the energy frame
And not the same.

Sleepiness at the switch also accounts for a blunder that occurred in May 1985. Amazingly, only one of my solvers sent a Gotcha. Were the rest suffering from spring fever? Here's the letter from P.L.B. of Lee's Summit, Missouri. Note that he wasn't sure that he had struck gold.

At times I feel your clues go to the outer limits of broad interpretation, but yesterday's went too far, in my opinion, with the clue for 31 Down, which was "worker."
Your answer in this morning's paper is DRONE. According to *Webster's New Collegiate Dictionary*, 1981 Copyright, page 346, the definition for drone is as follows: "*drone*—the male of a bee (as the honeybee) that has no sting and gathers no honey. . . . One that lives on the labor of others: parasite."

While we're on the subject of little creatures, I must tell you that Dr. H.F. in the Department of Invertebrates at the American Museum of Natural History earned an easy Gotcha certificate when he discovered that I didn't know a triton from a gecko.

I noticed an error in your crossword puzzle of about a week ago (see enclosed). Number 56 Down says "small lizard" and the expected answer is EFT. However, an eft is actually an amphibian, not a reptile (i.e., lizard).

For those who did not understand my triton-gecko sally, the former is an eft (amphibian) while the latter is a lizard (reptile).

In 1973, Ireland made some changes in its counties. Tyrone is one example. In 1982, I defined it as "a county in W. Northern

Ireland." Oodles of Gotchas informed me that it had been replaced by several new districts. And so, in 1984 when TYRONE
popped up in a puzzle again, my clue read: "Former Irish
county." Here's the scolding I received from W.R.H. of New
York City.

Having completed Wednesday's crossword, I'd like to point
out that Tyrone is in Northern Ireland and hence, still an Irish
county. Although part of the United Kingdom, it is assuredly
not an English, Scottish or Welsh county.

As even republican fanatics in Ireland still talk of the 32
counties, I think you should re-consider your designation and
not mislead your crossword fanatics, who probably still manage
to complete your, as usual, excellent puzzle.

Another example of my confusion is the Donegal situation.
Here's a 1989 Gotcha from A.M.G., president of the South Jersey
Chapter of the Irish American Unity Conference.

I write to bring your attention to an error in a clue which
appeared in the crossword which ran in the *New York Times* on
Saturday 20 May 89.

Clue 25 (Down) asks for a "County in Northern Ireland."
The answer, DONEGAL, is not a county in "Northern" Ireland,
although it is the northernmost county in Ireland. When the
British gerrymandered the island of Ireland in 1923, they re-
tained only six of the nine counties of the ancient province of
Ulster: Antrim, Armagh, Down, Derry, Fermanagh, and Tyrone. The other three, Donegal, Monaghan, and Cavan, were
returned to the Free State because their populations would not
guarantee a British electoral majority. So, while County Donegal is in northern Ireland, it is not in "Northern" Ireland.

And begorra here's another green Gotcha! It comes from
J.D.G.

The otherwise fine puzzle of *New York Times Magazine* July
31, 1983 was marred by one misleading definition I felt should
be brought to your attention: 6 Down—def: "Orangeman's
city;" solution: DERRY.

In fact, the city's name is *London*derry, *Derry* being the preferred usage only of Catholics there, very few of whom, I can

assure you, would style themselves "Orangemen." "Ulsterman's city" might have served instead.

Finally, my late Irish mother (Nellie Kelly from County Cork) would be ashamed to learn that her son once defined IRELAND as "Part of the United Kingdom." P.D. of New York City was one of the solvers who reminded me that the Old Sod is a republic and that only Northern Ireland is in the U.K.

As the reader may know, some countries have two capitals. For example, Bolivia's administrative capital is La Paz, but its official one is Sucre. Apparently, the same doubling exists in Crete. My attention was drawn to the situation by a 1983 letter from A.T. of New York City.

> I was just informed by my step-father that the crossword puzzle in *The Times* has, as 64 Across, the clue "Capital of Crete"—and so he asked me what was the answer (I'm the family's geographical expert). When informed that the answer was not either "Iraklion" or "Candia," but CANEA, my hands reached out for the atlas. Sure enough, the Fifth Edition of the National Geographic *Atlas of the World* (1981) shows Iraklion as the capital. What happened?

After receiving that inquiry, I called the Greek consulate and was told that Iraklion is the "unofficial capital" but Canea remains the constitutional one.

Here are additional "capital offenses." Dar Es Salaam is listed as the capital of Tanzania in *Webster's Geographical Dictionary* and other fine reference books. But sometime in the 1980s Dodoma became the capital even though Dar Es Salaam continued to be Tanzania's largest port. E.B.P. of Philadelphia won a Gotcha for informing me.

Also, T.M.H. of Loyola University apprised me that in 1985 Bangladesh had changed the English spelling of its capital from *Dacca* to *Dhaka*.

In the mid-eighties I ran into geographic trouble by consulting an old reference book. D.A. of Santa Monica, California, was the first to correct me.

You will hear from a number of your Hawaiian readers over this one.

The southernmost cape in the U.S. is South Cape, or Ka Lae, and not—as indicated in your puzzle today—Cape Sable in Florida. The former, on the island of Hawaii, lies just below the 19th parallel, while Cape Sable lies at the 25th.

Strangely enough, T.M.E. of New York City was the only solver to send me a Gotcha in 1988 when the clue for OCEANS was "Arctic and Antarctic." Of course, as he pointed out, there is no Antarctic Ocean. Incidentally, Mr. E. has a wry sense of humor. His communication ended: "But don't worry—no litigable damage was done to my psyche."

My reply should have been: "Suits me! I admit I was all at sea."

Another ocean tripped me up in 1989. B.R. of Rumson, New Jersey, was the first to notice that I had moved the Bahamas from the Atlantic Ocean to the Caribbean Sea. Since he had already challenged me on another clue, Mr. R. concluded his Gotcha as follows: "Don't be too mad at this pest."

Not only do I move islands but I also relocate cities once in a while. M.F.B. of New York City caught me in an unusual way. My clue for UNOS was "Ones in Orvieto." Ms. Browne reminded me that Orvieto was in Italy, where the plural of *uno* is *uni* (masculine) or *une* (feminine). She wondered correctly if I had temporarily mixed up Orvieto with Oviedo. I liked the conclusion of her Gotcha: "Keep up the good—the nearly perfect—work."

When crossword puzzles first became popular, the use of foreign words was frowned upon and a non-English entry was a *rara avis*. But expressions such as the one I have just used gradually crept into the pastime and opened the way for others like *adios, aloha, école, enero, iter, oro, uno,* etc. Even today editors tend to reject puzzles that have an abundance of foreign words. And when we let those strangers in, we must beware.

In 1989 my limited knowledge of French caused me to receive two Gallic lessons from J.D. of Providence, Rhode Island. The first came when I defined *onde* as "Wave on *la mer*." (*N.B.* Cassell defines *onde* as "wave; billow.")

In French, a wave on the ocean or on the sea is: *une vague*, and not *une onde*. No Frenchman would ever refer to it as *une onde*. It is true that *onde* is the general term in French for a wave. Thus, in physics you study *la propagation des ondes*. The subject matter might include electro-magnetic waves, as well as waves in fluids or solids. The latter would indeed include surface waves as well as waves in the interior. But when it comes to certain special cases the word *vague* is used instead.

The second lesson came a month later when *oter* appeared in a puzzle. Since one of the meanings for that French infinitive is "to take off," I assumed that it was a synonym for "to depart." Wrong! Here is a part of Mr. D.'s correction.

Perhaps I should tell you that I am born in France and only learned English later in life when I came to the U.S.

In any case, the clue for 66 Across was: "To take off, at DeGaulle." The reader presumes DeGaulle is the airport and that the taking off is done by an airplane with its passengers. In that sense, the French word is *décoller*.

You may be interested in knowing that I learned some of my English by doing the crosswords. French crosswords do not have a rule that the minimum number of letters per word is 3. This rule is very important and their crosswords are much less interesting as a result.

By the way, I should explain that the true meaning of *oter* is "to remove."

Italian plurals can be traps for the unwary. While making alterations on a constructor's 1979 puzzle, I came up with CITTE as an entry. Knowing that *citta* means "city" and that the plural of Italian nouns ending in *a* changes the last letter to *e*, I let *citte* remain and proudly defined it as "Milano e Napoli, e.g."

O terrible! A score of Italian scholars came out of the woods to tell me that *citta* was one of the nouns that do not change. Its plural is exactly the same as its singular spelling!

Since an old salt always uses the pronoun *she* when referring to a ship, in 1983 I had what I thought was a clever idea. The word in the puzzle was ESSA, which means "she" in Italian. Hence, I defined it as "Pronoun for the Pinta."

Señor M. wrote: "Shouldn't the answer be *ella* since La Pinta was a Spanish caravel?"

Monsignor A.V.M. put in his *due centi* as follows:

Mio Caro Dottore,

Questo giorno, per far onore al grand' uomo, Cristoforo Colombo, ci sono molte parole italiane nel cruciverba (m.); ma mi sembra che "essa" (17-D), pronome per la Pinta, deve essere la spagnola "ella," perche (se non mi sbaglio) le tre barche erano spagnole—senza dubbio "Nina" non e italiana!—e le due altre si scrivono lo stesso nelle due lingue. Ma veramente, non fa niente!

However, I ask the jury to picture Columbus talking about one of his ships. As an Italian, would he have used the pronoun *ella* or *essa?* The defense rests!

After studying Latin for four years in high school, I majored in the subject at college and taught it for three years. Such experience has helped to reduce the number of flubs in that language, but in drowsy moments over a period of fourteen years I have let a few creep into print.

For instance, in 1991 UTOR was misdefined as "To know, to Nero." R.G.C. of Philadelphia and M.D. of Brooklyn were among the first to remind me that *utor* means "I know." The infinitive of the verb is *uti.*

In 1987 Professor A.A.B., Jr., of Holland, Michigan, wrote as follows:

Two errors in recent *Times* puzzles prompt this letter. About a week ago the definition "part of i.e." appeared. The answer proved to be IDEM. But *idem* is no part of *i.e.,* which stands for *id est.* It didn't seem to be worth writing about at the time. Now today's puzzle contains the definition "Latin I word" (33 Across). The answer works out to be AMAT. But *amat,* while a Latin word, has nothing to do with the first person singular pronoun or the Roman numeral one, whichever the clue is intended to be. *Ego* is Latin for "I"; the word for "one" is *unus*. *Amat* means "he, she, or it loves."

Of course, the professor is correct concerning the *idem* lapse, but he misunderstood "Latin I." It stands for Latin One—the first course in the subject.

A typo generated the following would-be Gotcha from P.H., a recent graduate of the same high school that I attended in the thirties.

I write to register my horror at the depravation lately suffered by the Latin language under your auspices. I refer to the clue for 38 Across in the puzzle of Sunday, the 10th of July. The completed motto would read "Esse quam videre." This would be a perfectly good motto for a school for the blind, but not for an entire state whose inhabitants, presumably, cherish their sight. Surely you mean "Esse quam videri": "To be rather than to see*m*."

I expect more from a graduate of Regis. If, however, the mistake is not yours but North Carolina's, then please accept my apology. And I will begin proceedings to have them expelled from the Union.

Spanish also gives me trouble occasionally. Here are two letters that enlightened me. The first came in 1986 from D.C. and H.F. of Sunnyside, New York. The second Gotcha was sent in 1988 by N.S., Chairman of Foreign Languages at Neward Academy in Livingston, New Jersey.

In the puzzle of 18 October 1986 you had the clue "Villa, to Diaz," the answer to which was BANDITO. The clue suggests that the answer must be a Spanish speaker's word for "bandit." The word in Spanish is *bandido*. The *T* spelling is, as far as we know, an invention of 1950s American television; although, perhaps Mr. Safire could tell us more about it. *Bandito* appears in neither Webster's Unabridged Second Edition or the *Diccionario de la Real Academia Espanola*. It might appear in a dictionary of American slang; but in any case, the clue precludes its use in this cast.

Gotcha!

In yesterday's crossword, the clue for 45 Down was "Treat in Taxco." When such clues are given, the answers are always a word in the foreign language. However, the only answer that worked in yesterday's puzzle was TAMALE. No such word exists in Spanish; the word is *tamal* (plural: *tamales*).

Although this caused me grievous mental anguish, I shall continue to enjoy attempting your puzzles.

To conclude this section on linguistic lapses, let me quote part of a Gotcha from E.S. of New York City. Obviously, he is well-versed in Erse.

On behalf of the Irish language (aka Irish Gaelic) I would like to point out a grammatical error in the crossword of 10/18/87. According to 87 Down the Irish word MAC means "son of." Actually, *mac* simply means "son." When used in names it is followed by the genitive of a noun.

The other common Irish name prefix, *O* originally meant "grandson" but now indicates any member of the clan; it is also followed by the genitive.

My chief aim as a puzzles editor is to entertain. But secondary aims are to extend the knowledge of solvers or to refresh their memories. As a case in point, let me refer to FOE—a word that crops up often in puzzles. The easy and lazy way out is to define it as "enemy" or "antagonist." But *foe* offers a chance to review history. Here are some examples to clues I have used:

Howe, to Washington
Napoleon, to Wellington
Hannibal, to Scipio
Marius, to Sulla
Darius, to Alexander the Great

In choosing the Historical route, I open the way to errors. For example, when ANGLIA appeared in a Sunday puzzle, I could have settled for "Latin name of England" as the clue. Instead I elected to say: "England, to Caesar."

Two distinguished educators sent wise and witty Gotchas. The first comes from D.A.R. of City College of New York.

> Mary Virginia Orna's "Latin Rhythms" (August 8, 1982) would seem to have missed one beat. What was "England, to Caesar?" asks 114 Across, and answers ANGLIA. Now Caesar died in 43 B.C., having conquered Gallia and parts of Britannia; but the eponymous Angles did not arrive on those British shores—according to prevalent historical tradition—until 449 A.D. Evidently a case of inadvertent anachronism; or shall we say—to stay with the puzzle's latinate theme—of ex-temporaneity?

Mr. R. even suggested alternate clues such as: "England, to the authors of the Magna Carta" and "England, to St. Thomas Aquinas."

The second letter was sent by Professor G.J. of the College of Staten Island. Part of his correction reads:

> Caesar died in 44 B.C. There was no Anglia until the Angles, Saxons and Jutes invaded England five centuries later. Caesar was a wise man, but I don't think even the wisest of men could have known that the Britanni would be forced out of Britannia by the Angli in the fifth century A.D.

Professors seem to be on my case. Here's another Gotcha from the academician G.E.E. in Basel, Switzerland. A 1987 puzzle had defined COTTON MATHER as "U.S. clergyman-author: 1663–1728." My Swiss critic wrote:

> As the U.S. dates from the 1770s, the prescience of this Bostonian, Cotton Mather, is uncanny. Can one be a U.S. anything before there was a U.S.?

Touché, but all my sources describe Mather as an American. I used *U.S.* to save space. Perhaps I should have picked *Colonial* as the proper description.

• • •

Lizzie Borden is another historical American character. When AXE appeared in a 1989 puzzle, I opted for "Lizzie Borden's weapon" as an interesting clue. H.S. of St. Louis objected.

> Inasmuch as Miss Borden was found not guilty of axing her parents by her male peers, I think it is unfair to characterize her axe as a weapon.
> I know what people thought but if we were convicted by people's thoughts we would all be in jail.

When I asked Mr. S. if he knew why Lizzie was declared innocent, he replied at length. Here is a part of his answer:

> I believe she was acquitted because, although there was much circumstantial evidence, there was no "dripping axe" so to speak. Also, I think the twelve good men and true of the jury just couldn't accept the idea that a young lady in their community could do such a thing. They should live nowadays!
> The Lizzie Borden case was especially fascinating because of the patricide-matricide aspect and because the events were so well documented as to time. The time schedule was so tight that it seemed that no one but Lizzie could have done it. However, in the end, there was a tantalizing five minutes or so where it would have been possible for a stranger to slip in and do the job.

Sometimes history and geography intertwine. At any rate, W.K.S. of New York City caught me in an error when I described TOTEM as an "Algonquian pole."

> "Totem" is very omnipresent in native American usage—but a *pole* is rather unique to the Northwest. "Algonquian" does not extend, as I understand it, beyond the Rockies, being an Eastern/North Plains grouping.

How about a bit of French history? In 1987, I received an interesting letter from M.A. of Carlsbad, California.

In your puzzle "Dos and Don't" by Louis Baron of recent date, item 105 is "D'Artagnan's creator." This is true in a way, but Charles de Batz-Castlemore d'Artagnan was a real person, a Gascon in Louis XIV's service as a Musketeer. My ancestor Johan von Schmiedeberg, a Swedish soldier of fortune, was a Musketeer at the same time. There is an excellent book *D'Artagnan* in the libraries.

And now for some Greek history. In 1984 Mrs. N.R.F. of Yarmouthport, Massachusetts, sent me an informative letter.

I have a question about an entry in the Sunday *Times* Crossword of April 22. The clue for 93 Across is "Holy Statue"; the answer given IKON.

According to my Greek friends ikons are not statues but gilden and painted images, usually on wood. On a visit to Greece, we were told that Greek Orthodox churches have not had statues since the Turkish occupation, when soldiers rode their horses into the churches and smashed all the statues. To prevent such a thing happening again, they rebuilt their churches with ikons attached to the walls and with doors too small to admit horsemen.

No doubt a man as erudite as you knows all about this, but it was quite a fascinating piece of history to me. Possibly the Russian Orthodox churches have ikons which are statues, but I have never seen one.

Thanks, Mrs. F., for the compliment—but I'm still a learner, not a learned one.

K.B.F. of Floral Park, New York, gave more enlightenment on the *ikon* situation.

In the puzzle of Sunday, April 22nd, I came across something which surprised me. Number 93 Across said "holy statue" and the answer was IKON.

An icon is *never* a three-dimensional figure. It is absolutely forbidden to have a three-dimensional figure in a Byzantine Orthodox church and iconography is Byzantine by derivation. Icons are not even supposed to depict real people or events, but rather their *spiritual* values.

. . .

Sally Ride made history in 1983 when she ascended into the wild blue yonder, and I made a goof in 1986 when I described her as "First spacewoman."

E.B. of Dobbs Ferry entered the Gotcha Club when he pointed out that two U.S.S.R. female cosmonauts had preceded Ms. Ride:

> Valentina Tereshkova   June 17–19, 1963
> Svetlana Savitskaya   August 17–19, 1982

Despite my great interest in Sports, I am also vulnerable in that area. My first error came in the late seventies when I failed to notice the misspelling of the surname of a famous old baseball player. The typo read *Moranville* instead of *Maranville*. Sorry about that, Rabbit! Your kith and kin will be happy to hear that at least twenty Gotchas piled up on my desk.

T.S. of Ashland, Massachusetts, caught me napping on the status of another old-timer, Bobby Jones. I made him a member of the Professional Golfers' Association and forgot that the great golfer was always an amateur.

ERNE is a crossword repeater. The usual clue refers to a sea eagle. Sometimes the definition mentions a lake or river in Ireland. In an effort to be different, I once defined *erne* as "Former flyweight champion." No so! A.B., a boxing manager for 45 years, mailed me a Gotcha from Chappaqua, New York.

> Franklie Erne was lightweight champion of the world from 1900 to 1902, winning and losing the title to Joe Gans. Erne was born in Switzerland, and died in New York City September 17th, 1954. He had a total of 40 bouts, losing only 6. There was a flyweight champion with a four letter last name, however; he was Peter Kane of Ireland.

Just plain laziness caused me to go wrong on another Olympics star. In 1985, I called Eric Heiden a swimmer and received a Gotcha from E.C.S. of New York City.

By now you must have received too many reminders of the fact that both Eric Heiden and his sister are *skaters* and bicycle riders. It may well be that they both also know how to *swim*, but they are hardly noted for that skill.

My almanac mixed me up in 1990. I confused the New Mexico State team with the one at the University of New Mexico. The athletic director of the latter institution graciously invited me to be his guest at a football game so that I would never make the same mistake again. But it was even nicer to be able to bestow a Gotcha certificate upon P.J.F., a former pupil of a New York City school. For some unknown reason the young man had gone west. Here's what he wrote from Albuquerque.

Considering that you were Assistant Principal of P.S. 169 when I was a student there from 1948 to 1951, and in view of my long term residence in New Mexico, I feel compelled to correct the *gross error* I stumbled over in your Feb. 8 crossword puzzle. Referring to the clue for 33 Down, the (rather pathetic) Lobos are the University of New Mexico's teams, and hail from Albuquerque, not Las Cruces. New Mexico State University is in Las Cruces, and its teams are known as the Aggies.

Maybe I should have stuck to "timber wolves" as the definition for LOBOS.

Speaking of teams' nicknames, something strange is going on at Stanford University. Lots of letters came in when I made a non-singular slip. The following Gotcha from M.K. of New York City explains it all.

In the interest of Puzzle Purity, I'd like to point out an error in your puzzle of 11/28/86. Your clue 34 Down, "Stanford," calls for the answer CARDINALS.
The Stanford University nickname is "Cardinal." It is never written in the plural, regardless of the context.
I realize I'm nitpicking, but nitpicking is one of the joys of solving puzzles.

Fencing is not my cup of tea. Therefore, it was inevitable that I would fall into an EPEE trap. Consider the letter from M.J.S. of New York City.

> In the *Times* puzzle of September 21, 1987, the clue "Fencing foil" is given for 23 Across, EPEE. The foil and the epee are two different types of swords used in fencing. (The saber is a third.) The foil is flexible, with a rectangular cross section; the epee, a duelling sword, is rigid and has a triangular cross section. *Foil* is not a general term for "fencing sword."

I suppose dice games can be considered as forms of indoor sports. At any rate, my meager knowledge of such activities was evidenced in 1988 when FADES was defined as "Backs a dicer."

A.T.S., Jr., of Yonkers, New York, was among those who wrote "to *fade* is to *oppose* a dicer." I guess he's right. The dictionary's definition is so convoluted that I cannot comprehend its import.

C.K. of White Plains, New York, caught me when I stated that CLEAT was part of a baseballer's shoe. His letter ended as follows:

> Cleats are worn by footballers and soccer players. Spikes are worn by baseballers and golfers.
> P.S. Been plugging away for 19 years but this is the first time I've seen such an obvious mistake.

Webster's Sports Dictionary may have made an error when referring to baseball's GOLDEN GLOVE award. When I accepted their designation in a 1984 puzzle, P.N.B. of Glens Falls, New York, and several other solvers objected. Mr. Buchman wrote: "A *Golden Glove* tournament is held in boxing. A *Gold Glove* award is given in baseball."

Finally, I present a half-Gotcha from M.F. of Sioux City, Iowa. The clue for LAVER was "Four-time Wimbledon winner." My hawkeye harrier comments: "Rod Laver won 4 singles and one double, sort of a 4 ½-time winner."

Next let's consider the category of Amusements or Entertainment.

In 1981 the clue for SACK brought about a dozen Gotchas, I'm sad to say. Foremost in the initial barrage was the following letter from D.C.H.

> It has been a dream of mine to catch you in an error ever since I read a profile of you in which you admitted that, like the rest of us, you are human.
>
> Your clue in the puzzle of Sat., June 6, for 38 Across was "Mauldin's 'Sad' one." The answer was SACK.
>
> But the Sad Sack character was created by Sgt. George Baker. Bill Maudlin's characters were Willie and Joe.
>
> Thought you'd like to know you made the day of one puzzler, without really trying.

With regard to comics, a minor error caused J.H. of Philadelphia to be admitted to the Gotcha Club. In 1985 he wrote:

> I did enjoy your diagramless in the August 18th magazine. However, I think I detect a small error. Clue 46 Down, "Dogpatch character" is satisfied in the grid by PAW. While there are numerous "Paws" in the Hillbilly genre, I do not believe that any of them live in Dogpatch. Abner's father is *Pappy* Yokum, no? Does this qualify as a gotcha?

In 1987 I mixed up the comic-strip "Kabibble" with the musical one. A modest letter from D.C.S. of Wilton, Connecticut, corrected me. Part of it reads as follows:

> Ish Kabibble was a musician and comedy character years ago with the Kay Kyser band. I am almost positive that the old time comic strip that I remember, probably from the 1930s, was named "Abe Kabibble."

A comic book by Gaylord Dubois called Tarzan's son "Boy" and that name was also given to the child in the movie series. Foolishly, I assumed that "Boy" was really a character in the original novels penned by Edgar Rice Burroughs.

J.F.D. of Brooklyn is obviously a Tarzania expert. Here is his erudite, witty reaction to my error.

> Not to be picky; but one *must* at times pick. Refer to 3/31/83—54 Down: "Jane's son in Tarzan books"—answer duly indited as BOY. Be it henceforth known that one Jane Porter, born in Baltimore, Maryland, January 1, 1890, on Thursday, September 22, 1910, married one John Clayton, Lord Greystoke, aka Tarzan and on May 20, 1912, begat one John Paul Clayton at Greystoke House, London, England. He is called Jack, John Korak *but never* "boy." Later in 1912 John and Jane Clayton did adopt Tarzan's second cousin John Drummond, who was never called "boy."
>
> "Boy" was a fabrication, an intrusion of the ill-made movie series. Even in films the "boy" character was *not* Jane's son— the virginal demi-god figures avoided sex on all counts.
>
> This is meant to be creatively picky or pickilly creative. I hope it is taken in the spirit of humor.

In 1985 a diagramless puzzle got me in hot water. The constructor misdirected solvers concerning a film director, and we who control the switch fell asleep. But R.S. of Chicago was alert. He gave us a friendly warning.

> In Sunday's *Times* (12/08/85) Ms. Trombley's diagramless lists 21 Down as Martin Scorsese's "The ———."
>
> The answer was THE DEER HUNTER, but I believe she meant to credit the movie to Michael Cimino, *n'est-ce pas?*
>
> I'm not sure how Martin would take all this. I'd hate for him to come out with a movie entitled, "The Crossword Hunter." He's the kind of talent that when he gets down to it, he gets the message across.

Another unchecked "misdirection" got published in 1990. William Lutwiniak, a top constructor and a fellow crossword puzzle editor, mixed up two similar titles: (*A*) "It's a Wonderful Life" and (*B*) "It's a Wonderful World."

When Mr. Lutwiniak declared that Frank Capra had directed *B* my assistant and I failed to check his statement. F.C. of Venice, Florida, was the first of many solvers who pointed out that W.S. Van Dyke II was the *B* man and Capra got the *A*.

Literature is one of my fortes. Therefore, I am especially ashamed to admit that more than a dozen of my blunders relate to novels, plays, etc.

The most embarrassing error occurred on September 22, 1985, when the Sunday puzzle was my own creation. I had constructed it in connection with "Book Country"—a Sunday annually set aside by Gotham officials to encourage people to read. On that day Fifth Avenue is closed to vehicles between 50th and 60th Streets. Scores of publishers set up booths and display their wares.

Marjorie Longley, the then head of Public Affairs for the *Times,* had invited me to sit in the newspaper's booth. Puzzle addicts lined up to receive a free copy of the Sunday magazine along with my autograph atop the puzzle.

But that's not the story. Ms. Longley had arranged to have my puzzle blown up and printed on stiff cardboard. Three separate copies were tacked up on the sides and back wall of the booth. Fans were provided with magic markers to fill in the answers. Also, two young women were strapped with sandwich boards carrying the puzzle and passersby were urged to write the answers on the front or back. Wonderful ideas, but alas the puzzle had a literary error which some of the literate detected!

BRASS was an entry in the puzzle. My clue was "Novel by Frank Norris." One fan had scrawled on the right wall of the booth: "Charles Norris—not Frank!" My face reddened when the graffiti were shown to me. Hell's bells, I'd mixed up the brothers! But I must add that puzzle fans are a charitable breed. Those who knew about the error shook my hand and said things like: "Nobody's perfect. It happens to the best of us."

Giving credit to the wrong author is a trap I seldom fall into but a month before the *brass* blunder, I tripped up on the name of the *Borstal Boy* playwright. K.M.E. of Santa Monica earned membership in the Gotcha Club.

In your puzzle of August 5, 1985, you gave the name of Brendan Behan as the playwright of the play *Borstal Boy*. The playwright is Frank McMahon who won the Tony award and the Drama Critic's award for his play. The *book Borstal Boy* was written by Brendan Behan.

The above Gotcha reminds me that in my first year as an editor I made a common error by crediting Somerset Maugham for writing the drama called *Rain*. The truth is that Maugham's short story, "Miss Thompson," (1921) was dramatized as *Rain* a year later by John B. Colton and Clemence Randolph.

How did I find out? Simple! Mr. Colton's wife sent me a Gotcha.

In 1986, I let an egregious error get by in a Sunday puzzle and was amazed when only two solvers sent Gotcha letters.

B.K. of Wheaton, Maryland, wrote:

In today's crossword puzzle, the clue for 38 Across was "Bridge man," and the answer worked out to be HORATIO. The "bridge man," of course, was *Horatius,* while Horatio was Hamlet's friend.

J.B. was the other Gotcha man. Part of his letter reads as follows:

For 38 Across ("Bridge man"), I determined the answer to be HORATIO. If by this clue you refer to the Roman defense of the Tiber bridge against the Etruscans under Lars Porsena, the hero's name is "Horati*us*," not "Horati*o*." The story is best known in English literature from the first of Macaulay's *Lays of Ancient Rome*.

> With weeping and with laughter
> Still is the story told,
> How well Horatius kept the bridge
> In the brave days of old.

A tiny slip in a 1985 puzzle led to a fascinating Gotcha from J.D. of Scarsdale, New York.

What fun to catch you nodding! Perhaps everyone who ever took a course in dramatic literature and does today's puzzle will write to you on this one!

Hedda was not Mrs. Gabler, but Miss Gabler who became Mrs. George Tesman. She was General Gabler's daughter.

At Northwestern University, multi years ago, Dr. Lee Mitchell asked his class to create test questions rather than answer them. One of mine was: "Why is the title of the play *Hedda Gabler* rather than *Hedda Tesman?*"

It isn't a bad question, given the psychology of the lady, and it is fun for me to tell you about it!

Charlotte's Web is a bit of children's literature that I have never read. Hence, in 1989 I missed a constructor's goof re the characters. C.M. of Pleasantville, New York, set me straight: "Wilbur was not a rat (112 Across, Sunday, Nov. 12) but a pig. Templeton was the rat!"

Templeton? I thought he was a pianist. Wilbur? Isn't he a famous poet? Oh well, every day we learn something new.

It amazes me how quick some solvers are to spot small details that may be of importance. J.D.P. of West Warwick, Rhode Island, caught an error in a Sunday puzzle by Louis Baron.

> You have, in Number 65 Across, the clue "Like Samson at the end." The answer is SHORN. However, if you check the book of Judges, Chapter 16, Verse 22, you will see that the hair of his head had grown back—so that "at the end" Samson was no longer shorn; hence he was able to bring down the pillars on the Philistines.
>
> A message to Baron Louis, the peer, from one who is not much of a peri:

> Though the Philistines may jostle
> You won't rank as an apostle
> In the high conundrum band
> If you write down peccadilloes
> For your puzzle-loving fellows
> In your enigmatic hand.

Similarly, in 1987, a puzzle alleged that Othello strangled his wife. L.H. of Oakland, California, picked up on that detail.

Whoever wrote today's crossword puzzle forgot to consult his Shakespeare! Othello *smothers* Desdemona—he doesn't strangle her. Please check out Act V, Scene ii, line 84, which contains the stage direction "Smothers her."

Unfortunately, *strangled* and *smothered* are the same length.

That last sentence tells me why Ms. H. bothered to complain. If she used ink, I hope she had an erasable pen when she wrote "smothered." By the way, I recently witnessed a production of Verdi's *Othello* in which the Moor's fingers were clasped around the poor woman's neck as she took her last breath. I suppose it's called operatic license.

Bartlett's *Familiar Quotations* has a reputation for accuracy, but my edition misled me in 1988. Here's a letter from A.M.E. of New York City.

The puzzle on 11/16/88 featured a quote by Charles Kingsley which was not exactly as written by the author in "A Farewell to C.E.G."

It should not say "and let who will be clever," but "and let who *can* be clever," as printed in the *Oxford Dictionary of Quotations*.

I'd appreciate your comments—who's in the right?

Gadzooks! All my reference books except Bartlett cite "can" instead of "will."

My editions of Shakespeare quote Hamlet as saying "O, that this too too solid flesh would melt." E.K. of New York City claims that they are wrong.

With regard to the Saturday crossword puzzle clue 42 Across: you've fallen prey to the popular misconception that Hamlet says, "O, that this too too *solid* flesh . . ." In reality, he says, "*sullied*." Please check your edition of *Hamlet:* Act I, Scene II.

My source is *The London Shakespeare,* edited by John Munro, Simon & Schuster, New York, 1957. I would appreciate a printed correction should you find consistency in this error.

Since I don't have the original text, I'm not sure if Ms. K. is correct. All authorities on the Bard of Avon will please come forward.

And now let's plunge into the area of Spelling. Mark Twain once said that he had no respect for a person who could spell a word only one way. Tell that to the puzzle fans! But the truth is that many words can be spelled at least two ways. Sometimes it's a case of the American versus the British language. Examples are:

> color   colour
> analyze   analyse

Retention or loss of classical diphthongs is another reason for the either-or situation. Consider:

> aesthetic   esthetic
> oenologist   enologist

Folk usage is the chief cause of what I call "double spell." Puzzle fans are acquainted with *eerie* and *eery*. Also, there are *adviser* and *advisor; ambiance* and *ambience; all right* and *alright;* etc., etc.

Scots insist that their brand of alcohol can be spelled only one way—*whisky*. Other intoxicants of that ilk are subject to "double spell"—either *whisky* or *whiskey*.

Occasionally, in a sleepy moment, homophones will confuse me. M.R. of Quincy, Massachusetts, sent me a gentle, hesitant Gotcha in 1983.

> I'm surprised to see in this puzzle, which is in today's *Quincy Patriot Ledger,* that *panache* means "flare." I could have sworn the correct word is *flair.* My dictionary seems to agree with me.
> Perhaps you did it to see if you still have your faithful puzzle solver in Quincy.

The history of *panache* is fascinating. Its ancestor is the Latin *pinnaculum* ("small wing") and *pinnacle* is a relative. The original meaning of *panache* was "a tuft of feathers." Since such tufts were used as headdresses or ornaments on helmets, by metonymy the word came to be synonymous with the heroic flourishes of manner demonstrated by gallant knights prancing around on horseback. Thenceforth, it was easy for *panache* to become "flamboyance, swagger, verve, *flair*"!

Another bad case of "homophonitis" assailed me in 1987 when I defined *berg* as if it were *burg*. L.M., an erudite Gotcha Club officer, was the first to note the blooper. Part of his letter reads as follows:

> A one-horse town is a burg, inhabited by burghers. By no stretch of even the most "mountainous" imagination can it be spelled *berg*.

A substitute proofer and I also nodded in the summer of 1988 when a constructor defined IN ON as "Appraised about." E.S. of New York City and the ubiquitous G.H. of Los Angeles were the first to pounce. Here's Mr. S.'s Gotcha.

> I'm afraid you recently stubbed your toe on the confusion between *apprised* and *appraised*. In the puzzle for Wednesday, July 27, the clue for 3 Down should have read "apprised about," not "appraised about."

As noted earlier in this chapter, proper names are often liable to be misspelled. It's bad enough when the error pops up in a clue, but it's Heavens-to-Betsy time when it appears in the diagram! The clue was "Lardner's given name" and the answer was RINGOLD. The first fan who told me it should be *ringgold* was a man named H. RINGOLD. I kid you not.

But the worst monstrosity ever to befoul a *Times* daily diagram was MILLENIUM on August 9, 1985—a date that will live in crossword infamy. R.R.R., a Gotcha regular, from New York City was the first to inform me. He was quickly followed by A.N. of Merrick, New York. Oddly enough, only three or four others bothered to remind me that the proper spelling for "Paradisiacal period" is Mille*nn*ium.

At first I thought that so few deigned to write because the mistake was so obvious. But since then, while giving talks on crosswords to hundreds upon hundreds of people I have discovered that nine out of ten do not know how to spell *millennium*. If the reader doubts me, I suggest that my spelling demon be tried on friends and kinfolks. Honestly, you can win bets on it.

Since I was once a Latin scholar, I have no excuse for over-looking the constructor's boo-boo. *Millennium* literally means "a thousand years." The end of the word comes from *annus*, the Roman's word for "year." If *annus* had only one *n*, then the misspelling that appeared in the puzzle would mean "a thousand censored anatomical areas."

Let's proceed from the naughty to the nautical. In 1987 I described the LST as an "amphibious craft." H.J. of Philadelphia enlightened me.

No doubt an occasional LST wound up on land during World War II, but it was aground, not amphibious. Even its cargo wasn't amphibious. *LST* stands for Landing Ship Tank. LSTs had huge doors in front through which tanks were released after the vessel approached close to a beach. The ship itself never left the water.

According to my dictionaries, to be amphibious something must function as well on land as in or on the water. According to my recollection, an LST would function on land about as well as a flounder.

Gotcha?

Another vessel caused my downfall in 1987. The entry was STR.—an abbreviation for *steamer*. My clue was "QE2, e.g." M.L. of Syracuse was the first to give me the bad news.

Gotcha! (Gadzooks, what a nasty way to start a letter.)

Much to the chagrin of all England, *the QE2 was converted to diesel engines in 1986–87*. To add insult to injury, the work was done in Germany. The ship is no longer a steamship. It is now a motor ship.

L.S. of Manhattan College in the Bronx added more information. His "stationery" showed a picture of a Hudson River Day Line Steamer. Underneath were the names of famous steamers: Washington Irving, Hendrick Hudson, Alexander Hamilton, Robert Fulton, Albany, and DeWitt Clinton. Here's the Gotcha.

When I read your "Gotcha" article in Sunday's *Times*, I never expected to catch you in one, certainly not so soon.

Re 19 Across in today's puzzle: The *QE2* is no longer a STR. She left New York on last Oct. 20 for the last time under steam for a complete refit including replacing her steam engines with diesel. She's now an M/V.

By the way, the *QE2* seems to be my jinx ship. In 1992, the officials of that liner invited my wife and me to be their first-class guests on successive cruises between Southampton and New York City. My job was to give a total of four talks to crossword puzzle aficionados on board.

But a few weeks before our scheduled voyages the hull of the ship struck a ledge near Martha's Vineyard and our deal was canceled. Egad and gadzooks!

I was all at sea in 1989 and G.A.B of Wayne, Pennsylvania, was the first of many yachtsmen to catch this landlubber in an off-shore flub.

Your puzzles are excellent and, for the most part, correct. However, in the puzzle today a clue was "sheets for salts" and the answer worked out to be SAILS.

"Sheets" are *not* sails (although it seems logical) but are "lines" used in hoisting or lowering sails. Drop your lines and you're out of control—or "three sheets to the wind."

Nautically yours . . .

In 1990 I got my relationships confused when I stated that "unc.'s son" was a NEPH. The funniest Gotchas came from J.A.H. of Cinnamanson, New Jersey, and D.R. of Spring Valley, New Jersey.

Here's J.A.H.'s Hellenic spoof.

Phi on you! I think you delta bad clue. I Neph-er thought of my unc's son as anything but my cous. Of course my dau's unc's son is my neph, but that seems too relatively shifty from my perspective.

• • •

And now for D.R.'s rap:

I'LL BE A SON OF A MONK.'S UNC.

I hope I'm one of just a doz.
To say the answer should be "cous."
But to avoid having stubbed your semantic toe,
The clue should have been "son of a bro."

W.R.B. of Northport, New York, caught me lyin' there's no denyin'.

Gotcha!
In the puzzle in the *New York Times Magazine* of Sunday, February 15, 1987, there is a clue for 12 Down, "Kind of lion." The answer is BENGAL. However, I have been able to find no reference to a "Bengal lion" in any dictionaries or encyclopedias.
I believe the correct clue should have been "Kind of tiger," since *Bengal* is an accepted modifier for *tiger.*

Did I get mixed up by *bengaline*—a drapery and clothing fabric? The truth is that the composing room fellows changed *tiger* to *lion* according to my aide.

I'm grateful to D.T. for this instructive Gotcha.

The clue was "Emulate Dürer"; the answer, ETCH. But Albrecht Dürer (1471–1528) was a great engraver, and it is engraving for which he is best known. He tried etching, a new technique, but only executed five etchings vs. about 100 engravings because he was not satisfactorily able to control the acid requisite to etching. He also had difficulty with rust, because he etched on iron plates.
So, etch equals Rembrandt. To emulate Dürer, engrave.

A Gotcha regular, R.S. of Fresno, California, explained Big Ben to me in 1988.

I call to your attention the puzzle of August 5, 29 Across: "Westminster's Palace's clock." Now, everyone who is familiar with London knows that Big Ben is the name of the *bell,* not the clock. The clock has no specific name other than "the clock tower at Westminster."

It is the custom to give large bells names. Several years ago when the clock was out of order the BBC used instead the tolling of Great Tom, the bell at Christ Church Oxford.

W.K.S. of New York City added interesting information on the subject.

The famous bell of the clock tower (St. Stephen's Tower) at the Houses of Parliament weighs 13½ tons and was named after Sir Benjamin Hall, Chief Commissioner of Works, in 1856, when it was cast. Hall himself was called Big Ben on account of his size.

Well, it's fascinating to learn that the original Big Ben was Sir Benjamin Hall! Sometimes I'm glad I make an error because I learn so much.

J.A.M. of Long Beach, New York, sent an intriguing Gotcha on the proper way to give a date.

I would like to point out an apparent error in the daily crossword puzzle of July 14, 1987. For the clue of 45 Across ("First year after B.C."), the solution given, 1 A.D. is incorrect. This date should read "A.D. 1," as the year is always preceded by A.D.

This was pointed out several months ago in the Sunday *Times* by William Safire. Mr. Safire was an author of the plaque put on the moon by the Apollo 11 Astronauts. On it was inscribed in part "1969 A.D." Mr. Safire, in his article, hoped that a descendant would some day reach the moon and change the inscription to "A.D. 1969."

I also find this form in the dictionaries I have consulted.

A.R.S. of Long Beach, New Jersey, went to a lot of trouble to become a bona fide Gotcha Clubber. In 1988, he consumed several minutes in order to prove me wrong on a "timely" clue.

I would like to join the "club." In your puzzle of 7/2, the answer TWO TEN to the clue "Time when hands overlap (5

Down)" is erroneous. When the minute hand has reached ten minutes past the hour of two, the hour hand has advanced slightly towards the three. The hands will overlap at approximately 2:11. Kindly excuse my audacity in pointing an error out to you.

I enjoyed this Gotcha from J.D.P. of West Warwick, Rhode Island. Note his oblique pun in the last sentence.

In your puzzle of July 2, 1984, you refer to a shepherd in a manger (12 Down). If the shepherd were in the manger, he would not be much of an ADORER since he would be stepping on the Child. A manger is a small trough or food box, large enough for the proverbial dog, perhaps, but certainly not for a shepherd unless he were of the German breed. Perhaps one of the Magi could have pulled off such a bit of magic, or even a pinhead full of angels could have squeezed in, but shepherds, ancient or modern, have never been known for the miniaturization required for the feat described in your puzzle.

You could, I suppose, resort to synechdoche or metonymy, but that would be clutching at straws.

(I should have referred to a shepherd in a crèche.)

P.C. was one of several Australian-born solvers who contradicted *Webster's Third* in 1986.

I do love your daily crossword and I rarely have reason to doubt the wording of your clues, but as an Australian citizen, I must let you know that "Kia-ora!" (*New York Times,* July 11, 10 Down) is *not* an Aussie toast.

It is, in fact, a New Zealand expression. According to Australia's *Macquarie Dictionary*, the term, translated from Maori, means "good luck."

West Warwick's J.P. caught me again! But I do like his sense of humor.

I doubt that Daedalus would agree with your Sept. 22 Sunday Puzzle, 90 Down, which suggests CRETE for Daedalus' homeland. He was an *Athenian,* welcomed, at first, as a visitor to Crete because of his craftsmanship. He was eventually imprisoned in the labyrinths which he himself may have helped to construct. His aerospace adventures were part of the escape plan. Unless you wish to accept South Africa's definition of *homeland,* the term is misapplied in this context. Icarus may have been a bit of a cretin, but he and his pop were not Cretans.

Keep those verbal labyrinths labyrinthine.

This letter comes from S.B. of Sherman Oaks, California.

With reference to Crossword Puzzle No. 1222 which appeared in the December 22, 1990, edition of *The New York Times,* I extend my congratulations for the imaginative definition used to clue the answer to 2 Down: ENOS. It was a great improvement over old stand-bys such as "Adam's grandson" or "Slaughter."

However, in the interest of accuracy, it is my duty to report that the name used in the clue was misspelled and improperly styled. "Roscoe Coltrane" will not do. He should be identified correctly as he always calls himself: Sheriff Rosco P. Coltrane.

Incidentally, there are other colleagues and cohorts of the good Sheriff of Hazzard County whose names could well be used as clues or answers—namely: *Bo* and *Luke* Duke, Uncle *Jesse* Duke, Deputy *Cletus* Hogg, Mrs. *Lulu* Hogg, and last but I certainly hope not least, *Boss* Jefferson Davis (J.D.) Hogg.

Here's a Gotcha from a distinguished solver—the Associate Publisher of the *International Herald Tribune.*

First, you should know that *New York Times* puzzles have a substantial following of appreciative addicts in Europe and Asia through their daily appearance in the *International Herald Tribune.*

I myself am a particular fan of the Sunday puzzle which runs in our Saturday/Sunday paper. It's a wonderful, relaxing part of my every weekend.

That's why I can't help writing to point out a minor error in semantics in last weekend's puzzle ("The Anglo-Hebraic Way"). The clue to 80 Down is "Calais entree" and the answer turns out to be ROTI. Now, for a reason I have never understood, an "entree" in the United States describes the main course of a meal whereas, logically enough, in French it means a first course . . . a "starter," as the British would say. So, in all logic, an "entree" in Calais cannot possibly be a *roti*. It may be one at the Côte Basque, but never in Calais!

From now on my clue for ROTI will be "Mets in Metz." To clarify for some readers, *mets* is a French word for "food" and has no relation to a certain New York nine.

In 1989, V.C. of Staten Island sent me an interesting Gotcha.

Cease and desist, prithee! A lion is not king of the jungle, and its roar is not to be heard therein.

A lion could not live in the jungle, for it could not run at its prey in the dense undergrowth, and its mane could become entangled. Furthermore, its prey (zebras, elands, etc.) does not live in the jungle, so king lion would go rather hungry.

The lion, like its prey, lives in the grassy plains of the subtropics, so it may be called lord of the savanna. It may still be called the king of beasts.

That letter reminds me of a more recent blunder which a host of people caught. The word in the puzzle was MANED and the clue was "Having locks, like Elsa." Zounds! I forgot that only male lions have manes.

R.N. of Bedford Hills, New York, was correct in 1990 when he wrote: "About your March 14 puzzle, a koala is a marsupial, not a bear, for cryin' out loud!"

However, the koala looks so much like a cuddly little teddy bear that *koala bear* has become an entry in such dictionaries as *Webster's Third*. Incidentally, that lexicon also notes that the petite marsupial is sometimes called a *kangaroo bear*. But most lexicographers can't bear to recognize the faulty folk usage.

A 1985 puzzle ignobly stated that MILORD is the proper way to address a duke. Thomas Campbell of New York City was the first of many Anglophiles to suggest that I peer into some books on peerage.

RE: The Crossword Puzzle for Tuesday, 7th January: 35 Across. The correct term of address for a Duke is "Your Grace" never "My Lord" (or "Milord").

"My Lord" and "Your Lordship" are used for the other grades of the British peerage, i.e., Marquess, Earl, Viscount and Baron.

I enclose xeroxed pages from *Debrett's Correct Form,* Patrick Montague-Smith, editor, which is *the* authority on the subject.

Let me close this chapter with a funny letter from R.W. of Somerville, Massachusetts, and another from L.O. in which the joke's on me.

R.W. wrote:

A few weeks ago you matched up "nerds" with "jerks." I must disagree with this also. As a graduate student in electrical engineering at Tufts University I can tell you that the two are in no way synonymous. Nerds may be boring and wimpy but we are not jerks! Maybe we do eat quiche a bit more than desirable. Our clothes could also be snazzier. But we are polite, darn it! A real jerk would call you nasty expletives like a hyped up hockey player.

I have found many other errors solving your crossword puzzles. Unfortunately they are my own. I have to go now. My computer is lonely.

L.O. quipped: "The *New York Times* Crossword Puzzle of March 28, 1985, had the clue "Self," and the answer was SELF. I thought this was a rather 'self' explanatory clue!"

SQUAWKERS AND QUIBBLERS

There is a small but very vocal group of solvers who complain about matters over which I have no control. I call them the Squawkers.

Some Squawkers are left-handed. When the daily puzzle was printed on the left side of the page, these southpaws had no area upon which they could lean. Their elbow drifted out in space as they filled in the words. They pleaded with me to give them a break, and I kept sending their letters to the people in charge of layouts.

Maybe my intercession helped. Suddenly, without any warning to me or the fans, the puzzles appeared at the bottom-middle of the page. Furthermore, the style of printing was changed. Such double-dealing evoked a slew of other letters directly to me. They ranged from polite requests to angry protests. Here's an example of the former. It was written by C.C. of New York City.

This is a complaint. Several months ago you changed the typeface for the crossword puzzle. Why? Some of us are addicted to that daily feature. The change withdraws it from those who lack the sharpest eyesight.

The lighter print apparently gave trouble to many older people. Here's one from Col. S.P. of New York City.

Is it at all possible to darken your puzzles? I have become addicted to them. My failing eyesight combined with your faintness have caused me a hardship. Would you please alleviate my suffering now that I have attained the age of 91—I need all the help I can get.

P.J.H. of Valley Cottage, New York, had a complaint about the type of paper on which the Sunday puzzles are printed. In 1990, he wrote:

I don't feel the magazine section is the best place for your puzzles because:
a) the semi-gloss paper does not accept even a soft No. 2 pencil very well;
b) said semi-gloss paper reflects light significantly and causes glare.
I suggest therefore that the puzzles be put in another section of the paper in order to get around these drawbacks.
Many thanks in advance.

My suggestion to Mr. H. was that he purchase an erasable pen. As for the glare, one other solver requested that the puzzles be placed in the *Book Review* section, but that idea is not feasible because the thinness of the paper would result in rips when vigorous erasures are made.

To return to daily puzzles, the new position on the page also caused a furor. In that regard, the most interesting letter was sent by J.M. of Malvern, Pennsylvania. This is what he wrote.

I am an avid fan of your puzzles. I am also a creature of habit.
As an ex-New Yorker, I still use the "New York fold" when

reading the *Times*. I learned this while riding the 8th Avenue line over a period of years. The New York fold allows you to read the paper (or do the puzzle) in a crowded situation. As you probably know, the New York fold involves folding the paper on a vertical seam exactly in the middle of a page. This produces three columns of news from top to bottom of a page. More importantly, it also produces the puzzle in a perfect position. And, for even greater puzzle enjoyment, you can double fold the vertical section to an even more compact state.

All of this works fine, assuming the puzzle is printed along the right hand or left hand margin. (While less critical, it also helps if the puzzle is at the top or bottom of the page.) And, since this was the case for all of the years I have done the puzzle, this would have appeared to be a good assumption. But, then came July 2, 1990. For no apparent reason, the *New York Times* decided to move the location of the puzzle to the center of the page. Obviously, this made it impossible to do the puzzle while standing up or even sitting down, if you were accustomed to a neatly folded paper to work with. In my case, the misplacement of the puzzle caused me so much stress, that it has taken me a week to compose myself to write to you.

Once in a while, the printing on a solver's puzzle is blurred. On August 7, 1990, E.W.C. of Poughkeepsie discovered that the definitions for most of the vertical words were illegible. Undaunted, he completed the task of solving the entire puzzle, and he proudly sent it to me with the following letter.

You do, on occasion, present a challenging puzzle. This one proved for me just how challenging it can be. Deductive reasoning, plus some training in crossword puzzles, provided the basis for solution.

I realize, of course, that you don't control the printing. But this proved so unusual that I thought I would share it with you. And of course, tomorrow's paper will provide the truth of my deductions. Nevertheless, it proved to be more challenging than I anticipated when I got my paper.

Dr. J.B. of Fort Lauderdale, Florida, had a different kind of complaint. In 1990, he wrote:

Because I *remove* with scissors and try to solve your puzzle when the *Times* is delivered each morning I find that I am missing significant material *when I read the paper* (before reading the *Wall Street Journal*).

I would appreciate your *not* printing puzzles on pages that contain *important* articles on the reverse side since I read the paper thoroughly!

Actually, I don't believe that the *Times* can oblige Dr. J.B.; however, his request reminds me of a few others that did get sporadic results only because of a luncheon speech that I gave to *Times* advertisers in the mid-eighties. At one point, I mentioned several letters from non-solving mates of crossword addicts. All of them asked that an advertisement be placed on the back of the Sunday puzzle. I quoted a request from a woman in New Jersey. She said that after breakfast her husband tears out the puzzle, attaches it to a clipboard and locks himself in the bathroom.

Shortly afterwards, she said, the main article in the magazine often attracts her attention. But ten minutes later she discovers that the page on which the article is continued has disappeared. Where is it? In the bathroom!

After citing the above case, I said I wished I could get the attention of the person in charge of layouts for the magazine. Suddenly, I was interrupted by the official in charge of the luncheon. He sheepishly announced that he was the culprit and that his foul deeds would no longer be perpetrated.

Did he live up to his promise? Yes, most of the time. But he has recently retired, and now I must track down his successor.

In cases where both spouses are puzzle aficionados, a different kind of problem exists. I often receive letters asking that two identical copies of the crossword be printed. Naturally, I do not forward such requests to my bosses, lest I be sent to Coventry. People don't seem to realize how expensive space is: for example, a full-page ad in the *Times* can cost over $30,000!

One couple in Marin County, California, reported to me that they had bought a copying machine for the sole purpose of duplicating the puzzles. They figured out that in the long run they would spend more money if they bought a second copy of the newspaper every day. But they should know that photocopying the puzzle is a violation of copyright laws.

H.W. of New York City tells me that his local stationery store receives advance copies of the Sunday *Times Magazine* and certain other sections. Mr. W. pays the dealer for the entire newspaper and picks up the magazine on his way to work each Friday. He then uses the photocopy machine at the office to make an extra copy of the Sunday puzzle for his wife.

Since puzzle-solving is usually a private matter, it is not surprising to discover that most couples do not solve the puzzle together. Many prefer the method employed by my late wife and me. She solved the puzzle without my aid. If she had some blank spaces left (usually on sports) she asked me to finish it.

The mention of a photocopy machine a few paragraphs ago brings back the memory of a phone call from a clerk in a Manhattan office. She told me that she photocopied each daily puzzle and passed the copies around to her co-workers during the coffee break. Then they called out questions and answers to one another until the puzzle was entirely filled in or they were all stumped.

In another office, I was informed, the same photocopying procedure was used. However, the solving process was not cooperative. The first person to complete the puzzle (without help from others) stood up and received a round of applause.

In March 1988 the men in the *Times* composing room made a rare error. They printed the same daily puzzle that had appeared on the previous day! That mistake caused the phone to ring angrily all day and scores of letters to arrive shortly thereafter.

Among the communications, the most interesting one came from I.B. of Providence, Rhode Island. With his permission, I am happy to share it *in toto*.

You ruined a perfectly good restaurant lunch today by permitting an unprecedented gaffe on the puzzle page of today's *Times*—you reprinted the previous day's puzzle, thereby robbing me of a daily enjoyment that has become integrated in my midday ritual since I completed my first puzzle some 34 years ago at the tender age of 16.

Now I realize that age is usually recalled with more exotic, if not erotic, moments but for a young college student forced to ride the subways more than an hour each way up to City College from the depths of Brooklyn, the puzzle provided the one solace during that saturnine sojourn (two words, I believe, that I first ran across in my initial puzzle forays).

So you can imagine my discomfort at finding a day-old puzzle staring at me with almost the same intensity as the piece of salmon on my plate would have exhibited had it been similarly astonished.

I became addicted to the puzzles, particularly the Sunday effort, when I worked for a short time as a copy boy at the *Times* in the late 1950's. I was among the overlooked few who could obtain the magazine on its Thursday publication date, giving me a three-day head start over the rest of the literati (except, of course, for the Harvard drop-out who ran the mimeo machine while finishing his puzzle with one hand).

As V. Lenin asked in his famous tract "What Is to Be Done?" I suggest a simple solution—print an apology and then inform the puzzle addicts that to make up for this "typographical error," (are typos still possible in the computer age?) you will print two different puzzles on a future Thursday.

I expect no less from what most certainly must be the best puzzle editor in the nation. I don't want a refund and I refuse any credits or remonstrances. Just give me back my puzzle and my midday dreams.

To make up for the grievous goof, two puzzles were published on the next day.

In the first fifteen years of my editorship, only two *Times* solvers sent in a request that the answers be printed on the same day as the puzzle appears. In each case, I replied that the first *Times* editor, Margaret Farrar, had complied with solvers' wishes concerning the delay in publishing the answer and that the procedure has remained because fans don't want to be tempted to peek. Also, some are in competition with relatives or friends who might yield to the urge to cheat.

The advent of the "900 number" experiment in January 1990 eliminated the need to please a few impatient people. They could receive instant gratification via a Touch-Tone phone and a minimum of 75 cents. Apparently, the scheme was reasonably successful, but it did generate a host of letters from outraged fans who felt that the sanctity of their hallowed hobby had been violated. Most of the protests were sent directly to me in the belief that I had initiated the idea. The truth is that I was not involved in any way and had no share in whatever profits were made.

Here's a typical 900 squawk.

> Once again I take pen in hand, this time re: your new policy of supplying answers by a mere phone call. Do you realize that you have revolutionized the game? "The thrill of the chase" is gone! You have succumbed to society's new dictum—*Instant Reward.*
>
> No longer will friends call each other by noon on Sunday, because they can call *you* instead! No working and re-working Monday, Tuesday, Wednesday—what for? No longer awaiting the following Sunday to check answers—easily done any time!
>
> You've probably turned off as many as you've turned on. Was this ploy to increase circulation? Shame on you for capitulating! Coward!
>
> > Your former friend, M.A.B.

However, in an indirect way the 900-number plan helped me to enjoy longer hours of sweet slumber. Here's a typical scenario from the pre-900 era.

E.T.M.	(*answering the phone at midnight, and wondering who died*) Hello.
MALE VOICE.	Is this Dr. Maleska?
E.T.M.	Yes.
M.V.	Oh, good! I'm sorry to be calling you so late, but I need your help.
E.T.M.	Who is this?
M.V.	I'm one of your puzzle fans, and I can't sleep until I find out the answer to 49 Down.
E.T.M.	(*irritably*) How did you get my number?
M.V.	One of your friends gave it to me.
E.T.M.	Well, that person is no longer a friend of mine! Please hold the wire while I look up 49 Down.
M.V.	Oh, thanks! You're so nice!

Subsequently, the answer is given to the fan and the conversation ends as follows:

M.V.   (*with a sigh of relief*) Oh, so that's it! Thanks a mil-
          lion. Now I can sleep!
E.T.M.   But I can't! Good night!

One of my fellow Regis High School graduates once called me
on a weekday morning. He said he had made a large bet with
a friend that he could solve the *Times* daily puzzle perfectly, but
he would lose the bet if I didn't help him where 28 Across and
30 Down intersected. I wished him good luck and hung up
abruptly. I still wonder if he lost the bet, and I sort of hope so.

During the first month of my tenure at the *Times,* I received an
irate letter from a retiree in Miami. He said that he had scores
of friends who joined him in detesting my puzzles and that he
would lead them in a boycott if I didn't change my ways and
make them less difficult.

   In the same mail I received a letter from a gentleman who
lived on Park Avenue. He stated that Will Weng's puzzles always
gave him a challenge but that mine were so easy that he solved
them in less than half an hour.

   I tore off the address and signature of the Park Avenue letter
and mailed it to the man in Miami. Then I made the same
excisions on the "boycotter's" letter and sent it to the Gotham
critic. Neither was ever heard from again!

At the time when those letters were written, the managing editor
(Abe Rosenfeld) called me to his office. He said that he had
received lots of mail concerning the recent change. Half said the
puzzles were too easy; the other half said they were too hard.
He shook my hand and nodded: "Obviously, you must be right
down the middle. Keep it up!"

   As the saying goes, the beat goes on. Individuals who are
inexperienced continue to complain that I am some kind of ogre
who likes to torture people, whereas the mavens keep crying for
more difficult challenges.

   No puzzle editor can please all of the solvers all of the time.
Year after year, I continue to receive complaints that the puzzles
are too easy or too hard. More often than not, the squawkers

are good-humored. Here's an example. It came from R.R. of Santa Fe Springs, California.

> You and I have had breakfast together every Sunday for over 30 years.
>
> It all began at the Plaza Hotel's coffee shop overlooking Central Park. I would greet you with excitement and anticipation. Always with a pen (never a pencil!) in hand.
>
> After a half hour, you and I would leave the Plaza, find a sunny spot in the park under a tree, and begin to get serious.
>
> An hour later, our visit would be over. Sometimes, there were gaps in our thinking. But always, there was the educated guess and the joy of discovery. And always, you and your friend taught me something.
>
> On rare occasions, we agreed on every word. What joy there was then!
>
> But lately, you've become more distant, more remote. A case in point: "Bird botching." HILA, URIAL, ORDURE and the ever-lovin' 19th century emperor CHIEN are insurmountable obstacles!
>
> Even when we meet Chicken Little, Marten and Oaku, there's no way we can find a Hila and Urial, and thus no way we'll ever know Mr. Chien.
>
> Perhaps you're bored with the ups and downs of your job after so many years. You've become cross, wordy, unfair.
>
> I hope it's just a passing aberration. I pray that after 30 years together, you won't forget how much we've meant to each other. There has never been anyone to take your place.
>
> Please, please, Eugene, no more 19th century Chinese emperors. Give me back my self-respect. Give me back a fighting chance to win again on Sunday mornings.

As mentioned in Chapter 1, I try to gradate the daily puzzles from easy on Monday to difficult on Saturday. Similarly, some attempt is made to meet the vastly different abilities of Sunday solvers. About five times a year the featured puzzles are comparatively easy. On five or six other Sundays the 21-by-21 and 23-by-23 puzzles are real challengers. But most of the time the difficulty level is somewhere between simple and somewhat puzzling.

Does my easy-to-hard grading system please everybody? Not

on your life! I have resigned myself to the fact that squawks cannot be squelched entirely. Whereas numerous complaints about the "impossible" Saturday puzzles had been expected, many objections to the "too easy" Monday offerings had not been foreseen. A typical example of the unhappiness of my Monday-morning quarterbacks comes from K.W. of Hauppauge, New York.

> Seven days a week I read my *New York Times*. After I've finished reading about what's wrong in our world, I get excited about moving on to the crossword puzzle.
> I don't consider myself a crossword puzzle snob—I'm not that good. In fact, I often look up a word or two, but I don't consider that cheating. I even think it's acceptable.
> The main reason I'm writing is to register a minor complaint. The puzzles you print during the early part of the week, particularly on Monday, seem so simple that it would hardly present a challenge to a novice. There isn't much fun doing them unless there's some degree of difficulty. I'm sure you have a valid reason for doing this but I, for one, would like to begin my week with puzzles that take a little more time and thought to complete.
> I'm curious as to why the puzzles at the beginning of the week are so simple, but whether or not my letter causes you to revise your format, I will certainly remain a fan.

R.W. of Scarsdale, New York, has a seemingly simple solution to the difficulty problem.

> You have probably received thousands of letters saying the puzzles are too easy or too hard.
> The answer is: "Both of the above."
> Why not run *two puzzles* each day—one hard and one easy?

The powers-that-be at the *Times* are satisfied with the current system, but I am reminded of a dilemma faced by the chief editors of an upstate New York newspaper. They were publishing an easy daily puzzle supplied by a national syndicate. Because of constant squawks that the crosswords were too easy, they switched to the *Times* syndicate. Bad move! A storm of protests came from the other side of the fence. And so, they used the "R.W. Solution," and everybody lived happily ever after with the possible exception of the double-paying owner of the newspaper as he shelled out money to two syndicates.

Speaking of syndication, when the *Times* dispatches my puzzles to hundreds of other newspapers, occasionally a mistake is made either by the sender or receiver. At that point, I get the blame. For example, Mrs. C.W. of Geneva, Illinois, dashed off an irate letter to me when her local paper printed CLIY instead of CLOY as the answer to "surfeit." The fault was the sender's in that case.

But the receiver was culpable when the *Detroit News Magazine* mixed up several numbers for the clues. Ms. L.H. of Mount Clemens, Michigan, wrote to me: "Come on, Mr. Maleska. What has happened to quality control?"

The *Times* syndicate has a rule: receivers must wait at least a week before publishing a *Times* puzzle. Once in a while, either deliberately or inadvertently, a receiver breaks the rule, but the fans immediately inform me and I relay the news to the syndicate.

People ask me how much extra I am paid for the reprints of the puzzles in other newspapers. The answer is nil.

Sometimes the Sunday puzzle celebrates an occasion of note. For instance, in July of 1989 the crossword by Jacques Liwer was devoted to the bicentennial of France's Bastille Day. And on August 16, 1987, the puzzle centered on the tenth anniversary of Elvis Presley's death. That one generated a loud squawk from veteran solver L.M.K. of Hartsdale, New York. I admit that he had a valid complaint. Here is the node of his letter.

> . . . today's puzzle, which celebrates the tenth anniversary of Elvis Presley's death by giving us a puzzle impossible to approach unless you're a Presley fan, moves me to speak up.
>
> The crossword puzzle should be a "general interest" feature. Your themed puzzles are turning it into a "special interest" feature. And when the theme is as specialized as Elvis Presley's past movies, you're locking out a big part of your potential audience.

• • •

Sexism brings forth rebukes from women solvers. A brief, polite one was sent to me in August 1990. It was written by a female Certified Public Accountant.

Even the *New York Times* occasionally perpetuates sexual stereotypes. On August 2, a crossword puzzle clue was "numbers men, for short." The answer was CPAS. Enough said.

In a daily puzzle on April 4, 1987, CANON was defined as "Clergyman." The Reverend N.P., pastor of Christ's First Presbyterian Church in a New York town, objected.

Are you aware that many of us are not clergy*men* but *women?* Your use of the exclusionary term perpetuates an inaccurate stereotype. Clergyperson is acceptable although somewhat cumbersome. The term *clergy* is often used on its own.

I enjoy your puzzles and look forward to greater sensitivity on your part.

On another occasion I defined PRIEST as "Clergyman" and was gently scolded by the Reverend Beatrice B., a New York City priest.

D.J.S. lashed out at me and my "New Wave" critics. In September 1988 part of a long letter read as follows:

What is an 8-letter word for "vendor"? SALESMAN, of course. A 5-letter word for "Madison Ave. type"? ADMAN. And "Feds" are G MEN, while a "pieman" is a BAKER. These are traditionalist clues from *The Times* (the first two from August 5th and 10th, and the last two from September 13th).

The New Wave offers its own sexist clues: in the sample that accompanied the referenced article, a 4-letter word for "man of action" is a DOER.

It is unfortunate that no progress has been made in crafting these clues. As any student of etymology knows, the words we use represent how we think. In excluding women from being called doers and Madison Avenue types, we preclude women from being seen in these categories.

What is a 12-letter word that describes this situation? *Narrow-minded.*

As early as 1981, I got into trouble with the feminists. Worse yet, my wife wrote "Hear! Hear! I'm with her" alongside the following letter from a promotion copywriter for *Psychology Today.*

I am an avid, accomplished *Times* crossword enthusiast. While I normally praise the *Times* for providing a challenge for my compulsive addiction, in this instance I cannot. This time I'm truly puzzled.

As you can see, I did not complete this recent puzzle. When I read Clue 42 Across I was horrified to find such blatant sexism. There are many clues for EVE—i.e., "The Three Faces of ____," "Christmas ____," or simply "Arden"—all considerably less chauvinistic than "Rib outgrowth." As editor, I hold you responsible for this offensive oversight. There is no reason to remind your male audience of the mythological origins of women that portray us as subservient, second-class creatures who were an afterthought of a male God.

In the future, I would hope your pricked conscience will guide you to use more equitable clues. And I look forward to your personal response—an apology I will share with fellow *Times* crossword puzzlers.

Since the above letter was addressed to Mr. Hugh Maleska, I could have disclaimed any responsibility for the offensive attempt at humor.

Another female writer got into the act in June 1987. Here's the letter from C.L.G. in New York City.

In last Sunday's (June 21st) crossword puzzle, one of the Across clues was "Org. for Mom." I hoped that the answer wasn't PTA, but, much to my shock and dismay, it was. First of all, the clue is simply incorrect; *PTA* stands for *Parent Teacher Association,* not *Mother Teacher Association.* Assuming that this is a well-known fact, the clue given implies that only mothers are involved in the PTA despite its name, which to my mind is a sexist and untrue implication. Not being a parent myself I do not know what the percentage of fathers in the PTA is, but I'm sure that there are enough to warrant it being called the PTA and not the MTA.

I enjoy the *New York Times* Crossword Puzzle and one of the reasons is that I feel that I can count on it *not* to be offensive. In mass-market crossword puzzle magazines I would expect, and indeed have found, clues like the one I am discussing, but I was disappointed to find this in the *Times*.

As a puzzle editor, I find that the sensitivities of women are multiple in nature. This one comes from M.P.M. of Port Washington, New York.

In a recent crossword puzzle (June 17 *Magazine* [among others]) we were asked in 40 Across for a word for "old womanish." The answer, as all good crossword-puzzle-solvers know, is ANILE.

I find the words *old womanish* and *anile* most offensive. To quote the dictionary in part: *anile* [L *anilis;* Fr. *anus* old woman; akin to OHG . . .]. I am not aware of a word for *old mannish*. If one doesn't exist, may I suggest *buttile*. To quote the dictionary again in part: *ass* [ME . . . akin to OHG and OM *ars* buttocks . . .].

Alternatively and preferable, I would prefer to eliminate the expression *old womanish* and any debasing terms of reference.

There are three Latin words spelled *anus:* (1) the fundament, (2) a ring, and (3) an old woman. The third has no etymological relationship to the other two.

The Latin word for an old man is *senex.* From it, we get the adjective *senile.* Unfortunately, that adjective is also applied to aged females.

Mrs. W.H.K. of New York City has another axe to grind. She wrote:

In the crossword puzzle in today's *Times,* there was a distinctly denigratory tone! e.g., 17A: "Fast woman's dating list," ans.

TOM, DICK AND HARRY; 36A: "Fast woman's benefactor," ans. SUGAR DADDY; and so on. Not nicely done!

Of course, I know that you only *vet* the correspondents' puzzles, but this time, as a long-time devotee of the puzzle, I may say that I think you ought to have *put* this one very firmly *down!* Or were you trying to put something *across* to your female solvers?

In the same vein, along came a letter from A.G. of White Plains, New York.

Your crossword puzzles have given me hours of enjoyment over the months; my colleagues and I have become somewhat addicted to them.

Yesterday's puzzle was an exception. I was very surprised, disappointed and hurt to discover the word SLUT being called for with the clue to 26 Down.

The word *slut* is misogynist in nature, origin and current usage. There are no such mean-spirited words to describe slovenly, loose men. Hearing or reading the word *slut* is jarring and upsetting; it calls to mind the painful double standard in existence for women, one which continues to damage both sexes.

Mr. Maleska, I realize that language is often slow to change and that a crossword puzzle may seem an odd place to start, but all forms of media have considerable power. I would be happy to find no more anti-women sentiments, be they conscious or not, on view in your puzzle. Thank you.

It is fascinating to note that words like ROUE and RAKE constantly appear in the puzzles. Also quips about LIBERTINES who are "gay deceivers" and "participants in orgies" have been published—but not one letter of protest from a male has ever been sent to me. To echo Andy Rooney, *why is that?*

Of relevance is the fact that I used to receive complaints from a few men every time the word *sissy* cropped up in a crossword. The two definitions in an average dictionary are:

1. an effeminate man or boy
2. a timid or cowardly person

Neither clue pleased certain individuals. Then, thank Heaven, the movies provided me with *Sissy* Spacek. She put an end to my problem.

One of my severest critics is C.S. of Ridgewood, New Jersey. She not only writes long objections to me but she also sends copies to my bosses. Here's her latest sally.

As you may recall, I wrote to you in 1981, when I was employed by the New York State Office of Mental Retardation as the Director of the Client Rights Unit, to criticize the use of a word derogatory to persons with handicapping conditions in a daily crossword puzzle. Your prompt response assured me that such a word as *moron* would no longer be used in puzzles to describe such persons with low I.Q. scores.

Unfortunately, I find myself having to write to you a second time, to criticize your use of the word *cretins* to describe "certain handicapped persons" (clue number 47 Across) in the daily puzzle of October 15, 1985. The word *cretin,* like the word *moron,* while it may be correct in terms of dictionary usage, is no longer considered an appropriate word to describe persons with handicapping conditions. Again, as I pointed out in 1981, it is a socially stigmatizing and extremely derogatory word which those of us in the field are trying to remove from everyday usage. Indeed, such a word as *cretin* is as harmful and as distasteful to us as calling a black person a "nigger," a Jewish person a "kike," or an Hispanic person a "spick." You would never dream of including such words in your puzzles, yet you continue, even after I pointed this concern out to you, to use such words as *cretin* in them.

I would suggest that in the future you more carefully edit your puzzles so that words such as *moron* and *cretin* do not appear in them. Their inclusion in the *New York Times* is in very poor taste and is extremely injurious to the rights of all persons with handicapping conditions to live dignified and normal lives. Thank you for your attention to this matter.

Ms. S. has a point because words like *moron, idiot,* and (less often) *cretin* are sometimes bandied about in a derogatory manner. Hence, although many people would say that the woman is supersensitive, I have found inoffensive clues:

Moron	City in Argentina
	Town in Cuba
	City in SW Spain
Idiot	Dostoevsky's "The ——"
	Kind of board, box or card
	Type of servant

However, *cretin* poses a different problem because I cannot find a geographical or literary reference to get around the direct definition. Recently, *cretin* appeared in a puzzle sent to me for the daily *Times*. Luckily, I was able to change it to *Cretan*. But what will I do when alterations are impossible? To quote Scarlett, "I'll think about it tomorrow."

By the way, *cretin* is derived from *Christian*. When the first infants suffering from the mental deficiency were discovered in the French Alps, the term was used to indicate that the unfortunates were indeed humans despite their deformities.

CABAL appears often in the crosswords. It means "intrigue or group of schemers." In 1981 when I published the word in a puzzle, Rabbi W.F. gave me a lesson in history.

> I am most disturbed by the unfortunate perpetuation in your puzzle of April 13 of a little-known but pervasive religious slur. I refer specifically to your word [for] 5 Across, CABAL, defined as "Pernicious plot."
>
> The word *cabal* is derived from *Kabbalah* (sometimes spelled *Cabala*), the Jewish mystical tradition. Because traditional Judaism and—even more—traditional Christianity attempted to suppress the teachings of the Kabbalah, and because mystical teachings—of whatever faith—have traditionally been shrouded in mystery and secrecy, these teachings were thought of as a secret, dangerous, and evil body of arcane knowledge associated with Satanic rituals. This distorted view of the Kabbalah has left it mark on the English language in the word *cabal* denoting any conspiratorial and subversive group.

Several rabbis took me to task early in the eighties when a top constructor named Jordan Lasher defined PHARISEE as a "hypocrite" and I let the clue stand because it was verified by all my dictionaries. One rabbi sent me copies of about a dozen pages of a book extolling the Pharisees for their scholarship and piety.

All the rabbis agreed that the ancient sect had received an undeserved bad reputation in the New Testament writings by Saint Matthew and Saint Luke. In Chapter 23, for instance, Matthew quotes Jesus as saying: "Woe unto you, scribes and Pharisees, hypocrites!"

Apparently, the rabbis are losing this particular battle. I have just acquired two newly published dictionaries. In both books, *pharisaical* is defined as "hypocritical."

In April 1990 a Sunday puzzle by Maura B. Jacobson was called "Mideast Monkeyshines." Mrs. Jacobson is noted for her puns, and the crossword in question was no exception. Here are some of the main entries and the answers:

Clue	Solution
Polluted waters at Port Said?	THE SEWAGE CANAL
Donne's geographical error?	OMAN IS AN ISLAND
Valentino?	A WOLF IN SHEIK'S CLOTHING
Title for an aged Islamic rancher?	IMAM AN OLD COWHAND
Mideast mecca for stargazers?	KUWAIT WATCHERS

The puzzle evoked an angry letter from a Rochester professor.

Occasionally I have been forced to my knees by the *New York Times'* Sunday magazine puzzle and have not completed it, but the puzzle you saw fit to print on Sunday, 22 April, was the first I stopped working on because it was morally and ethically objectionable—in fact, in every sense of the word, poisonously anti-Semitic and smelling of the grossest religious prejudice.

"Mideast Monkeyshines," Mr. Maleska? Indeed. Turn a couple of the choicer definitions around: 50 Down, "Drowning Sabra's cry," or 75 Across, "Title for an aged Hassidic rancher." Print one of *those* and you and I know how long you would continue to edit the crossword for the *Times*.

Whatever Ms. Jacobson's dirty little secret thoughts, they have absolutely no place in any part of the *Times*, and if you didn't recognize this, you are not doing your job. I am, by the way, neither Arab nor Moslem, but I know hatred and sniggering

ethnocentrism when I see it, and you and your newspaper owe
an apology to your readers. I for one do not wish to have my
stomach turned on a quiet Sunday morning by this sort of
shameful nonsense.

Here's a copy of my reply:

If the April 22nd puzzle were as offensive and objectionable
as you say it is, then why was your letter the only complaint of
that nature? Why is it that *no* Arabian delegation has stormed
the *Times* and is demanding an apology?

Puzzle solvers are used to puns on names of people and
places. People like Jack Lemmon (*lemon*) Lucille Ball (*bawl*) et
al. are subjected often to paronomasial quips. Does that mean
we have singled them out for abuse? In the past, we have used
words like Czeckmate and we have defined Chinese checkers
as "Peking supermarket employees." Are we, therefore, having
dirty little secret thoughts about Serbs, Croats, and people of
the Far East?

You'll be interested to hear that there was one other letter
stating that we are anti-Semitic. It referred to 74 Across. The
clue read: "___ Yisrael (Palestine)." We were accused of failing
to recognize Israel!

Since you are obviously an intelligent person, I will not state
that you lack a sense of humor. Instead, I will assume that on
April 22 you got up on the wrong side of the bed.

Of special interest in the Rochester letter was the use of *anti-
Semitic,* meaning "against Arabs." Many people seem to forget
that the word *Semite* includes both Jews and Arabs.

Having a sense of humor has plunged me into hot water on
several occasions. For instance, in April 1988 I published a daily
puzzle in which constructor Kenneth Witte had used the following phrases as a theme:

A. GO OFF HALF COCKED
B. JUMPED THE GUN
C. TRIGGER HAPPY
D. SHOOT FROM THE HIP

Mr. Witte's quartet involved *impetuosity,* but in an effort to alert
the solvers to the fact that the phrases also involved firearms,

he brought the National Rifle Association into the act. His clues for the foregoing phrases were:

A. "Act impetuously, N.R.A. style?"
B. "Acted impetuously, N.R.A. style?"
C. "Impetuous, N.R.A. style?"
D. "Act impetuously, N.R.A. style?"

I suppose I should have realized that the references to the N.R.A. in such a context might be considered offensive by members of that group, but my mind was on the need to tip off the solvers concerning the specific nature of the rashness in all four instances.

Sure enough, protests poured in. Here's a typical one.

> I am highly offended, as an N.R.A. member, [by] these *false* derogatory remarks about the N.R.A. I don't believe that you should permit these cheap-shots to be incorporated into the crossword puzzle. I know many N.R.A. members and none of them act like these four phrases indicate.

Some nicknames can also bring out a breed of Squawkers. As a case in point, when a constructor defined GAOL as "Limey lockup," I liked the alliteration but I was afraid that the designation might be disparaging. First, I consulted *Webster's Third* and *New World*. Those lexicons merely declared that *limey* was a slang word for an English sailor or Englishman. Then I called the British consulate. The person who answered assured me that the sobriquet was not offensive.

And so, I let the clue get into print. Bingo! From Northvale, New Jersey, came an objection by L.N.S.

> I have been doing your puzzles in the *New York Times* for years and I want to let you know that I take exception to something in one of your recent puzzles—probably one day at the end of July. 25 Across—"Limey lockup."
>
> I am an English woman, and I must say I am surprised at you—can you imagine the flak you would get if your clue was "wop" lockup or "nigger" lockup—rightfully so??
>
> I must say I am very surprised at you and at the *New York Times* for allowing you to get away with this. I trust you will be more sensitive in future.

• • •

Similarly, in 1987 the word OKIE appeared in a puzzle. Since I had read Steinbeck's *The Grapes of Wrath,* my definition was "Dust Bowl refugee." That clue angered L.F. of Carmichael, California. He wrote:

> Just as Blacks do not like to be referred to as Niggers, so Whites from the Oklahoma area do not like to be referred to as Okies.

Now when OKIE crops up in a constructor's contribution, I try to change it to OBIE or OPIE. If alterations are impossible, I publish the puzzle anyway—but not without a twinge of regret.

The Okie problem reminds me of YAHOO. Here's a squawk from P.H. of Flushing, New York.

> I found the puzzle "Kitchenware" by Alfio Micci (*New York Times Magazine,* 10/29/89) in poor taste. Citing *yahoo* as a synonym for *bumpkin,* as in 36 Down, is inexact and pejorative. I think Mr. Micci owes his audience an apology, particularly rural dwellers.

Methinks Mr. H. is tilting at the windmills of common usage. In *Gulliver's Travels* by Jonathan Swift the Yahoos were a race of brutes. Eventually they became a part of our language. Synonyms given by modern lexicographers are *uncultivated or boorish persons, louts, philistines,* and *yokels.*

But Mr. H. does have a point. As far back as the ancient Egyptians and the Greco-Roman civilization, urbanites have treated rural people with linguistic disdain. As just one example, consider the fact that the word *villain* comes from the Latin noun *villa,* meaning "farm."

City people who control the media have looked down their cultured noses at *yokels, rubes, hicks, hayseeds, bumpkins, chawbacons,* etc. and probably will continue to do so until the end of time. Is it incumbent upon crossword puzzlers to censure such words?

• • •

Sometimes when constructors and editors are on strange ground, the dictionaries mislead them into the use of offensive words. Take *Kaffir,* for example. In *Webster's Second* or *Webster's Third* that word appears as part of the definition for IMPI. Ask any puzzle addict, "What's an impi?" and you'll be told: "A body of Kaffir warriors."

People like me embraced *impi* as a component of good, old crosswordese and ingenuously used the *Webster's Second—Webster's Third* definition. Little did we know that *Kaffir* was a disparaging term. My friends and I assumed that impis were subgroups of an African tribe called the Kaffirs. And so, in 1984 I was greatly surprised when I received an admonishment from A.S., Jr., of Mills College in Oakland, California.

> Your crossword puzzle in the Feb. 8 *New York Times* contains what in my view is a lapse of judgement or taste, in the form of Clue 58 Across: "Body of Kaffir warriors." Since the answer to the clue is IMPI it is clear that you are referring to South African history (rather than, say, Arabic, whence the term de-rives). You should be aware that the term *Kaffir* is used by South African whites to give the most calculated and deep offense to South African blacks. It is the equivalent to, and as emotion-laden as, such derogatory terms as *Abo, Wog,* or *Nigger,* none of which would I believe be likely to make an appearance in your puzzles. *Kaffir* should in its turn be banned as a word not only likely to offend, but intended to offend.

You may have noticed that Mr. S. mentioned ABO and WOG in his letter. The former is a disparaging Australian term for the aborigines on that continent. Here again, the Merriam-Webster dictionaries are at fault for not warning readers that the short-ened form is offensive. I must confess that I unwittingly let the denigration appear in a *Times* puzzle before I discov-ered its contemptuous intent. Today I use a long-winded defi-nition for ABO. It's the Swedish name for Turku, a seaport in Finland.

Wog has two meanings. As an offensive word, it is a British term for a black person of Arabian background. Its origin is probably *golliwog,* a grotesque black doll created in 1922 by il-lustrator Florence Upton.

The other *wog* is chiefly an Australian term for a certain injurious microorganism and is believed to be the shortened form of *polliwog*.

In the spring of 1986, one of my best constructors submitted a puzzle containing WETBACK, which was defined as "Illegal border crosser." Feeling that the word was offensive, I decided not to publish the crossword. But after consulting *Webster's Third* and *New World* (my two latest dictionaries at the time) I changed my mind. Neither lexicon gave any hint that *wetback* was a no-no.

Predictably, a Squawker surfaced. L.K. of Miami wrote:

> It is sad when one of my daily pleasures is ruined. To wit: the answer to 30 Across, "Illegal border crosser" is WETBACK.
>
> I fail to understand how any pejorative or racist term can be allowed into the crossword puzzle. I have never seen racist labels for Blacks, Jews, Puerto Ricans, etc. used in the crossword. Do you not feel that Mexican immigrants deserve the same respect?
>
> In my work with Haitian refugees, we constantly struggle against stereotypes and strive to emphasize individuals and their needs. It is obvious that all refugee groups deserve the same treatment—not only from their support groups, but more importantly, from such widely read newspapers as the *Times*.
>
> One of the greatest impediments to refugees gaining their due rights [is] racist and xenophobic thinking. Using the term *wetback* in the crossword adds to the problem by legitimizing racist terms.
>
> I am sure you will agree and endeavor to remove these terms no matter where they occur in your newspaper.

Interestingly enough, when *Random House, Second* was published two years later, the lexicographers agreed with Mr. K. They designated *wetback* as "Disparaging and offensive." Hence the word will never appear again in a Maleska-edited puzzle.

M.P. of Morristown, New Jersey, is a Double Squawker. In 1989, her subject was a reference to an outmoded and cruel form of punishment.

> As a long-standing member of your Gotcha Club, may I take the liberty of complaining about 35 Across in today's crossword

(Monday, Dec. 11, 1989, p. C-17). "Feathers' partner," as a definition for TAR, has often appeared in the crosswords, and has irritated me every time I have seen it. It is meant to be light and humorous, but the practice of tarring and feathering was *not funny*. As a form of degradation and punishment, it was akin to lynching. It is unseemly to be resurrecting it over and over again in the crosswords with a light-hearted definition. Tear up the card already that has that definition of *tar,* or remove it from your computer program, I respectfully request.

Then in 1990, M.P. lectured me on a puzzle that contained offbeat references to liquor, such as an allusion to the battle of Brandywine.

Once again, I'm afraid I have a "cross word" for you—a poor return for all the daily and Sunday pleasure that your many wise, witty, and literate puzzles have given me!

Yesterday's "Skoal!" puzzle amazed me in its cheerful, innocent evocations of alcoholic liquors and associated words. It's bad enough that the *Times Magazine* section is full of liquor ads, but it was jarring yesterday to see the crossword reminding solvers of peach brandy, Scotch (several times), bourbon, aqua vitae, vodka, cold duck, mash, brandy, wine, ale, bottles, tokay, grenadine, shot, lime rickey, bar, beer, malt, sherry, pubs, whiskey, gin, rye, nip, rum, mixer, jigger, screwdriver, vat, keg, etc., etc.,—and even a brand name, "Jack Daniels," for whiskey.

Thinking of the thousands of lives lost or maimed by accidents or crimes connected with alcohol, and the tragic effects of alcohol on users' health and on their children, as well as the thousands of members of Alcoholics Anonymous and similar organizations who are struggling to abstain from serious addiction, I was shocked to see your puzzle blithely offering all the words connected with such addiction, as a form of amusement!

You wouldn't do it with drug abuse words, I hope, or Holocaust words, or sado-masochism words?

In our constant search for new definitions, the constructors and I sometimes inadvertently touch the sensitive nerves of some solvers. A prime example of this problem occurred in 1990 when DEAF received an unusual clue. Instead of typing "Unable to

hear," the constructor chose "Unwilling to hear"—a secondary
definition that appears in all unabridged dictionaries. The illus-
trative phrase that is sometimes cited is "to turn a deaf ear to
pleas."

At any rate, B.P.H. of Massapequa, New York, took up the
cudgels. Here is part of her letter.

> I must write this time for all those in the silent world you
> may have insulted by lack of sensitivity. I refer to the weekday
> crossword puzzle which included the clue "unwilling to hear"
> with the "correct" down response DEAF.
> Had you ever been among the deaf, you would know that
> there is nothing that a hearing impaired person wants more
> than to be a part of the hearing world. To imply that deafness
> is a matter of willingness is to negate the years of being called
> dumb and social ostracism that hearing impaired people live
> with.

B.P.H.'s point has some merit. Unfortunately, there *are* some
obtuse people who are blessed with good hearing and are prone
to believe that deaf individuals are deliberately closing their
minds to others' opinions.

Even the best of golfers fall into traps now and then. Crossword
puzzle editors have the same problem. Each clue that we publish
is like taking a swing, and we are not always perfect. For example,
back in 1987 I allowed SMUTS to be described as a "South African
statesman." A well-deserved rebuke came from C.W.B. of Dor-
chester, Massachusetts.

> Shame on you for permitting your subjective bias to creep
> out in the definition of 33 Down! Perhaps your acceptance of
> the semantic form *statesman* to describe Smuts of South Africa
> should be excused on the grounds of ignorance or insensitivity.
> Whatever the reason, the use of the term is inexcusable since
> governing without narrow constraints of partisanship is an in-
> tegral factor in the concept of statesmanship. You should have
> used a neutral term, e.g. "south african leader." The number
> of spaces would not permit me to indulge my bias and ink in
> the name Mandela—so, could we call a truce and settle on a
> neutral definition where South Africa is concerned—or, for

that matter, wherever racism (covert or overt) rears its ugly head.

Because horizontal and vertical words cross in a puzzle, certain niceties concerning diacritical marks in other languages cannot always be observed. For instance, if *soupçon* appears in the diagram, we do not show the cedilla in the solution because the letter *c* in the crossing word invariably does not require the special marking.

Similarly, we omit the tilde for a word like *señora* unless, by a 1000-to-1 chance, it happens to cross with another Spanish word also requiring the mark over the *n*.

The chief problem with regard to the above comes when the word *año* crops up in the diagram. If topped by a tilde, it means "year," but without the mark it means "anus"!

Whenever I omit cedillas or tildes, the solvers of Gallic or Hispanic background remain silent or send me gentle reproofs. But failure to include the umlaut usually evokes a storm of Teutonic choler. For example, in 1990 when GOTTERDAMMERUNG was the answer to a definition concerning the Wagnerian Ring Cycle, the letters from the Germanic contingent were didactic and accusatory. In no uncertain terms, I was instructed that the proper English spelling is GOETTERDAEMMERUNG. It was hard to resist a testy reply such as: "Don't be so lazy, *mein Tadler*. Fill in your own umlauts!"

Somewhere between the Squawkers and Leapers are those correspondents that I call Quibblers. Some are nitpickers; others are pedants; many have not kept up with folk usage. Let's start with an example of that last category. The letter came from S.K. of Newark, New Jersey.

I am writing with regard to the crossword puzzle which appeared in *The New York Times* on November 4, 1986. The clue for 49 Down was given as Russian port. The answer to that clue was ODESSA. Odessa is not a Russian port. It is part of the Ukrainian S.S.R. making it a Ukrainian port. Alternatively, it is a Soviet port, Soviet being the encompassing modifier, rather than Russian. Only cities, etc. which are part of the Russian Republic are Russian. You have made errors such as this one before. Since I am a daily puzzle addict, I would appreciate it if you were more careful about your usage. Not only do I find such errors personally offensive, but why make factual mistakes?

You are not by any means the only party to make this error repeatedly. Your newspaper is probably more sloppy than most. For instance, there is an article on page C13 of the same issue entitled "Russia gets Boris from Maine." The very same mistake is evident.

Technically, S.K. is correct. But *New World, Random House, Second,* and other recent dictionaries recognize the fact that millions of educated Americans equate Russia with the former Union of the Soviet Socialist Republics. Similarly Georgians, Ukrainians, et al. are often described as Russians.

Here's an interesting letter from K.W. of Claremont, California.

Because I maintain a strong interest in the country of Portugal, I must take exception to the clue 19 Across in the puzzle "Fraidycat!" Actually, the answer should be the city of *Porto,* not *Oporto.* Americans have mistakenly renamed the city in American English as "Oporto" because the Portuguese people say "voy o Porto," meaning "I go to Porto," the *o* being equivalent to our "to." We would not look favorably upon foreigners calling our cities "Tonewyork" and "Tolosangeles"; therefore we should practice correctly calling the city *Porto.* Thank you for your time.

My sources seem to indicate that K.W. is correct. The Portuguese name for the city is Porto, and in Caesar's day it was called Portus Cale.

The following excerpt from a letter sent by S.S. of Berkeley, California, might be considered a quibble, but I regard it as a reminder to be consistent.

Down 54: The Tagus is one
Answer *Rio*??
The *Tajo* is a *Rio*

The *Tagus* is a *River*
This is in keeping with your very (usually) good way of elic-
iting foreign terminology.

E.C. of Port Angeles, Washington, wrote me a provocative letter
when I stated that James Duane was the first mayor of New York
City (1784–89). Her source (*Americana Encyclopedia*) declared
that in 1689 Peter de Lanoy became the first elected mayor of
New York. Ms. Clark demanded to know who is right.

Well, chronologically her authority wins. However, de Lanoy
was elected by Tories while New York City was still part of a
British colony. Duane got the job after the Revolution.

In 1986, G.E.H. objected to an anatomical definition.

While I still disagree with *Webster's New World Dictionary* defining *Dame* as wife of a knight, rather than merely a female
knight, I now have found a new solecism in the puzzle for
January 8. Definition No. 56 Across says "hamstrings." This is
a specific term for the tendons adjacent to the knee (the ham
being the thigh). The word called for is ACHILLES TENDONS. The
Achilles tendons are at the heel, and anatomically, there is absolutely no relation between the hamstrings and the Achilles
tendons. They are not even tendons of the same muscles.
Therefore, the definition given is wrong. I have checked this,
to see if there could be alternate definitions, in two major unabridged dictionaries, and find support for my position and
none for the position taken in the puzzle.

I guess we should have been more specific. *Horses'* hamstrings
are Achilles' tendons.

Sometimes I deliberately court criticism by choosing a secondary
or controversial synonym for a word in the puzzle. In 1989,
ENORMITY was one of the entries in a daily puzzle. I consulted
Random House, Second and found "monstrousness" and "hei-
nousness" as the primary definitions. But I chose No. 3, "huge-
ness," even though the lexicographers noted: "Many
people . . . continue to regard *enormity* in the sense of great size
as nonstandard."

My choice caused a spate of objections. The kindest one came from M.A.S. of Westport, Connecticut.

> The word ENORMITY seems to be the answer sought for item 10 Down, "hugeness." According to *The American Heritage Dictionary of the English Language*, "enormity is not used acceptably when it is applied to indicate mere size, without the accompanying sense of outrageousness, wickedness, or evil." *Enormity* is not the noun for *enormous*.

Every year I receive an average of three letters from tradesmen or professionals who have never heard of a word that applies to their line of work. They insist, therefore, that I am mistaken. My only recourse is to refer the complainers to the dictionary in which the item was found.

The following letter from W.D. of Sherman Oaks, California, is an example. (In my response, I asked W.D. to consult *Webster's Third*.)

> Every Sunday the puzzle page of the *Times Magazine* gives me an hour or two of enjoyment. It has become for me, and I'm sure for many others, something of a habit.
>
> "I'm often puzzled, which is, of course, the point, and resist until the last moment the urge to go to reference books. From time to time I have certain quibbles about clues. Last week was one of those times.
>
> 87 Down, as I recall, of the May 4 puzzle. The clue was "Movie set worker." The solution was POLEMAN. I have worked in the Hollywood film business for almost ten years. I have heard of "boom-men," and "lead-men," and "Best Boys," but I've never heard the term *Poleman*.
>
> Where did your puzzle maker get this clue? How is it that so many people actively involved in the motion picture business, people who frequent "Movie Sets" on a daily basis, had never heard of such a "Movie Set Worker" as a *Poleman?*
>
> We weekly willingly endure puns and conundrums that would tax saints. When you invade our profession with abstruse clues such as this, we have a right to protest.

It's possible that some Quibblers are consciously or subconsciously trying to show me that they have outdone me in keeping

up with current events. Consider this 1987 communication from
W.K.K. of Rego Park, New York.

> In a recent crossword puzzle the clue was "Shields at Prince-
> ton." The answer worked out to be COED. Ms. Shields was grad-
> uated in June and she is no longer a *coed* but rather an *alum* or
> *grad.*
> I think I gotcha!

Actually, Ms. Shields' graduation made no difference. When
she attended Princeton, she was indeed a *coed.* It's like defining
cadet as "Eisenhower at U.S.M.A."

In *Random House, Second, slo-mo* is given as a shortening of *slow-
motion* used by people in TV and movies. Good! Now we puzzlers
have a new clue for SLO. In the past, our only recourse was the
abbreviated road sign, which elicited an objection by W.J.R.

> We have yet to catch you in error with the possible exception
> of a clue which we have noted twice in recent weeks (e.g., 43
> Across in 3/4/86 edition), the clue being "Road sign" and the
> answer being SLO.
> We have consulted the Motor Vehicle Law of the State of
> New York and the Rules of the New York State Department
> of Transportation and we find no authorization for the use of
> such a road sign. I would appreciate your shedding some light
> on this issue.

I do not have proof that "SLO" is painted on some pavement
in the U.S.A., but I remember seeing "GO SLO" on a rural road
in New Jersey. Whenever we passed it, my father would say:
"We are now entering the town of GOSLO."

P.M.W. of New York City practically admits that his objection
to my alliterative clue is a quibble.

> A minor comment, concerning the puzzle of May 24, 1989,
> 12 Across: "to live, to Livy." I would have thought this to be
> *vivere,* instead of ESSE. Perhaps the desire was to have the def-
> inition be something that sounded more like "Livy." The Latin
> dictionary of Cassell saves you, but only barely.

• • •

B.W. of Annandale, Virginia, wasn't really quibbling when he corrected my clue. He was right!

> Your puzzle of last Friday seemed to me to be one of the most difficult of the year, and I congratulate you on it.
>
> I should, however, like to raise a question of accuracy. Item 44 Down says: "Tails for bulls and hills." The proper answer, it turned out was OCKS. This threw me for quite a while.
>
> The question I raise is whether the clue should not have read: "Tails for bull and hill." It certainly does not make sense to put *ocks* on the end of *bulls* and *hills*. This looks like a dual typo to me, and I should appreciate having your opinion.

In 1983 D.P.C. of Haverford, Pennsylvania, sent me an objection that cannot truly be called a mere quibble.

> Having just completed your Thanksgiving Day crossword puzzle, I find myself moved to protest. In reference to 13 Down, your clue "British hippies" for MODS is utterly misguided. The mods are characterized by short, well-kempt hair and very neat clothing. They attempt to express their dissatisfaction with middle-class values by taking middle class virtues such as neatness to an extreme, thereby parodying the targets.
>
> While the mods share with hippies a disenchantment with established society, I think you will agree that the characteristics associated with the two groups are far from similar.

My clue inexactly equated hippies and mods. Although both groups felt alienation from conventional mores, their modes of protest were vastly different.

In a 1985 puzzle SPORES was defined as "Sori." If A.P.C. of Brookhaven, New York, is not a lawyer, he has missed his profession. Here's his "quibbulous" letter.

> I have referred to my *Webster's Third New International Dictionary* and have found the following: a sorus is a cluster of reproductive bodies . . . ; a clump of sporangia . . . a mass of spores . . . and a cluster of gemmae . . . What finishes each

clause is probably irrelevant. In effect you have made *sorus* synonymous with *sporangium, spore, gemma* and *reproductive body.*

So it occurred to me that one could have a word like *gulungus* which would be defined as a herd of cows, a brace of pheasants, a pod of whales or a murder of crows. Would then it be appropriate to make *gulungus* synonymous with *cow, pheasant, whale* or *crow?*

Let me conclude this chapter with an item that bothered dozens of solvers in 1988. The following letter is typical of the protests that poured in when I defined *gerontological* as "senile." The dissatisfied solver is from the School of Nursing at the University of Pennsylvania.

For shame to use the word SENILE for "Gerontological" in the Crossword April 11th! Gerontology deals with aging and the problems of the aged. Senile has a negative connotation and is almost always used to indicate a loss of mental faculties associated with old age.

Actually when I started the word with *sen* . . . I thought it would be *senior* although the other possibility did occur to me.

I love the puzzles and hope that my coming gerontological state does not include my becoming senile so that I can no longer complete my morning obsession.

It is true that in popular usage *senile* is associated with deterioration in the later years of one's life, but I was trying to remind the solvers that the adjective is derived from the Latin word *senilis*, which merely means "old" and has no negative connotations.

Also, in dictionaries like *Random House, Second, gerontological* and *geriatric* are given as synonyms for *senile.*

OUR PUZZLING LANGUAGE

Any foreigner will affirm the idea that English is a very difficult language to learn. There are many reasons.

First of all, as H.L. Mencken pointed out in *The American Language* (1919), it is divided into two parts—English and American—and the latter has become the dominant part. For example, a Londoner's *elevator* is a *lift;* the *hood* of his car is a *bonnet;* the automobile's *trunk* is a *boot*—but most foreigners who study the American tongue learn that a *lift* is what a hitchhiker hopes to get, a *bonnet* is a woman's head covering, and *boot* has many meanings not associated with cars. In fact, as *boots* ("novices"), they may get a *boot* ("thrill") out of going to a baseball game and seeing the opposing shortshop *boot* one.

As intimated above, a second problem presented by our language is American slang. What used to be a rivulet seeking to flow into the mainstream but often blocked by purists is now a roaring cataract. During the course of the twentieth century it became more and more fashionable for educated speakers and learned writers to latch on to the latest slanguage, as if to say, "I'm no fuddy-duddy; I'm with it!"

The interesting phenomenon is that a great deal of yesterday's slang is replaced by new lingo. You were hep to the jive in the forties, but you weren't hip if you used *hep* in the fifties. Similarly, the drips and twerps of yesteryear have yielded to the nerds and wimps of today (and by the time this book is published other terms for stupid, weak, unattractive, and ineffectual people may have replaced the ones in vogue as I write).

Lest it be inferred that I am against the influx of slang, let me say in a mixed metaphor that those who wring their hands in despair are crying down a rain barrel; slang adds panache to our language. Furthermore, by a process of natural selection the barbarism that isn't really needed is ephemeral but the argot that fills the bill will survive. My favorite example is *blizzard*. According to some lexicographers, this perfect word for "a prolonged, intense snowstorm" may have come from *blizzer,* a word in Midlands dialect.

Another of my favorites is *pizazz,* or *pizzazz*—a noun which has an onomatopoetic flavor and can mean anything from "energy" to "attractive style, dash, or flair." Here's its history in some of my dictionaries:

Webster's Second (1954)	Not listed
New World (1988)	Colloquial
Random House, Second (1988)	Informal

A third problem that our language poses is the tremendous effect of folk usage. It holds sway over spelling, grammar, diction, and the meanings of words. It also causes havoc among purists, lexicographers, writers, puzzle solvers, and editors of crosswords.

What "folks" are we talking about? Well, essentially they are not merely the group that Aristotle called "the judicious" but they extend to a large variety of people ranging from high school graduates to college presidents. In other words, if multitudes of people (including individuals who have earned respect) pronounce *harass* as *har-AS'* instead of as a rhyme for *Paris,* then *har-AS'* becomes the proper pronunciation. Again, note the changes:

Webster's First	*hár-as* only
Webster's Second	*hár-as; har-aś*
Random House, Second and	*har-aś; hár-as*
New World	

My theory is that the prudish Victorians subconsciously eschewed the accent on the second syllable because it sounded indecent!

Now let me give some instances of my correspondence with fans because of folk usage. An interesting one occurred because of a clue for s.o.p. that I borrowed from *Random House, First*. When a New York City solver objected to the clue, I referred him to my esteemed source, and he promptly wrote the following to the editor of the dictionary:

Dear Sir:

According to a usually reliable source of usage of language, I am being informed that the *Random House Dictionary* gives the definition of "standard operating procedure" to the well-accepted abbreviation of *SOP*.

The acronym in question derives from its usage in the military services and has always been used to stand for "standing operating procedure" as, still to this day, is listed in the official Army Regulation (AR) 310-25, titled "Dictionary of Army Terms."

Indeed the expression has been misused, but I would expect that a serious reference work like your dictionary would set it straight and avoid the perpetuation of an obvious mistake which, of recent, has even appeared in the *New York Times* daily crossword!

Please reassure me that future editions will set the record straight. Thank you and best regards.

Here's the reply:

Dear Dr. R.:

Just a note to thank you for your recent letter about the meaning of *SOP*. The next revision of our dictionary will show both "standing" and "standard" in the expansion of the abbreviation. This may well be an example of a case in which usage, perhaps originally incorrect, has now become so widespread that it has to be acknowledged by showing both versions of the expansion. Thank you again for taking the trouble to write.

Sincerely yours,
L.C.H.
Managing Editor
Random House Dictionaries

(Incidentally, the editor fulfilled her promise in *Random House, Second*.)

Dr. P.H.P. of Reseda, California, is another opponent of those who yield to folk usage. What stirred him up was the appearance of NO IFS, ANDS OR BUTS in a 1981 puzzle. Here are some excerpts from his letter:

Webster, not for the first time, is all wet and a corrupter of the language.

If *ifs* and *ans* were pots and pans
There'd be no work for tinkers
(Old nursery rhyme)

An is a synonym for *if*, which has gone out of use since the seventeenth century together with the correct and elegant use of the subjunctive or conditional tenses. In former times (in Shakespeare, for example) sentences would start: "An it be your wish, I shall attend to the business," or "An it were possible. . . ." Commonly one hears today the phrase "*Ifs, ands* or *buts*," which is another misusage.

I feel sure that you would be the first to agree that clear thinking depends very much on correct usage (and *vice versa*). People seldom seem to analyse the sense of catch phrases they commonly use. For example, "I could care less" means exactly the opposite of what it is intended to convey.

After all this, I must confess that my own everyday speech falls far short of the ideal, but I still cherish that ideal.

As for old Noah, he has, in my opinion, been vulgarizing the language from the beginning. Probably his first sin against elegance was in dropping the *u* from words like *honour* and *labour*, thereby turning a subtle diphthong into a simplified *or*. But that is a mere peccadillo by comparison with his steady course of surrender to slang and regionalisms. To hell with the *koine!*

• • •

For those readers who are not familiar with *koine*, a definition from *Webster's Third* is: "a dialect or language of a region, country or people that has become the common or standard language of a larger area and of other peoples—compare *lingua franca*."

On the whole, I try not to admit trademarks into the puzzles, partly because it might look as it one product is being favored over another. But the general public has adopted some names so extensively that they are included in the latest dictionaries. *Kleenex* and *Saran* are prime examples—also *Orlon*. When that fiber appeared in a *Times* crossword, a DuPont executive demurred concerning the clue. He wrote:

> As an avid struggler to solve your crosswords, it was a pleasure to find one of our products as an answer in your 5/29/87 puzzle. However, Orlon is a trademark for DuPont's man-made acrylic *fiber*. Orlon acrylic is not a man-made *fabric*.
> Thanks for thinking of Orlon acrylic fiber.

I saved a copy of my reply. Here it is.

> Thanks for your interest in the puzzles and for taking the time to write. As for ORLON, you are like the little Dutch boy who put his finger in the dike to stop a flood. In this case, you are up against folk usage.
> Because so many people have erroneously designated the *fiber* as a *fabric*, modern lexicographers have been forced to accept ORLON as a *fabric* as well as a fiber.
> Among other lexicons, I refer you to *Webster's Third New International Dictionary* and the *New World Dictionary—Second College Edition*.

Quite often the puzzle fans who object to certain definitions are technically correct, but all that is right and proper has been superseded by the mistakes of millions. Dr. C.H.P. of New York is one of the individuals who refuse to give in to the masses.

Your crossword edition of January 1, 1990, contains a misleading and erroneous clue (57 Across). Jan. 1, 1990 is not the start of a decade. It is only the last year of the decade that began Jan. 1, 1981. The start of the next decade is Jan. 1, 1991. The start of the next millennium will be Jan. 1, 200*1*. When we count to 10, we start with 1, not zero.

In my response, I mentioned several excellent dictionaries that essentially say the same thing as *Random House, Second,* which defines *decade* as "A period of years beginning with a year whose last digit is zero: the *decade* of the 1890's."

The ten-year problem is only a reflection of the hundred-year debate. *Webster's Second* states the following under *century*: ". . . the *first century* (A.D. 1–100 inclusive); the *nineteenth century* (A.D. 1801–1900)." But the latest *New World* recognizes that when people rang in the year 1900, they were celebrating the start of the twentieth century. The text reads: ". . . in common usage, a century begins with a year ending in 00 and runs through 99. . . ."

One of the chief differences between scholars and John Q. Public is that the savants make fine distinctions but John Q. is not so choosy. In 1987, G.M.S. of Belmont, California, wrote:

The clue for No. 19 Across in today's puzzle was "friar." The answer expected was MONK.

There is, as I understand things, a qualitative difference between a friar and a monk. In fact, the Franciscan and Dominican orders of the 13th century, composed of friars, arose in distinction to the enclosed life of monks.

When I pointed out to Mr. S. that modern lexicographers have been forced to face the fact that most people equate *friars* with *monks,* he graciously replied:

Thank you for your kind note. As an aging professor, I have the luxury of keeping my finger in the dike, even if I sometimes think I'm fighting at Dunkirk instead of at Chalons.

Ad multos annos!

• • •

STUNG was the word in the puzzle. The clue was "Bitten by a bee." Professor D.J.S., Chairman of Entomology and Economic Zoology at Rutgers University, sent me a correction:

> We continue to enjoy the puzzles, especially when clues and answers are entomological. However, the March 11, Friday puzzle had an error in 8 Down. Bees don't bite, at least not the kinds we know. Of course, some sting, an act associated with the posterior end of the insect. Certainly that's not equivalent to a bite, delivered by mouthparts at the anterior end.

Many years ago the good professor had a point that could not be disputed. But so many citizens have moaned about being "bitten by a bee" that the experts now allow *bite* as a synonym for *sting*. One of the definitions in *Webster's Third* is "to pierce with any of sharp-pointed buccal organs (as the proboscis of a mosquito or the fangs of a snake)." *Random House, Second* declares succinctly that *bite* can mean "to sting, as does an insect."

To all entomologists: Please remove the bees from your bonnets.

As noted earlier in this chapter, even slanguage cannot be trusted to mean the same as the years elapse. Now listen to S.S. of New York City:

> In yesterday's Xword (27 Across) the definition is "chutzpah" and turns out to be MOXIE, which is as gross an error as I have ever seen in any of your puzzles (and you have had some exotic beauts on your editorship).
> *Chutzpah* is the Yiddish for "nervy" and implies very bad manners. *Moxie* has always meant strength or courage. Where in heaven's name is the alleged connection?
>
> Anxiously awaiting your reply.

In this case, the fan is probably right. Most dictionaries describe *moxie* as a synonym for *courage* or *pep*. *Webster's Third* agrees but also states that it can be the same as audacity or nerve.

I am old enough to remember that a drink called Moxie was sold at ice cream parlors. (Ah, where are those parlors of yesteryear?) The ads for the beverage hinted that it would give you lots of energy. After a few years of being brainwashed, people would make statements like, "I don't know where that boxer got the *moxie* to go fifteen rounds with a slugger like Dempsey."

It's easy to see how vigor was transposed into courage or guts—or maybe even nerve of the *chutzpah* type. By the way, have you heard the anecdote that defines *chutzpah*? A young man does away with both his parents and then throws himself on the mercy of the court because he's an orphan. Now that's *chutzpah!*

Sometimes, while searching for the proper nomenclature, folks don't change the definition for an old word—they expand it.

D.W. of New York City wrote the following letter in 1984:

> Usually I find your crossword puzzles most enjoyable and challenging. I know I can rely on you to provide accurate clues, though cleverly disguised at times. However, I must question 29 Across of your February 8 puzzle, "leader of a singing group." The answer turned out to be CHORAGUS—the leader of a Greek chorus! Since when is a Greek chorus a singing group? To the best of my knowledge, they recited, not sang. The term *chorus* deals with the collection of voices as in "to recite in chorus," not with music.
>
> Nevertheless devotedly yours . . .

Yes, the original Greek chorus was not a singing group, but a *choragus* today could also be the leader of all those altos, tenors, et al.

The plural of *choragus* is *choragi* or *choraguses* or *choragoi*. If that's not bad enough, the singular may be spelled *choregus*.

The expansion of the meaning of a word is also exemplified by *tempo*. First I present a letter from M.M. of Boston. The second paragraph is the part I really like!

> In your January 10 crossword puzzle you have TEMPO as the answer to the clue "rhythm." Surely tempo is the pace at which music is performed—measured, since Beethoven's day, as the number of quarter notes per minute—while rhythm is the pattern of the notes.
>
> While it is enjoyable to keep an eye out for petty slips of this

kind in your puzzles, the real fun comes from the double meanings, twists, and other forms of wit you apply to the clues. They
keep the puzzles, which are after all not hard to solve, lively,
and they are what make the *Times'* daily crosswords the only
ones for me.

Within the precincts of music, Mr. M. is correct; but for many
years people have been using *tempo* in a nonmusical sense and
making it a synonym of *rhythm*. Even *Webster's Second* editors
admit that enlargement. One of their examples is "The *tempo* of
an eight-oared shell."

One aspect of folk usage is "back formation." *Typewrite* is a
good example. The *typewriter* came first. Also, the *butler* did it
when he gave us the verb *buttle*. Why not *butle*? The answer
probably is that such a spelling would cause the word to sound
like a rhyme for *futile*.

But the best instance of back formation is the verb *grovel*. It's
the stepchild of *groveling*, which was originally an adverb meaning "prone" or "face down." Because it looked like a participle,
people created a verb meaning "to creep on the earth, or with
the face to the ground." And as *grovel* became a popular verb,
its new participle took on such meanings as "cringing, fawning,
acting abjectly."

Recently, a TV comedian commented that Miss Universe was
misnamed: She's Miss Earth. Well, here comes folk usage again!
"The inhabitants of earth" and "this earth" are two of the definitions for *universe* in *Webster's Third* and other dictionaries.
Maybe those statements will be expunged when Martians, Ven-
utians, Neptunians, et alii began competing with Earthlings.

Cohort is a word that has expanded and changed drastically. In
Caesar's day a cohort was one of ten divisions within a legion,
and it consisted of three hundred to six hundred soldiers. In
my *Webster's Second* (copyright 1954) it was described as above
and the only addition was "a band of armed warriors."

A.M.G. of New York City must have been using *Webster's Second*
or some other vintage dictionary. In 1987 she wrote:

I realize that you did not construct the puzzle in today's *New York Times*, but as Editor you are supposed to prevent erroneous definitions from being printed.

Today, 102 Across asked for a "Cohort of Cornwallis" and the answer called for was TARLETON. Banastre Tarleton was not the cohort of Cornwallis or of anyone else, as a cohort is a band of armed men, part of a legion. It is *not* someone in the same profession, holding the same rank, at the same time.

It really is amazing to observe what has happened to *cohort* in the span of less than four decades. Whereas it had been strictly a collective noun, it also evolved into a synonym for *accomplice* or *conspirator*. Finally, as *Random House, Second* says, it came to be "friend, comrade, fellow, chum, pal, buddy."

Most interesting among the definitions for *cohort* is "A subgroup sharing a common factor in statistical survey, as age or income level."

Just like *cohort*, the adjective *jejune* has undergone tremendous expansions in its meanings—especially in recent decades. Let's start with a letter from J.T.M. of Lake Forest, Illinois.

Concerning your January 22 puzzle titled "Kerchoo."

The clue for 67 Across is "naive." The answer appears to be JEJUNE. None of my dictionaries show any connection in meaning between these two words. Can you explain? Thank you.

The Roman adjective *jejunus* meant "empty." It was related to the *jejunum,* a division of the small intestine.

In English, the idea of emptiness continued. "Lacking nourishment" was a primary definition. In the 1950s the additional meaning was "void of interest"; a critic might call a novel "jejune." Other meanings in *Webster's Second* were "barren, meager, dry, insipid."

But somehow in the past thirty years, the word has become associated with *juvenile*, perhaps because of its sound and general appearance together with the sometime association of insipidness with ingenuous adolescents. And so, the next step was to make *jejune* a synonym for *unsophisticated*—and finally, *naive*.

When I was in college, a Bing Crosby hit was "June in January." A fellow sophomore broke us up by singing "It's je-June in je-January." Je-jumping je-Jehoshaphat!

• • •

The mention of the *jejunum* reminds me of a letter from Dr. L.W.L. of Beloit, Wisconsin.

> In a recent Sunday *Times* puzzle entitled "Age 35: Aaugh!" the clue for 133 Down was "spleen" and the answer was BILE.
> I believe that this is in error, since bile is produced by the liver and not by the spleen.

Technically, the good doctor is correct, but so many people with a nonmedical background have confused *bile* with *spleen* that the interchange is accepted in such dictionaries as *American Heritage* and *Webster's Third* when the intended meaning is "anger, irascibility or ill-humor."

Now here's a letter to my editor from W.M., an alderman in Hamilton, Ontario.

> The last occasion I wrote about the Sunday crossword puzzle was a couple of years ago when Mr. Maleska was looking for an E-BOAT; the clue was "a small fast *British* warship"—it was of course not, it was "a fast small *German* warship." Be that as it may.
> This time (Sunday, June 12), it's 84 Down: "Black watch garb." The answer he is looking for is obviously TARTAN. But, tartan is not a garb; it is a patterned length of cloth. When a piece of tartan is made into a kilt or a plaid, then it becomes a (Scottish) garb, Black Watch or otherwise.
> Technically, tartan is a woven material, generally of wool, having strips of different colours and varying in breadth. The arrangement of colours is alike in warp and weft (length and width)—this forms the different patterns, which are called "Setts."
> Calling a tartan a garb is like calling a bolt of blue serge a suit.

While W.M. was adhering strictly to the original meaning of *tartan,* millions of others were stretching the fabric into the garb itself—and that example of synecdoche is accepted in up-to-date dictionaries.

What's synecdoche? Listen to the editors of *New World:* "a figure of speech in which a part is used for a whole, an individual for a class, *a material for a thing, or the reverse of any of these.*" (The italics are mine.)

Some examples of synecdoche are:

bread for *food*
copper for *penny*
the army for *a soldier*
fifty sail for *fifty ships*
Croesus for *a rich man*

Metonymy is a relative of synecdoche. At one time, there was a distinction between the two. One meant "using the whole for the part," and the other meant "using the part for the whole." The terms were applied to linguistic tricks employed by poets. But today, because of folk usage, they are considered interchangeable.

Professor R.S. from California State University in Fresno is another specialist who wishes folks would stop messing up the meanings of new words in our language.

I must bug you about today's puzzle. Clue 44 Across is "genetic duplicate" with the only possible answer CLONE. You have hit a very sore point with geneticists. We emphasize to our classes that a clone is a *group* of genetically identical individuals, not an individual which is a copy of another.

You will notice that this is borne out by *Webster's Third.* I might also cite two dictionaries of genetics: Robert C. King's *A Dictionary of Genetics:* "a *group* of genetically identical cells or organisms . . ." and R. Rieger et al., *Glossary of Genetics and Cytogenetics:* "a *population* of cells or organisms. . . ."

It is true that many half-educated yuppies seem to labor under this misapprehension, but neither one of us is in the business of perpetuating error. Regards, . . .

I must confess to Professor S. and the rest of the world that I have not only been perpetuating the so-called error in my role as editor but have been helping to create it in daily conversation—and I'm relieved to report that lexicographers have recently sanctioned my obtusity. By the way, changing the group into an individual is another example of synecdoche. Class dismissed.

A fan named R.F. sent me the following set of couplets. I think it's a very clever piece on the effect of slang on changes in the meanings of words.

PSYCHEDELIRIUM TREMENS

Remember when HIPPIE
   meant big in the hips,
And a TRIP involved travel
   in cars, planes and ships?
When POT was a vessel for
   cooking things in,
And HOOKED was what Grand-
   mother's rug might have been?
When FIX was a verb that meant
   mend or repair,
And BE-IN meant simply
   existing somewhere?
When NEAT meant well organized,
   tidy and clean,
And GRASS was a ground-
   cover, normally green?
When lights and not people
   were SWITCHED on and OFF,
And the PILL might have been
   what you took for a cough?
When CAMP meant to quarter
   outdoors in a tent,
And POP was what the weasel
   went?
When GROOVY meant furrowed
   with channels and hollows,
And BIRDS were winged creatures
   like robins and swallows?
When FUZZ was a substance
   that's fluffy like lint,
And BREAD came from bakeries,
   not from a mint?

When SQUARE meant a 90 degree
    angled form,
And COOL was a temperature
    not quite warm?
When ROLL meant a bun, and
    ROCK was a stone,
And HANG-UP was something you
    did to a phone?
When CHICKEN meant poultry,
    and BAG meant a sack,
And JUNK trashy cast-offs
    and old bric-a-brac?
When JAM was preserves that
    you spread on your bread,
And CRAZY meant balmy, not
    right in the head?
When CAT was a feline, a
    kitten grown up,
And TEA was a liquid you
    drank from a cup?
When SWINGER was someone who
    swung in a swing,
And a PAD was a soft sort of
    cushiony thing?
When WAY OUT meant distant and
    far, far away,
And a man couldn't sue you for
    calling him GAY?
When DIG meant to shovel and
    spade in the dirt,
And PUT-ON was what you would
    do with a shirt?
When TOUGH described meat too
    unyielding to chew,
And MAKING A SCENE was a
    rude thing to do?
Words once so sensible, sober
    and serious
Are making the FREAK SCENE like
    PSYCHODELIRIOUS.
It's GROOVY, MAN, GROOVY, but
    English it's not.

Methinks that the language has
gone straight to POT!

And now we come to the troublesome subject of Transliteration. Relatively speaking, few problems arise when translating from Latin or such Romance languages as Spanish, Portuguese, and French. Their alphabets are the same as ours. German causes some difficulties because of differences in capitalization, plurals, and idiomatic expressions, but at least the alphabetic basis is identical. Greek, Sanskrit, Arabic, Russian, Hebrew, Chinese, and Japanese are among the many languages that use writing systems dissimilar to ours—and there's the rub! The transliterators must depend on their perceptions of the sounds of the characters in the original language, and they must also take into account the vagaries of our own tongue.

Here's an example. The first letter of the Hebrew alphabet becomes either *aleph* or *alef* when carried over into English because *ph* and *f* sound alike to us.

Some other instances are:

tepee versus *tipi* or *teepee*
taboo versus *tabu*
hara-kiri versus *hari-kari*

As a result of the quirks of transliteration, I receive Gotcha letters from solvers whose reference books give spellings different from the one in the puzzle. For instance, if the solution to "Rural Russian log house" is ISBA, some fan is sure to inform me that the correct orthography is *IZBA*, even though either spelling is acceptable.

Geographic places are especially vexatious: consider *Iraq* versus *Irak*. And then there's *Nis*, a Yugoslavian city known to most crossword puzzlers. But it's also *Nish*, and was once known as *Naissus* or *Nissa*. And nearby in Bulgaria is the river *Nisava*—or should we write *Nishava*?

Here's an interesting aside on the geographical problem. The following letter from Mrs. W.S. of New York City does not concern transliteration. Instead it involves an objection to Anglicization.

Hesse is not a German state; it is a citizen thereof, just as Kansan is not an American state, but a resident of Kansas. Thirty-seven years ago, from Wiesbaden, I wrote to the *Times* style editor pointing out that there is no place called Hesse, at least not in Germany, but who listens to me?

Many German place names, names of states, provinces and countries, end in *-en.* Cf. Preussen, Bayern, Schwaben, West-falen, Sachsen; also Norwegen, Italien, Spanien, Albanien. In English we like *-ia* as an ending, and *-ian* is another: Prussia, Prussian; Hessia, Hessian. Who scared Ichabod Crane, a head-less Hesse?

Puristically yours, . . .

Here's my reply:

Thanks for your interest in the puzzles and for taking the time to write. If you had your way, nobody would refer to Florence but would be forced to say Firenze, and Lyons must only be Lyon. Anglicizing foreign names would be verboten. But you are tilting at the windmills erected by folk usage and supported by all the lexicographers and encyclopedists. It's a tainted world where purists are a small minority whispering into the wind.

Transliterated names of foreign leaders can also be problemat-ical. R.D. of Booklyn, New York, objected to OLAF as a spelling for a Norwegian king. In 1987 she wrote: "Even though a final *v* is pronounced as an *f,* the name of Norway's king is spelled *Olav.*"

My reply was that all my dictionaries give both spellings. Sim-ilarly, in correspondence with S.C.E. of Lake Worth, Florida, I had to defend the use of REZA Pahlavi as shah of Iran, instead of *Riza.* Either vowel is okay.

Mrs. H.V.S. of Tappan, New York, inquired about the spelling of another foreign leader's name. Here's her letter:

In the puzzle of Thursday, September 29th, the clue for 43 Down was "Egyptian King" and the answer was shown as RAMSES.

I have always seen the spelling as "Rameses" and I checked

my dictionary which shows no other spelling than "Rameses." However, since my dictionary is almost as old as said Egyptian king, there may now be an alternate spelling.

I have also been to Egypt where I was lucky enough not to suffer with "Rameses Revenge," which is the local term for traveler's diarrhea, and the pronunciation is in three syllables.

I would appreciate hearing from you in this regard. Thank you.

My two most modern dictionaries are *New World, Third* and *Random House, Second*. Both give *Ramses* as the first spelling and *Rameses* as the variation.

Incidentally, *Random House, Second* also lists an Egyptian city called *Raamses*, which the enslaved Israelites were forced to build. It was there that the Exodus began.

In connection with the above, I am delighted to share with you an interesting passage from one of William Safire's "On Language" columns in the *Times*.

It would be easier to get our allies to agree on overflight rights to a bombing raid on terrorists than to forge a consensus on a way to spell the name of the strongman of Libya.

Jack Gescheidt of New York City puts the problem succinctly, to the tune of the 1937 Gershwin song, "Let's Call the Whole Thing Off."

> The News says, Khadafy
> The Times says, Qaddafi
> Time says, Gaddafi
> Newsweek, Kaddafi;
> MOO-a-mar
> Mo-AH-mar;
> LIB-ya
> Lib-ee-a;
> Let's blow the whole thing off.

There is no "corect" way to spell Qaddafi. When we use Western characters to signify sounds of the Arabic language, we are free to paint the page any way we like.

Chinese is an especially difficult language to transliterate. In 1989, PUY popped up in a puzzle. I was glad to discover that

Henry Puy was the last Emperor of China, but B.H. of Wilmington, Delaware, was sure he had earned a Gotcha certificate. He cited several book titles in which the spelling was *Pu-yi*. No award was given. Most lexicographers accept either *Pu-yi* or *Puy*.

Another reason for trouble with Chinese-to-English is that each new revolution seems to bring a change in the original spelling of the names of people and places in that ancient land.

The latest Chinese puzzle stems from the decision of the People's Republic to use Pinyin (literally, "phonetic sound") as the official system for translating Chinese ideograms into the Latin alphabet. As a consequence, here are a few of the many spelling changes:

Amoy becomes *Xiamen*
Mao Tse-tung becomes *Mao Zedong*

When transliteration problems are combined with the caprices of Greek mythology, mix-ups occur. D.N. of Newton, Massachusetts, insists that *Kronos* was the father of Zeus—not CRONUS, as stated in a 1988 puzzle. My sources state that *Kronos*, *Cronus*, and *Cronos* are the same Titan who sired the Olympic honcho.

Greek also caused orthographic trouble with regard to a breed of compact, finely shaped horses. In 1988 D.B.V. of Petersburg, Pennsylvania, inquired:

My Enc. Brit. spells *lippizaner* lipizzaner. Interestingly enough neither of my dictionaries listed this horse. Could you give me your source of the spelling used in the puzzle?

Both *Random House, Second* and *Webster's Third* give *Lippizaner* as the first spelling. Other combinations are *Lipizzaner, Lippizana*. The town near Trieste whence the steed originated is *Lippiza*— or is it *Lipizza?* Choose whatever strikes your fancy.

Hebrew and Yiddish can also cause many a dispute in the realm of orthography. Let's look at various spellings for the Jewish months, as listed in *Webster's Third*.

 1. *Tishri, Tizri*
 2. *Heshvan, Hesvan, Cheshvan, Chesvan*
 3. *Kislev, Chislev*
 4. *Tebet, Tebeth, Tevet, Teveth*
 5. *Shebat, Sebat, Shevat*
 6. *Adar*
 7. *Nisan, Nissan*
 8. *Iyar, Iyyar*
 9. *Sivan, Siwan*
10. *Tammuz, Tamuz*
11. *Ab, Av*
12. *Elul, Ellul*

Interestingly enough, the one that gives transliterators the least trouble is a crossword puzzle favorite—ADAR. But whenever I define it as "the sixth month of the Jewish year," someone is bound to send me a letter stating that it's the twelfth month. The problem is that Adar is No. 6 in the civil year, whereas it's No. 12 in the ecclesiastical year.

Note the *Ab-Av* problem and the same ambivalence at No. 4 and No. 5. It has relevance to the following letter from S.S. of Cumberland, Maryland.

> I wrote to you once before, but I was in error. So glad you corrected me! Now—in October 20th's puzzle 22 Across—SHI-BAH ("mourn in Israel")—I don't know if it was a misprint, but I do believe it is *sit shivah*. I will quote from Leo Rosten's book, *The Joys of Yiddish:* "Pronounced SHI-VAH, to rhyme with a Southerner's pronunciation of 'river.' From the Hebrew 'seven.' The seven solemn days of mourning for the dead, beginning immediately after the funeral, when Jews 'sit shivah' in the home of the deceased." I am Jewish, so I am familiar with the pronunciation and spelling. Enjoy the puzzles—I am learning from them all the time—only twice have I completed the entire puzzle—I really can't believe it.
>
> If you check *The Joys of Yiddish* there is more of an explanation.

Mr. Rosten is probably correct, but so is *Webster's Third*. That lexicon gives *shibah, shivah, shiva*. The definition is: "A traditional 7-day period of mourning that follows the funeral of a close relative and is observed in the home by Jews."

To S.S. I say: "May you live to be 120 and never have to sit *shibah*. Shalom!"

• • •

The letters of the Hebrew alphabet are subject to the same transliteration predicament. In a 1983 puzzle SAMEK was the answer
to a clue, and P.W.F. of Manchester Center, Vermont, was
stumped. He wrote:

> In the Oct. 16th *New York Times* Crossword Puzzle there is a
> "question" 7 Down which asks for the Hebrew letter after *nun*.
> The correct answer is *samekh* for which there are insufficient
> spaces allowed. What gives?

Webster's Third also gives *samech* as a possible spelling.

My last story on the transliteration situation concerns a Malay
outrigger canoe that all crossword fans have known for decades
ever since the word PROA appeared in *Webster's Second* as far back
as the thirties. But when *Webster's Third* was published in 1961,
proa was considered a variation of *prao*. Soon afterwards in a
Times puzzle the four-letter answer to the "Malay canoe" clue
was PRAO instead of PROA.

With tongue in cheek, A.K.B. of Oak Brook, Illinois, wrote:

> Re 44 Across in today's puzzle, I find that I have been mis-
> spelling that word for years. Oh well, as Elroy Hirsch* once
> said "There is no use maoning over spilt milk."

Mr. Burke's letter caused me to do some research on the transliterated spellings of the canoe. I found *proa, prau, prao, prahu,
prow*, and *praw!*

Sometimes ambiguities concerning foreign words have no connection with transliteration but stem from other sources. Consider *aula,* for instance. In *Webster's Second* and *Webster's Third*
that noun is defined as "the assembly hall in a German school
or university." When I used that definition as a clue for *aula*,
E.T. of Providence, Rhode Island, objected strongly. She said
that the *aula* is an Italian assembly hall, and she was right. Were
the two dictionaries wrong? No!

*See Chapter 5, "Gotcha," re Mr Burke's sly reference to Elroy Hirsch.

Aula comes down from the Greeks, via the Romans. In Cicero's day it meant "a forecourt, a court or a hall." It's easy to see how the Italians inherited the word, but the German connection is difficult to trace. Perhaps it is the result of Caesar's conquests in Europe.

The Bible can be perplexing, too. P.K. of Sanibel, Florida, sent me the following letter in 1985:

> Regarding the puzzle on March 17th! I ran into a heap of trouble! In the lower left hand part of your puzzle the definition was: "Prophet who was fed by a raven." I knew it was *Elijah* but it certainly didn't fit. In desperation I concluded that it was either an error or some kind of weird poetic license and I spelled it ELIAS. Looking at the solution yesterday, I had evidently taken the right tack. When did Elijah change his name to Elias? A new translation perhaps? Please fill me in. I can hardly wait for an answer.
>
> Your truly devoted crossword puzzle fan,

The nub of the problem is Old Testament versus New Testament. In Kings the prophet is called by his Hebrew name (Elijah), but Matthew used his Greek name (Elias).

Nonage can be tricky because there are two separate words with the same spelling (just like *arete* and *arete* in a previous chapter). The first is pronounced *no'-nage* and means "the ninth part of movable goods of a decedent, formerly paid to a clergy." The second is pronounced *non'-age* and is more widely used today. It means "legal minority; immaturity."

In 1987, A.C.A. of New York City wrote:

> As a regular crossword solver (I once corrected your clue when you put a *fret* on a violin), I always thought that nonage was like dotage—90 with the same root as nonagenarian! But you are right according to the dictionary! How come?

The answer to A.C.A.'s question is that *nonage* carries the literal sense of "not of age." Therefore, a teenager is not in his dotage but in his *nonage*.

Now let's talk about spelling. At one time I was an instructor at Hunter College, and later at the City University of New York. My students were teachers and future teachers. In one of the courses, "Methods of Teaching Language Arts," I would always give the class a two-word spelling test and assure them in advance that nobody would get 100 percent. Amazingly, my predictions were correct every time!

The two spelling demons were *all right* and *Pharaoh*.

Because most people do not have occasion to write about the Egyptian ruler, his title still remains orthographically unsullied. But millions of educated people have been shortening *all right* into *alright* (probably because of the subliminal influence of *altogether, already,* and *almost*). Consequently, the lexicographers have been forced to allow *alright* as an entry. Naturally, they print disclaimers in order to placate the purists, but you can bet that in the next century, *alright* will be A-O.K.

G.G.H. was either a former student of mine or a friend of one. Here's what he wrote in 1988.

When I [was growing] up . . . there was acceptable spelling and unacceptable spelling. And the most common misspelled word in the English language was *all right*.

I love doing your crossword puzzles daily and Sunday and find my most difficult problem is the fact that I am a terrible speller.

So it is with chagrin [that] I find *all right* spelled *alright* in the August 15th *New York Times*, 27 Across, "O.K."

Has Webster's and Maleska, a [former] English teacher, each capitulated?

It should be underscored that my definition for ALRIGHT was "O.K." That was my way of matching one colloquialism with another—a style I often use in an attempt to be fair to solvers.

• • •

Of course, I knew I was taking a chance when I published AL-
RIGHT, but the person who sent me that puzzle was one of my
best constructors and I hated to reject the crossword for stick-
in-the-mud reasons.

The same thing happened in 1989. Gayle Dean, a fine puzzler,
sent me a clever crossword, but it contained TUMERIC. Luckily,
Webster's Third accepted that form as an alternate, and I decided
to give it a whirl. About twenty "spicy" letters chided me. Here's
one of the first, by H.B.R. of New York City.

I am sure you have heard from others with regard to the
Tuesday, December 5, crossword puzzle, and your answer for
5 Down, TUMERIC. Both of the dictionaries that I consulted, the
Concise Oxford Dictionary and *Webster's New Collegiate Dictionary,*
spell the word "Turmeric" and do not list an alternate spelling.
Webster's does list a second *pronunciation* which eliminates the
first "r," but does not eliminate it in the spelling.

Mr. R.'s dictionary apparently was not published by G.K.C.
Merriam. Since the name *Webster* is in the public domain, any
group can attach the name to the dictionary they put out, but
most scholars agree that Merriam-Webster lexicons are of high
quality.

Also, note the reason for the fact that so many people shortened the spelling of *turmeric.* The first *r* had become silent in
thousands of kitchens!

As mentioned above, pronunciation can often affect spelling.
That delicious Italian coffee, *espresso* (literally "pressed out") has
been mispronounced by so many millions of Americans that the
latest dictionaries carry *expresso* as a valid second spelling.

Furthermore, *Webster's Third* allows *ecstacy* as an alternate for
ecstasy. And so, if a pen pal tells you "One drink of *expresso* sent
me into *ecstacy*," emulate the Beetles and let it be.

Folk usage affected *lagniappe,* too. That French import pleased
so many poor spellers that they gratuitously tipped the scales
(puns intended) in favor of *lagnappe.* When I allowed the second

spelling in a puzzle, Mrs. J.F.P. of Short Hills, New Jersey, gave me what for.

In the daily crossword of April 7th, 40 Across "gratuity" is *not* spelled as you have it. Any dictionary will show it *should* be *lagniappe*.

Shame! How can mere mortals be expected to work the puzzles when the editor can't spell??

My asinine answer went like this:

> A lady who lived in Short Hills
> Delved in crosswords up to her gills;
> Then she spotted *lagnappe,*
> Gave Maleska a slap
> For his lack of orthography skills.
> "Dear Madam," was Maleska's reply,
> "In *lagnappe,* the drop of the *i*
> Was accepted by those
> Great linguists who chose
> Both spellings—I know not why."

M.M. of Westwood, New Jersey, sent me a succinct letter when REPELLANT appeared in a 1987 puzzle.

Have spelling rules changed since I learned them some sixty years ago?

14 Down, May 31, 1987 should be *repellent,* I always thought.

All my dictionaries accept the *-ant* ending, because so many people misspell *repellent.* Then why is *existent* unchanged? My guess is because so few people put the word in writing. But lots of Americans make notes about buying those substances that keep insects away.

At this point, I should also explain that the puzzle constructors do not prefer second spellings, but sometimes they use them when the first spelling will not fit. Their feeling (and mine) is that permission is given by the lexicographers who allow such deviations into their dictionaries. Why should a puzzlemaker spend extra hours eliminating an entry just because some pedant might not like it?

• • •

Changes brought about by the onward march of time are ex-emplified in the following letter from G.P.F. of Chatham, New Jersey.

> In the Sunday *Times* of August 9, 1987, there was an incorrect definition in the crossword puzzle titled, "Antilogous Words" by T.W. Underhill. The clue for 110 Across was "Blur, in print-ing." This is a *mackle,* not a MACULE.
>
> The unabridged edition of *Webster's Third New International Dictionary* gives the following definitions: *mackle*—a blur or dou-ble impression on a printed sheet; *macule*—a patch of skin ex-hibiting altered coloration, but usually not elevated above the general surface that forms a characteristic feature of various diseases (as smallpox).
>
> Nonetheless, I enjoy tackling the Sunday *Times* crossword puzzle each week and especially the bi-weekly Acrostic puzzle. Keep up the challenges!

As noted before, *Webster's Third* was published in 1961. Ap-parently, folk usage since then has prevailed enough to have *Random, Second* concede that *mackle* and *macule* can both be blurs on printed sheets. *Random House, Second* was published in 1988.

If you live in Olean, you're a New Yorker; if your home town is Fond du Lac, you're a Wisconsinite—but is a native of Mobile an Alabaman or an Alabamian? The answer is "take your pick." The same suffixes apply to citizens of Arizona, Florida, and Louisiana. Interestingly enough, North and South Carolina choose only the *-ian* ending.

Two states attach an *-er* to identify the natives and one state merely adds an *-r.* They are respectively Maryland, Vermont, and Maine.

Michigan adds *-der,* but citizens who don't wish to look anserine prefer Michiganite or Michiganian.

Other people that can't make up their minds are the Illinois-ans, or should we say Illinoisians? Either is okay, but one group prefers to be called Illinoians. The question that arises is why that third contingent would rather be thought of as pests than considered to be cacophonous.

Some residents of Salt Lake City believe in brevity. While the rest call themselves Utahans this group settles for Utahns.

Dwellers in such cities as Passaic and Newark are ambivalent. Some are New Jerseyans and others are New Jerseyites. And both camps usually drop the *New* part.

There are New Hampshirites, but no New Hampshirans. Instead there are New Hampshiremen. One wonders what the women of the Granite State think of that designation.

Some Tennesseans call themselves Tenneseans for some inexplicable reason, but Delawareans are unanimous in their choice.

My sources for this topic are *Webster's Third* and *Random House, Second*. In the former, Connecticuter is listed, but the newer dictionary omits it. Does this change imply that residents of the Constitution State do not like to look cute?

The people of Massachusetts stand alone. No *-ites, -ans,* or *-ians* follow them around. And the only use of *-ers* comes when they declare themselves Bay Staters.

All of the above was generated by F.T. of Cincinnati. When a 1987 Sunday puzzle contained OHIAN, that alert Buckeye sent me clippings from his home state showing that *Ohioan* was the proper nomenclature. His contention was supported by *Random House, Second,* but *Ohian* does appear in *Webster's Third*.

The mention of *Michigander* above reminded me that citizens of Glasgow are Glaswegians and those who live in Liverpool are Liverpudlians. And let's not forget the natives of Cambridge, either here or abroad. They are Cantabrigians! Incidentally, that's why Harvard students are called "Cantabs."

M.C.T., who lives on *Roast Meat Hill Road* (I kid you not) and is a "Connecticuter," knows a lot about proper orthography but is perceptive enough to realize that many other folks not only can't mind their *p*'s and *q*'s but also don't know their *e*'s from their *w*'s. Here's her letter.

Knowing that my ensuing observation will probably not gain my entrance to the "Gotcha Club," I nonetheless submit my *beef* concerning this week's (May 25th) puzzle: as far as I know, there is no such synonym for *knickknack* as *geegaw;* the word is *gewgaw.* My authority on this is *The American Heritage Dictionary of the English Language,* copyrighted 1976. As this is obviously outdated, *geegaw* may be cited as second preferred in more recent publications.

Some reactions:

1. The italics for *beef* are mine in view of the fan's address.
2. She knows how to spell *knickknack,* and I'll wager she can do justice to *bookkeeper,* too.
3. *Geegaw* has been accepted as an alternate spelling in *Random House, Second.* Both *Webster's Third* and *New World, Third* call it a variation.

The foregoing mention of "mind their *p*'s and *q*'s" reminds me that a solver once asked me to elucidate the source of that phrase. "Why pick those letters?" he asked. I couldn't find the answer; and so I turned to my colleague William Safire. He replied:

Dear Gene,

The etymon for "mind your p's and q's" is lost in antiquity— best speculation is the confusion between the p and the q, which are mirror images.

Best,
B.

Well, I'll buy that guess. It had never occurred to me that when you look at a *q* in a mirror, it does resemble a *p.* Only recently, in a book by Jimmy Breslin, I learned that old-time printers picked letters from boxes and often chose a *q* when intending to select a *p.*

Spelling, grammar, and diction are all affected by folk usage. For example, here's a letter from R.S. of Brooklyn, New York.

Methinks I found an error in the Sunday puzzle of 3/8/87.

The clue for 10 Down is "other than." The answer in the puzzle is BESIDE (no *s*). A check with my Webster's dictionary confirms my opinion—"other than" defines *besides. Beside* (no *s*) can be defined as "alongside, or on a par with."

R.S.'s dictionary is probably aged. Modern lexicons state that *beside* is often "other than." *New World, Third* gives this example: "Who *beside* him is qualified?"

R.G.K. of Bellerose, New York, questions my diction.

I admit that the definition "More inferior" (14D) in today's crossword puzzle is better for WORSE than "More inferiorer" would have been, but just plain "inferior" would have been more better. I was tempted to write *worser* for the answer, had there been enough space.

Well, R.G.K., I can see your point. But a *Random House, Second* definition of *bad* is "inferior." Hence, *worse* can mean "more inferior." An example is: "Your grade on the test was *bad*, but mine was *worse*" ("more inferior").

Usually, I try not to offend the purists, but occasionally I send up a trial balloon to see how many strict observers of the old rules are out there and how virulent they are. A case in point is the *less* versus *fewer* situation. Years ago when I taught English, I made a big point about the difference between the two comparatives. My favorite examples were:

There is *less* sugar in the bowl than there was yesterday.
There are *fewer* cars on the road today than there were
   yesterday.

The point, of course, was that sugar comes in a mass and it's difficult to distinguish one grain from another whereas cars are separate entities.

In this case, folk usage has vacillated. Centuries ago, people talked about "less men" or "less books." Then the grammarians led the way in making distinctions. Today the pendulum has swung back to the days of yore. You will hear educated speakers talking about "less cars" or "less children," etc. As a result, *Random House, Second* accepts the usage.

At any rate, in the spring of 1989, I decided to define LESS as "not so many." Amazingly, only a dozen letters of protest arrived, but I can picture how many other solvers silently shook their heads in sorrow. The reaction of Mrs. J.J.B. of Milford, Connecticut, was reported by her "lesser" half.

> Daily, my wife sits across the breakfast table, engrossed in doing the *New York Times* crossword puzzle. At times the silence is punctuated with mumbles that often are recognizable as your name. Once in a great while the mumbles turn to shouts of glee at the possibility that "Maleska made a mistake!"
>
> My wife had a taskmaster of an English teacher when she was in school and I suffer from the lessons she learned there. How many times have I been corrected when I have misused the words *less* and *few*. "Less should be used for amounts and few for numbers," I have been told over and over.
>
> In today's puzzle with 59 Across, you are the one to receive the benefit of her many hours of English class.
>
> She still gloats over the fact that *your* wife told you that there was such a place as Grand Central *Station,* even though true New Yorkers know that it is proper to call it Grand Central Terminal.

My rebuttal to that last sentence is: That's a quibble, Mrs. B. The *terminal* is also a *station.*

Mrs. J.H.H. of New Rochelle, New York, wrote:

> Some guardian of the purity of English you are! May 15 puzzle: 59 Across "Not so many" turns out to be LESS!!
>
> I tried to squeeze in *fewer* but no go! Are you getting careless?

Gosh, Mrs. H., were you one of my students way back when?

My constant correspondent, R.K., took a pedagogic stand and gave me a lesson on the difference between "not so many" and "not so much." I told her I was not *enthused* about the latest trend and it *aggravated* me, but I'd decided to go with the flow.

Another point I used to raise when I taught English was the difference between *likely* and *liable* or between *apt* and *liable*. The latter adjective, I pointed out, has a negative connotation. Consider *liabilities* (debts).

But once again I discovered that modern usage has blurred the differentiation. Then I went fishing and defined APT as "liable." The publisher of *50 Plus* magazine took the bait. He wrote:

> The crossword 50 Down on 6/24/87 is APT. Its synonym is *likely* not *liable*. One is apt or likely to make a mistake but liable for punishment in committing a crime.

In rebuttal here's a sentence used as an example in *Random House, Second:* "The Sox are liable (or likely) to sweep the Series."

English is not the only language in which the usage situation is a factor. In 1985, I defined ENTRE as "Among, in Cannes." That clue evoked a note from Marvin F.P. He maintained that *parmi* meant "among"—not *entre*, which means "between."

But so many Frenchmen have extended the meaning of *entre* that the latest edition of Cassell's *French-English Dictionary* gives "among" as a second meaning. Sorry about that, Marvin!

Several years ago, a puzzle constructor sent me a crossword containing the word *venery*. Because I knew that the word meant "sexual intercourse," I wondered whether I should take a chance and publish the puzzle. But I received a pleasant surprise when I looked at the constructor's definition: "Art of hunting." Thus, I would duck the outrage of puritanical people while simultaneously using a different word with the same spelling as the one I had previously known (again, something like *arete* and *arete*).

Naturally, I was curious about the respective origins of the "twins." The sexy *venery,* I discovered, was a descendant of *Venus;* the other stemmed from *vener,* a medieval French verb meaning "to hunt."

The *venery* coincidence also reminds me of another pair of look-alikes with altogether different backgrounds:

demean	To conduct or behave oneself
demean	To lower in dignity, honor, or standing

On the subject of the S word, here's a polite letter from P.N.B. of Glens Falls, New York:

In your Wednesday, April 8, 1981, crossword puzzle you defined 34 Down (SEXY) as "sensuous." I think that is a little inaccurate and misleading. While *sensuous* and *sensual* both relate to providing pleasure through gratification of the senses, *sensuous* more accurately implies delight in beauty in color, sound, texture, or form (no sexual implication), while *sensual* stresses indulgence of appetite especially for sexual pleasure (I have used Webster's). I suggest that *sensual* was perhaps what should have been used.

M.B. received a Gotcha certificate. Actually, the error was the constructor's and I overlooked it.

Overlook! Now there's a double-dealer's word! It means "to fail to notice" or "to supervise" or "to look down upon, as from a hill."

Priceless is another fooler. If compared with *worthless* or *harmless*, it should mean "without cost." Instead it means "very costly." But if you analyze the word, you can see that it connotes the idea of having such a value that a price cannot be put on it.

Coming back to the look-alike words, here are three pairs that almost fill the bill:

alligator	Broad-snouted crocodilian; caiman
allegator	One who makes a statement without proof
erotica	Literature or art dealing with sexual love
*exotica**	Foreign or unfamiliar things
torturous	Pertaining to or causing suffering
tortuous	Full of twists, turns, and bends

Stephen Barr of Woodstock, New York, has called my attention to the vagaries of pronunciation that are faced by foreigners trying to learn how to speak English. As examples, he cites:

laughter versus *slaughter*
should versus *shoulder*

*Somewhere recently I came across *neurotica*. The word is not listed in any of my dictionaries but it seems to mean "collections of experiences related by psychiatrists."

My own lists come from the *-omb* and *-ough* families. Consider the following:

> *bomb, comb, womb*
> *bough, cough, dough, rough*

Worse yet, *slough* has three different pronunciations. As a swamp, it rhymes with *how;* as a condition of despair, it is pronounced *slew;* and as a synonym for *molt,* it rhymes with *rough.*

B.S. of Jamestown, Rhode Island, also felt the urge to write to me after reading *A Pleasure in Words.* While discussing rebuses, I cited: "I C U R YY 4 ME." Mr. S. countered with a rebus his father had taught him.

> ABCD goldfish?
> L, MNO goldfish!
> SDR, SDR!

Well, even without rebuses or other forms of wordplay, most people agree that our language is indeed a puzzlement!

CHAPTER 8

OLIO

When I was sixteen, I made my first attempt at solving a cross-word puzzle. At that time, *olio* was not part of my active or passive vocabulary. I learned that word and thousands of others while pursuing a fascinating black-and-white hobby. And so it pleases me to use "Olio" as the title for the final chapter of this book.

Among the synonyms I could have chosen are *gallimaufry, mélange, omnium-gatherum, potpourri,* and *salmagundi*—all of which were either initially planted in my mind via crosswords or were reinforced in my memory by the puzzles. But *olio* is a brief, solid, unpretentious word expressing the fact that this last chapter is a mixed bag. Parts of its contents are items which belong in previous chapters but only recently were sent to me; then there are some fan letters from the past that fell between the cracks. Other sections deal with new developments such as crossword clubs and individual feats by solvers or constructors. Finally, several pages are devoted to celebrated solvers.

· · ·

Let's begin with some recent inquiries. The first one comes from
A.J. of Philadelphia.

> I recently ran into a road block in your Large Type February
> 29 issue wherein I was unable to supply the answer for "Can-
> ape"—No. 55 Across—and so was not able to complete the
> puzzle.
> I was perplexed when I saw the answer in the succeeding
> March 7 issue of the Weekly.
> The answer was SOFA!
> Is that an acronym for *canape?*

Here's a copy of my reply:

> Your letter and fifty others awaited me on my return from
> a sixteen-day vacation.
> As for *canapé,* please consult any good, unabridged diction-
> ary. *Canapé* literally means "sofa" in French: A Gallic sofa in
> Louis XV style is a *canapé.* The word is a cousin of *canopy.*
> The popular meaning of *canapé* comes from the fact that a
> bit of bread is the *seat* for the delicacy placed atop it.

Speaking of sofas, C.B.K. must have imitated Rip Van Winkle
on one. Almost three years after tackling a *Times* Sunday puzzle,
she wrote:

> Friends and I have been puzzled for a long time about the
> significance of the answer to Question No. 94 Across. The an-
> swer is: I SING THE SOFA, which possibly is a play on words?
> William Cowper is given as the source of the quotation.
> No one can come up with a sensible explanation. If it is a
> familar work, we have not heard of it. Please help! Thank you.
> My library reference service could not help either.

The answer is that Cowper actually wrote "I sing the Sofa."
It's the first line of his opus called *The Task,* and obviously *so-fa*
lends itself to a pun on two notes of the scale. By the way, lounge
lizards and couch potatoes may be interested in reading Cowper's
poem.

• • •

A 1991 inquiry from M.J.L. of New York City reads as follows:

> Can you explain to me, please, how you came up with RALLYES
> as the plural in your Saturday, Jan. 18, 1991, puzzle?
> My well-worn Webster gives the plural of *rally* as "rall*i*es."
> The clue—20. "Certain auto races."
> Really scary—this sort of thing.

Unlike my New York City inquirer, I'm not frightened—nor
am I surprised. Innovations and changes in spelling, diction,
grammar, and pronunciation crop up so fast in this modern era
that the aberration by the fans of the Unsers and A.J. Foyt and
other auto racers is almost inevitable. Readers who still doubt
rallyes are advised to consult *Webster's Third* or *Random House,
Second.*

Sometimes an inquiry stems from a lack of interest in a certain
area. For instance, S.A.W. of Chicago is clearly not a baseball
fan.

> In one puzzle the clue was "Spahn and ——— and pray for
> rain." The answer was SAIN. I use the expression "pray for rain"
> often in my classes on the eve of an exam. Could you possibly
> give me the reference? Who are Spahn and Sain? What's it all
> about?

For the benefit of others who are lacking in diamond lore, in
the 1940s and early '50s Warren Spahn and Johnny Sain were
star pitchers for the Boston Braves in the National League. But
the other pitchers for the team were mediocre. Hence, the city
had a saying that fitted the situation.

Leapers continue to jump to their stationery in recent years.
Here's an example from J.T. of Scarsdale, New York.

> No doubt dozens of people have complained to you about
> an error in last Sunday's main puzzle, "Children's Hour," by
> John Samson, but in case they did not, I am venturing to draw
> your attention to it.

Clue 67 Across reads "Deserts." That conjures up visions of sand, drought, desolation, Sahara, Negev KTA.

The author meant "Reward": he should have written "Desserts."

It is a very small point, but it caused a certain amount of delay and frustration.

Ms. T.'s error is a common one. For the reasons she gives it does seem logical that *rewards* and *desserts* should go together. Incidentally, Ms. T. was kind enough to permit me to publish her letter, but she could not resist an *obiter dictum* on the lexicographers.

I am honoured that you would wish to include my note in your book, and give my consent.

I hate to say it, but in this instance the dictionaries are wrong. Their compilers have forgotten the origin of the term *dessert*, and simply are perpetuating slothful inaccuracy. [Them's fighting words . . .] The term arose during the nineteenth century. Dinners consisted of several courses such as soup, fish, meat and *pudding*. Pudding was the sweet course, and among really aristocratic speakers in England, remains the current term.

After dinner [and pudding], dried fruit and nuts were passed, often with the port. Dried fruit etc. was known by the French expression *des-serts*, two words. *Sert* describes the dry characteristic.

Sorry for the long diatribe, but it is such a luxury to be able to ride a hobby horse, sharpen an axe and feel righteous all at once!

In connection with the above, *Webster's Third* and *Random House, Second* state that *dessert* comes from the French verb *desservir* ("to clear the table").

Once in a while, a Leaper's letter has an angry tone. This one is from J.L.C. of Philadelphia.

Your continuing errors are most annoying. This one is blatant: 19 Across ("Has a Drink") should be "*Whet* one's whistle" *not* "*Wet*. . . ."

This is from common knowledge, but you may also consult

Mr. William Safire, who has written authoritatively on this phrase in your very own newspaper.

The accusation troubled me, especially since *Random House, Second* gives "wet one's whistle" under both *wet* and *whistle,* but fails to mention the phrase under *whet.* I decided to write to Bill Safire. Shortly thereafter, a reply from Mr. J.M., a researcher for Mr. Safire, arrived.

> William Safire asked me to check the files for you concerning *wet* (vs. *whet*) *one's whistle.*
> I can find no reference to this topic in our files. Neither does it appear in the index of any of the *On Language* collections.
> I assume that the puzzle fan has confused Mr. Safire with someone else.

I was especially delighted by Mr. M.'s P.S. He wrote: "I've taken much pleasure in *A Pleasure in Words* as well as your puzzles."

Mention of Mr. Safire reminds me to share with you a paragraph that closes one of his "On Language" articles. After discussing pedants and sticklers for outdated rules, he concludes:

> Let me tell you about the very grammatical. They are different from you and me. They get their habits ingrained early, and it does something to them, makes them rigid where we are flexible, and cynical of usage where we are trustful, in a way that, unless you were exposed at an early age to a severe English teacher, it is very difficult to understand.

Those words from an eminent modern authority on language caused me to recall a statement by the Great Cham of Literature, lexicographer Samuel Johnson. When pointing out that linguistic precepts can never remain stagnant, Johnson referred to "the immutable law of mutability."

As indicated in previous sections throughout this book, I am amazed by the number of puzzle fans who resist any changes in our language. They hold firmly to rules taught to them by some English teacher (like me once) in the distant past and act as if those pedagogues' old yardsticks were made of solid gold. As one who was once an ultraconservative, my advice to such people is: "Get with it!"

•   •   •

Sometimes an inquirer or critic gets confused when the same word can be either a noun or verb. J.F.B. of Brooklyn, New York, wrote in 1991:

> . . . for 39 Down, you give the word "tear," which is present tense. Yet, in today's solution you give the word RENT, which is past tense. Am I correct or missing something? Would you be kind enough to clarify?

Mr. B. apparently forgot that as a noun, *rent* is synonymous with *tear* although as a verb it is also the past tense of *rend*.

Next comes one from H.F.G., Jr., of Morristown, New Jersey. Somehow this 1989 letter got lost for several years.

> Just got around to doing your diagramlesses for 4/23/89, namely the one by A. Kaufman. 52 Down—"Spanish baby boys" is not and never was *nenes,* Hawaiian geese, but *niños.* Alas, such laxity. (Where is Will Weng?)
>
> About two months ago you omitted the *O* in *Oenology* in *another* diagramless. Unfortunately, so few good diagramless puzzles are extant (Dell's are nothing) that yours are still the best. Keep the standards up. We're watching.

I had saved a copy of my reply. Here it is.

> Thank you for your interest in the puzzles, but I must tell you that you are among the fans whom I have called *Leapers* in my recent book, *Across and Down.*
>
> *Enology* is the accepted spelling in the *New World Dictionary* (which is the "Bible" of the *Times*) and in *Webster's Third.*
>
> As for *nenes,* see Cassell's *Spanish Dictionary.* Also, according to most lexicons, the plural of that Hawaiian goose is *nene*— not *nenes.*
>
> Anyway, thanks for your kind words about the puzzles in general.

The Germans have an inside joke about their beloved ex-chancellor, Konrad Adenauer. They refer to him as "der Alte"—an expression which literally means "the old woman."

Since all short words beginning with vowels are grist for puzzler's mills, the *Alte* nickname has been appearing in the crosswords for the last three decades. M.H.R. of New York City is probably a new solver. At the end of 1990 he sent me an objection to the *der Alte* combination. After receiving my rebuttal, he wrote a long and congenial letter of apology. Part of it reads as follows:

> Too late, I went out to consult the authorities: Langenschneidt's *German-English Dictionary,* a couple of German grammars, and the nice lady with the German accent who works in the local hardware store. They all agreed. After the definite article *der* the weak form of the adjective is used (*alte*). But note that after the indefinite article the correct form is *ein alter Mann.*
>
> But I can take some consolation from Mark Twain. He, too, was baffled by the German language. He was keenly disappointed when he found out that the accent on *damit* was on the wrong syllable. However, he concluded that all you really need to know in German were three words: "Kellner, noch zwei!"

Did I boot one? J.H.C. of Montclair, New Jersey, thinks I did so in 1991 when I described a U-BOAT as an "Untersee menace."

> It might have been more accurate to have allowed the German spelling of the clue for 61 Across, "untersee . . . ," to carry over into the solution, which you have as U-BOAT, but which should be *U-boot.*

In late 1990 another quibble came from R.M.L. of New York City.

> With regard to the "Startling Statements" puzzle by Dorothea E. Shipp (*New York Times Magazine,* 12/9/90), 98 Down, "Nope's opposite" is not YEAH, but *Yep.* The opposite of *Yeah* is, of course, *Nah.*

My answer should have been: "Is zat so?"

I suppose a case could be made on behalf of Bayonne's Dr. M.T.M. if I called him a quibbler. At any rate, here's his letter.

I'm crushed! Disappointed beyond relief! HAILSTONE for "Winter pelter" (17 Across on 3-10-89)? I was sure that you had something wonderful up your sleeve and *knew* that hail is formed not by seasonal cold weather, but by strong, convective air currents rising within towering cumulus clouds, much more typical of summer.

Perhaps 17 Across should be *sleetsone,* but I can't seem to make it fit . . .

Thanks for the puzzles; they're the best part of the paper.

From now on, HAILSTONE will be defined as "helter-skelter pelter."

Here's a clever 1991 Gotcha from Stu S. of Los Angeles.

In your puzzle of this date, the clue for 55 Across is "Mo Udall's Brother." The answer is apparently STU. Please be advised that the TBSC (True Blue Stu Crew) takes a dim view of this matter. The Secretary of the Interior during the Kennedy and Johnson administrations was S*tew*art L. Udall (1920–   ), which is customarily, and properly, shortened to "Stew," not "Stu."

I hope this settles the Stu Stew.

*Stu*diously yours, . . .

I guess I'll have to stick with actor Erwin, who died in 1967 or lexicographer Flexner, who passed away a few years ago. The only other recourse is "R-V connection"—a stale clue.

Orthography has always been one of my fortes ever since grammar-school days when I won all the spelling bees. Hence, I was shocked to receive the following letter from J.M.G. in December 1991:

As an avid *New York Times* crossword puzzle devotee I feel compelled to point out a continuing error I observed in your puzzle.

The week of December 1st featured two puzzles which included clues for the word *dietitian.* Unfortunately, it was spelled *dietician* instead of *dietitian.*

Webster's spells it *dietitian* with *dietician* as [an] acceptable spelling alternate; however, more than 60,000 members of The American Dietetic Association (ADA) use *Dietitian* exclusively. The ADA is the largest organization of nutrition professionals in the world.

All the dietitian crossword enthusiasts I am sure join me in requesting you to join us in our use of *T* over *C*.

Thank you for your attention in this regard.

That letter gave me food for thought, especially after a search through all my dictionaries proved that J.M.G. was right. Now I must inform my *physitian, electritian, optitian,* and various *polititians.*

The above matter reminds me that I met a professional dietitian at a party. She seemed like such a snob that I took a stab and asked: "Where did you study sitology?" Ah, a hit, a very palpable hit! My parvenu looked at me as if I had just come from Mars.

"Sit what?"

"Sitology, the study of dietetics and nutrition."

"Oh yes. My, my, this room is noisy." She crept away.

Now folks, if you meet any uppity dietitians, try *sitomania* and *sitophobia* on them. The former is an abnormal craving for food and the latter is the opposite.

Now we come to the final Gotcha of this book. About a year ago A.B.U. of Bronxville, New York, sent me a correction.

In the puzzle of Saturday, August 3, the definition "Stand like Druids of ———; Longfellow" was given for what turned out to be the word OLD. As my memory of reading *Evangeline* as an eighth-grader told me, and as subsequent research proved, the Druids were "of *eld*," not "of old."

The story behind that mistake is that *eld* had appeared in a puzzle a few months previously and I had used the "Druids of eld" definition. My proofer, however, told me I was wrong and she referred me to page 622 of the Fourteenth Edition of Bartlett's *Familiar Quotations*. Wondering if my mind was playing tricks on me in my advancing years, I dutifully used another clue for *eld*.

Ms. U.'s letter caused my proofer to visit the main branch of New York City's public library. There she found the original publication of Longfellow's poem. *Eld* was correct; Bartlett was wrong. Egad!

By the way, Bartlett's Sixteenth Edition repeats the error!

Next we turn to humor, either conscious or unconscious, in editor-fan confrontations. We'll start with a bombshell caused by a typo in a definition for SLEET in a Simon & Schuster puzzle. The clue was supposed to read "Partly frozen rain" but the printer had changed the *P* to an *F*.

When S.P. of Carteret, New Jersey, called my attention to the error and asked for a reply to his complaint about scatology, I said: "The answer, my friend, is blowin' in the wind."

Puzzle editors never know what kind of bizarre request will come in next. Here's an example from a member of the English Department at the University of Washington in Seattle.

A long time ago, probably sometime between 1968 and 1975, *The New York Times* ran a crossword puzzle that had, as a clue for 5 Across, "hard-hearted girl," and as a clue for 7 Across, "Claire of films." Is there any way for you to tell me what the date of this crossword puzzle was? In addition, I'd appreciate receiving a copy of the puzzle, both solved and unsolved. I'll be happy to pay for any research and mailing costs. Thank you very much.

I half-suspect that the professor was tugging at my lower limb with glossa in gena. But if you think he gave me an impossible mission, consider the fact that a young New Yorker, D.G., had the *chutzpah* to ask me to devote a daily puzzle to his crossword-crazy father as a birthday present. He even told me Dad's favorite book, his occupation, and other personal facts to include in the diagram. I dashed off a little fill-in type of puzzle and sent the rough copy to young Mr. G. along with a suggestion that he enlarge it and prepare a neat copy. Such filial devotion, however ingenuous, had to be rewarded.

• • •

That incident reminds me of the time cosmetician Lauder's first name appeared in a Sunday puzzle. Nearby nestled the word MONO, described as a "howling monkey." A few days later a long set of verse arrived from the vice-president of the Madeleine Mono cosmetics company. The gist of the good-humored rhymes was that if ESTEE could get free billing, his boss deserved better treatment than to be called a ululating simian on the same page. The letter impressed me so much that the next time MONO cropped up, it was defined "Cosmetician Madeleine ———."

Along with a delightful expression of thanks from Ms. Mono, I also received a letter from a consul for the Republic of Chile.

> Congratulations [on] your raising Madeleine Mono to the pantheon of crossword puzzledom. As I know from personal experience with my friend and fellow cross-worder U.S. Federal Judge Magistrate Marianne B. Bowler, "Madeleine," her signature perfume, is far and away one of the most entrancing and attractive perfumes ever made.

I should explain that before I gave publicity to the Mono people, I checked with the Better Business Bureau to find out if the company was reputable and not a fly-by-night organization. On the whole, I try to follow Margaret Farrar's policy that the black-and-white squares are no place for free advertisements. When a choice is evident, I select the noncommerical word. DIAL, therefore, is never described as a soap lest all the detergent companies rightfully demand equal time. Similarly, I usually choose "Mountain range: Comb. form" as a clue for OREO rather than a certain cookie. Of course, the slang definition concerning blacks who adopt the values and attributes of whites should be avoided, as must all other words that are offensive or in poor taste.

But as far as commercials are concerned, it's important not to be too rigid. I remember the time I received a daily puzzle and was horrified to see DUZ at 1 Across. My first impulse was to reject the puzzle, but upon close examination I discovered that the constructor had used a remarkable number of words containing the letter Z and it was impossible to remove DUZ without losing its Z and several others in the crossing words. I winced a bit but let it go through. Simultaneously, I worried that new constructors might think that the trademark ban had been lifted for all puzzles. That's a problem facing any conscientious editor. If special circumstances override a rule, will puzzlemakers think that the regulation has been abolished completely?

To get back to D.G.'s request, sometimes I do receive inquiries concerning personalized puzzles for relatives who are crossword addicts. The callers realize that they will be charged a certain fee and that they must supply far more details than will be used. In such cases, I always assign the puzzle to a constructor who has an abundance of time and a scarcity of money. As an aside, I must say that personalized puzzles make great birthday gifts.

Sometimes a person is honored in a puzzle by coincidence. For example, on September 17, 1991, one of my daily crosswords contained the following placement of two entries:

A N I T A
P E A R L

Immediately after the publication of the puzzle, I received an interoffice memo from a woman in the Classified Ads Department of the *Times*.

I just couldn't let this strange coincidence pass unnoticed. Thank you for the mention. I realize that the true sign of fame is to be the clue—not a chance answer—to the crossword.
. . . but what a delightful way to begin!

Honest, folks, neither the constructor of the puzzle nor I had ever heard of Anita Pearl. But it was nice to learn that we had accidentally given a solver a unique thrill.

D.E., a puzzler from Sylmar in California, sent me a startling article published on October 11, 1990, in her *Daily News*. It describes a puzzle that had appeared in the quarterly newsletter of the Women's Prosecutors of California. Here are some of the entries in the crossword:

Clue	Solution
Slime bucket	DEFENDANT
Defense witness	LIAR
Lawyer who knew a governor	JUDGE
Twelve uninformed people called upon to make an important decision	JURY

The president of the Women's Prosecutors group responded to criticisms by stating that no offense was intended—it was just an attempt at humor.

I have also seen booklets of "dirty puzzles" on the stands and crosswords have appeared on shower curtains, beach towels, coffee mugs, T-shirts, and even toilet tissue. Apparently, there is no end to the variety of purposes and uses for the leisure-time activity that Arthur Wynne invented in 1913 during his tenure as an editor of the *New York World*.

Speaking of newspapers, I am reminded that the *Times* spurned the crosswords fad until February 1942, when its Sunday *Magazine* published a large puzzle by Charles Erlenkotter under the editorship of Margaret Farrar. Then (in February 1992) the newspaper celebrated a half-century of entertaining solvers. The Erlenkotter puzzle was reprinted along with about a dozen gems from the past. Some were examples of new departures such as punny puzzles, rebuses, humorous themes, and quotations—including my own invention, the Stepquote. Also an article by Dick Shepard described the influence exerted by editors Farrar, Weng, and myself.

In December 1991 M.L.G. of the Computer Science Department at Stanford University sent me an amazing puzzle that was the result of his first attempt. Every entry in his 23-by-23 crossword contained a quotation from Shakespeare. When I returned the puzzle, I told M.L.G. that it probably would have taken up three whole pages in the *Times*.

It's always delightful when fans respond to unusual puzzles with clever letters mirroring what has just baffled or intrigued them. For example, in October 1991 a *Times* puzzle featured a trick.

Clue	Solution
UUU	EMPLOY (synonym for *use*)
YYY	SAGE (synonym for *wise*)
TTT	RIB (synonym for *tease*)
CCC	GRAB (synonym for *seize*)

D.D. of New York City sent a retort that gave me a chuckle: "UUU guise really make me CCC up when UUU UUU tricks like DDD in the puzzle—GGG wood UUU plEEE EEE up?"

I should add that in reply to my query concerning his "CCC up," Mr. D. said that it means "be annoyed."

One of my cleverest fans is Claire G. of Port Republic, New Jersey. Recently, when a puzzle featuring clichés appeared in the *Times,* Ms. G. retorted with the following animalistic piece.

CLAIRE'S CLICHÉS
à la CAR

Since confession is (said to be) good for the soul, I'll admit to my red light vice. It's this: while I'm waiting for that amber-turned-red to green, I think about the birds and beasts and how lucky they are with no traffic problems.

That's when I dredge up phrases that indicate how closely we are allied to those creatures. Sometimes, if the light is a long one, I put the clichés together. I'm mad as a wet hen and cross as a bear. If I'm sly as a fox and strong as an ox, quick as a cat, bold as a lion and maybe fierce as a tiger, I'll be busy as a bee and never get fat as a pig by being greedy as a hog.

I'm not free as a bird, much less wise as an owl, but I don't *think* I'm crazy as a loon nor mad as a March hare. I may wind up poor as a church mouse, but I'll be happy as a lark and loose as a goose.

Before one of us gets sick as a dog, I'll stop. There's that red light again.

As mentioned in a previous chapter, one method of looking at words is to find those that alternate consonants and vowels. Using such words is a trick of puzzle constructors—especially tyros. For instance, examine the following seven-letter words.

```
M  E  N  A  C  E  D
O  V  E  R  A  G  E
M  A  T  A  D  O  R
```

Note how the three-letter vertical words make sense. Of course, puzzle fans know *Ara* Parseghian, the famous ex-coach of Notre Dame teams, and *Der* is familiar to opera fans who like *Der Rosenkavalier* and to others who remember Crosby as "Der Bingle."

Constructor Kevin Boyle and I have been playing around with longer alternating combinations. My contributions are ALABAMA SENATOR (14 letters) and DELAWARE SENATOR (15 letters), but Kevin topped me with UNITED ARAB EMIRATES (18 letters).

My hope is that a man named EBENEZER OHARA will someday be elected to the Senate by the citizens of the Blue Hen State. Twenty-eight consonants and vowels would alternate!

Seriously, Kevin Boyle and I would like to know if any reader can top his record with a legitimate alternating combination. The first to reply will receive a free book of Simon & Schuster crossword puzzles.

An interesting phenomenon has occurred in recent years. Crossword puzzle clubs seem to be springing up in various places. The first one to come to my attention was formed at Cornell. An alumnus of that university told me that an article in a campus newspaper described a Maleska Club formed by a group of students who convened every Sunday to have a go at the *Times* puzzle.

In 1991 I heard from J.F.E., president of the Jolly Roger Puzzle Club in Marco Island, Florida. Here is part of a letter that he wrote to me on November 24, 1991.

The club started about five years ago. We had all done the puzzle individually for quite a while. One happy hour, as we were sitting in the now defunct Jolly Roger, the thought occurred—why not have a club with a scheduled meeting to discuss the clues and answers? And thus conception.

The puzzle comes out on Wed. in the Marco Island *Eagle* and we have until Mon. to complete it. We have an official "Checker" who corrects them. If they are all right, we get a gold star. We keep records—the star sheet. You'd think the pages would be full of stars but alas no. All sorts of reasons why—from inadvertently leaving a blank, to just plain carelessness.

Personally, I'm intrigued by the cleverness of the authors. If you recall "Anglo-Hebraic Way" (about a year ago), that one gave most of us fits. Some got it right but still didn't get the gist of it.

J.S., a member of the club, sent me a letter stating that he hopes to construct puzzles as well as solve them. He sent me a copy of a quatrain that he had found in some newspaper.

DRAWING BLANKS

The crossword puzzle I've just done
Had quite a novel twist:
It called only a couple of times
For words that don't exist.

D.E.

Another congenial puzzle club has existed since 1985 in Indianapolis. Here is a letter from their treasurer, S.P.H.

We have only one condition for membership and that is the obligation to construct a puzzle from time to time on a rotating basis. Because of the difficulty in constructing a puzzle according to *New York Times'* criteria the club has only ten core members. Special meetings like the one scheduled for April 3rd can increase attendance to as many as 30.

In lieu of dues at monthly meetings, the puzzle presenter provides lunch for all who attend.

At each regular meeting we race to see who can finish the daily *Times'* puzzle first. The puzzle presenter than presents an original puzzle which we all solve independently, then critique.

No prizes are awarded; however, the best of the originals are often published in *The Indianapolis Business Journal.* The club has been in existence for approximately 6 years and although we do not solve the *Times* Sunday puzzle at club meetings, most of us have a go at it on our own over the weekend.

The president of the club, a filmmaker named Michael Maurer, made his debut in the *New York Times* with a daily puzzle on May 4, 1992. A month before that event, my wife Carol and I were guests of the club for a weekend.

Here's a protest sent to me in 1992 by the "TGIF Crew" of the Legal Aid Society of Minneapolis.

> Except for your puzzle, Friday is a great day! We have worked a long 40-hour week and are at the end of our patience and brainpower—but only 4 more hours to work. We want to relax—we want to wind down—we want to be mellow as we leave the office. We want to fill in all the blanks. But we are not relaxed, we are wound up even tighter, we are definitely not mellow and we haven't filled in all the blanks.
>
> Therefore, we ask for a different order of the puzzle, to give us the hardest puzzle on Wednesday, the easiest on Friday and save the sanity of our office place.

My tongue-in-cheek reply read as follows:

> Although I understand your problem, I feel that you should all consult a psychiatrist. The Friday puzzle should not cause tension; it should engender expectation. Over the weekend you can finish it at home in your individual dens or on Saturday morning at your local library. It will serve as a warm-up for the rough Saturday puzzle and the Sunday challenger.
>
> Also, millions of solvers have become used to the gradual increase in the difficulty of the puzzles from Monday to Saturday each week. Can you imagine the havoc that would be caused by a Wednesday toughie? Armageddon would be upon us.

Interviewers and fans often ask me if I know of any famous people who are crossword puzzle addicts. By hook or crook, I have gathered quite a list, beginning with President Bill Clinton and Queen Elizabeth. The former likes the *New York Times* puzzles, but the latter restricts herself to the British cryptics.

But my list of celebrated solvers is not limited to national leaders; well-known sports figures, Hollywood luminaries, and many other public personalities are among those who enthusiastically tackle crossword puzzles. Actor Walter Matthau and his wife are said to be ardent solvers, as is, Margaret Farrar once told me, Celeste Holm. Crosswords are also a favored pastime of both Andy Rooney of "60 Minutes," and noted TV critic Judith Crist. Lee Iacocca is known to test himself on the black and white squares with some frequency. And Hall of Fame pitcher Tom Seaver even used to pore over the *Times* puzzle in the dugout.

In 1925 poet Stephen Vincent Benet and dramatist Robert E. Sherwood participated in a solving contest at the Roosevelt Hotel, and to this day quite a few literary lights remain crossword aficionados. Nora Ephron and Robert Katz, author of *The Cassandra Crossing* as well as a puzzle constructor himself, are among them.

I do not know for sure if Robert Ludlum is a puzzle fan, but the following paragraph from *The Aquitaine Progression* makes me think that the author cuddles up with a crossword now and then:

> The folded *New York Times* resting on his knee, Stone inked in the last two words of the crossword puzzle and looked at his watch. It had taken him nine minutes, nine minutes of relief; he wished it had been longer. One of the joys of having been station chief in London was the London Times crossword. He could always count on at least a half-hour when he could forget problems in the search for words and meanings.

Often it is a bit of correspondence from celebrities themselves—something I receive surprisingly often—that prompts me to lengthen my list. My first such fan letter was a 1942 postcard from the noted screenwriter and short-stories editor, Ben Hecht. He referred to my daily puzzles for the *Herald Tribune* and said that he wanted to thank me for being the only constructor constantly defining BEN as "Writer Hecht" rather than "Franklin."

Many years later, I added Beverly Sills to my list when I received a phone call from her secretary in the late seventies. It seems that the soprano was about to give concerts in the Far East where the *Times* is not available. Consequently, would it be possible for me to send her the Sunday puzzles for the next three weeks before she took off?

Ordinarily, I would never grant such a request, but in this case I yielded—maybe because I'm an opera buff. A month later I received a sweet thank-you from the soprano; I was given "hugs and kisses." (Ms. Sills is not the sole Met soprano crossword fan: Both Shirley Love and Irra Petina have sent me fan mail.)

On occasion, my response to a celebrity's letter will lead to another letter, and before long we'll have struck up a regular correspondence, all due to our common interest in crossword puzzles. In this way, I've even developed some genuine friendships with the likes of actor Joseph Cotten, a big fan of Stepquotes, which I invented; author John Hersey, whose *A Bell for Adano* appears often in crossword puzzles; screenwriter Ernest Lehman, of *The Sound of Music* and *North by Northwest* fame; and Pulitzer Prize–winning poet Richard Wilbur (whose son Nathan, by the way, married my daughter Merryl).

A final luminary whose passion for crosswords has led to a fine friendship is Frank Sinatra. Indeed, in 1984 Ole Blue Eyes hosted a dinner in my honor at a restaurant in New York City. Most of the thirty guests were crossword mavens. Among them were Arlene Frances and her husband, the late Martin Gabel. Also present were ex-mayor Robert Wagner and his wife Phyllis (widow of Bennett Cerf), Kitty Carlyle Hart, and several tycoons.

Incidentally, Francis Albert shares with President Clinton a feeling of pride about an acquired ability to solve the puzzles in ink. Both curl up with a pen and a crossword during their many flights on private planes. Aides and friends dare not disturb their efforts to cross 21 Across with 16 Down.

Let me add that I also prefer ink over pencil when tackling a puzzle. But because I have a tendency toward rashness, I use an erasable pen.

And so, we have come to the end of a book that I hope has given some measure of pleasure to the readers. For me, it has been a delightful experience because most puzzle fans are gentle, courteous, intelligent people. Discussing my correspondence with them has therefore been very enjoyable.

But let me not sound like a pollyanna. Editing puzzles has its seamier side. For example, a small minority of solvers can be classed as selfish egotists who expect every puzzle to be geared to their particular ability and experience. They disregard the fact that a million other people are tackling the crossword; they demand custom-made puzzles for the price of a newspaper.

Then there are the two percent who rake me over the coals whenever a typo occurs. They cry "For shame!" and say they are "shocked" to see such a terrible error in a *Times* puzzle. They actually expect infallibility from another human being. Maybe I should be honored; perhaps they think I'm some kind of deity. Hey, out there, I'm just another member of *homo sapiens*—and I can be just as sappy as the next person in my weaker moments.

Pax, amor et felicitas!

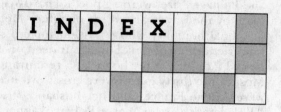

INDEX

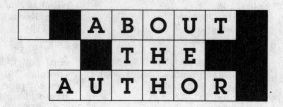

ABOUT THE AUTHOR

Eugene Maleska was the crossword puzzle editor of *The New York Times* for sixteen years. He also edited puzzles for Simon & Schuster for approximately thirty years. After graduating from Montclair State College in 1937, he taught Latin in New Jersey and then became an English teacher in a Harlem junior high school. While rising to various principalships, he pursued a hobby as a crossword puzzle constructor and eventually became one of the top wordsmiths in that field.

Dr. Maleska earned an Ed.D. degree at Harvard University after having been granted a fellowship in 1952. He taught education courses at Hunter College, City College of New York, and the University of Vermont. After serving as Community Superintendent in District 8 in the Bronx, Dr. Maleska retired in 1971. A brand-new middle school in the East Bronx was subsequently named for him.

Dr. Maleska published over a hundred poems as well as a book of verse (*Sun and Shadow*) sponsored by the Poetry Society of America. He was also co-author of *The Story of Education*. For Simon & Schuster, he wrote *A Pleasure in Words* (1981), *Across and Down* (1984), and *Maleska's Favorite Word Games* (1989).